The Economics of Information in the Networked Environment

Edited by

Meredith A. Butler
Bruce R. Kingma

ASSOCIATION OF RESEARCH LIBRARIES
1996

The Economics of Information in the Networked Environment

Proceedings of the Conference:
Challenging Marketplace Solutions to Problems in the Economics of Information
Washington, DC, September 18-19, 1995

Edited by

Meredith A. Butler
Dean and Director of Libraries
University at Albany, SUNY

Bruce R. Kingma
Assistant Professor, Department of Economics
School of Information Science and Policy
University at Albany, SUNY

Library of Congress Cataloging-in-Publication Data

Conference: Challenging Marketplace Solutions to Problems in the Economics of Information (1995: Washington, DC)
    The economics of information in the networked environment: proceedings of the Conference: Challenging Marketplace Solutions to Problems in the Economics of Information, Washington, DC, September 18-19, 1995 / edited by Meredith A. Butler, Bruce R. Kingma.
        p.   cm.
    Includes bibliographic references.
    ISBN: 0-918006-29-5 (alk. paper)
    1. Academic libraries--Data processing--Economic aspects--United States--Congresses. 2. Library information networks--Economic aspects--United States--Congresses. 3. Digital libraries--Economic aspects--United States--Congresses. 4. Universities and colleges--Data processing--Economic aspects--United States--Congresses.
    I. Butler, Meredith A.   II. Kingma, Bruce R.   III. Title.
Z675.U5C728 1995
025.04--dc20
                                                                  96-21222
                                                                   CIP

∞ The paper used in this publication meets the minimum requirements of the American National Standard for Information Sciences–Permanence of Paper for Printed Library Materials, ANSI Z39.48-1992.

© Copyright 1996, Association of Research Libraries

Permission is granted to reproduce and distribute the contents in any media, provided that such reproduction is for not-for-profit, educational, or library purposes and credit is given to the source. All other rights are reserved to the authors or their designees who should be consulted directly for permissions.

Association of Research Libraries
21 Dupont Circle, NW, Suite 800
Washington, DC 20036
202-296-2296 (phone)
202-872-0884 (fax)
pubs@cni.org

TABLE OF CONTENTS

Part I
Challenging Marketplace Solutions to Problems in the Economics of Information

Conference Themes.. 1

Welcome and Introduction.. 7
    Meredith A. Butler
        Dean and Director of Libraries
        University at Albany, SUNY
    Deanna Marcum
        President
        Council on Library Resources
    Duane E. Webster
        Executive Director
        Association of Research Libraries

Information Technology and the Transformation of the University.............................. 15
Keynote Address
    David P. Roselle
        President
        University of Delaware

Costs and Benefits of Investments in Technology:
How Can Technology Serve the Public Interest?.. 17
Keynote Address
    Mario Morino
        President
        The Morino Institute

Part II
The Andrew W. Mellon Foundation's Program in the Economics of Information

JSTOR and the Economics of Scholarly Communication.. 23
    William G. Bowen
        President
        The Andrew W. Mellon Foundation

Part III
Economic Modeling of Investments in Information Resources at Academic Institutions

The Economics of Information.. 37
    Roger Noll
        Professor, Department of Economics
        Stanford University

The Economics of the Internet and Academia.. 43
    Hal Varian
        Dean, School of Information Management and Systems
        University of California at Berkeley

The Economics of University Investments in Information Resources............................ 53
    Michael McPherson
        Professor, Department of Economics
        Dean of Faculty
        Williams College
Questions and Discussion.. 56

Part IV
Case Studies in Transforming the Scholarly Process: Costs and Benefits of Cooperation

Funding Social Science Data Archiving and Services in the Networked Environment.. 61
    Richard Rockwell
        Executive Director
        Inter-university Consortium for Political and Social Research

Building the Distributed North American Collection for Foreign Languages... 79
    Burkart Holzner
        Director, University Center for International Studies
        University of Pittsburgh

Questions and Discussion.. 90

Part V
Alternatives to Current Access Models in Research Libraries

The Economics of Resource Sharing, Consortia, and Document Delivery................ 93
    Meredith A. Butler
        Dean and Director of Libraries
        University at Albany, SUNY

The Economics of Access versus Ownership: The Costs and Benefits of Access to Scholarly Articles via Interlibrary Loan and Journal Subscriptions.. 99
    Bruce Kingma
        Assistant Professor, Department of Economics
        School of Information Science and Policy
        University at Albany, SUNY

Questions and Discussion.. 108

Part VI
Can E-Journals Save Us?

Can E-Journals Save Us?—A Publisher's View... 115
    Lorrin R. Garson
        Chief Technology Officer
        American Chemical Society

Can E-Journals Save Us?—A Scholar's View... 123
    James O'Donnell
        Professor, Department of Classical Studies
        University of Pennsylvania

Questions and Discussion.. 127

Part VII
Economic Considerations for Digital Libraries

**Economic Considerations for Digital Libraries,
a Library of Congress Perspective** 131
    Hiram Davis
        Deputy Librarian of Congress
Cost Centers and Measures in the Networked Information Value-Chain 137
    Paul Evan Peters
        Executive Director
        Coalition for Networked Information
**This Little User Went to Market, This Little User Stayed Home:
What Users, Potential Users, and Nonusers Can Tell Us** 143
    Ann P. Bishop
        Assistant Professor, Graduate School of Library and Information Science
        University of Illinois at Urbana-Champaign
Questions and Discussion 149

Part VIII
The Economics of Information Access in Higher Education

NCLIS Remarks 153
    Jeanne Simon
        Chairperson
        National Commission on Libraries and Information Science
Measuring Costs and Benefits of Distance Learning 157
    James H. Ryan
        Vice President for Continuing Education
        Pennsylvania State University

Part IX
The Limits of Marketplace Solutions and the Need for Collaboration

The Need for Collaboration to Build the Knowledge Infrastructure 167
    Richard P. West
        Vice Chancellor, Business and Finance
        California State University System
Questions and Discussion 173

Part X
The Economics of Information and the Need for Collaboration–Creating a Research Agenda

Panel
    Karen R. Hitchcock 186
        Interim President
        University at Albany, SUNY
    Clifford Lynch 189
        Director, Library Automation
        University of California
    Timothy Ingoldsby 192
        Director of New Product Development
        American Institute of Physics

Colin Day... 194
    Director
    University of Michigan Press
Malcolm Getz... 197
    Professor of Economics
    Vanderbilt University
Richard Ekman.. 200
    Secretary
    The Andrew W. Mellon Foundation
Deanna Marcum... 202
    President
    Council on Library Resources
Duane Webster.. 203
    Executive Director
    Association of Research Libraries

Appendix
    Conference Sponsors.. 205
    Conference Advisory Committee.. 207
    Conference Participants... 209

Part I
*Challenging Marketplace Solutions to
Problems in the Economics of Information*

Conference Themes

Funding the knowledge infrastructure—the development, expansion, and maintenance of the network, computing resources, the electronic library, electronic classrooms, and faculty development—has become an issue vital to the long-term viability of today's research universities. The current national climate is focused on greater privatization and marketplace solutions. The current economic climate demands greater economic efficiencies in the production of scholarship and the distribution and use of scholarly information. Today's students and faculty demand greater breadth, scope and ease of information access, and user-centered organizational cultures in which economic costs are balanced against user benefits. Academic officers and university administrators planning the delivery of educational services are asked to reconcile these competing and confusing forces. They are asked to make economic decisions which may have significant long-term impact and short-term viability.

This conference brought together academic officers, chief information officers and other administrators, economists, and other interested faculty, librarians, computing professionals, and representatives from higher education associations, to examine issues related to the development of the knowledge infrastructure and their economic impact on higher education. Participants explored the role higher education can play in the public policy debates on the economics of information access and delivery. Participants examined case studies in the infrastructure, including print and electronic journals, library consortia, delivery options, and network resources, and services for research universities.

Keynote Speakers

David Roselle, President of the University of Delaware, spoke about the university's experiences implementing new technology. President Roselle related the experiences of the university in providing students with electronic access to their university records, enabling students to have the answers to many frequently asked questions over the university network. The university also began a program to subsidize the purchase of computers by faculty and students and an upgrade of the local computer network. President Roselle outlined the costs and benefits of the University at Delaware's investment in information technology and services, and noted that improvements in service and access for students and faculty came at an increase in costs.

The second keynote speaker was Mario Morino, President of the Morino Institute, who spoke of impending change he foresaw coming in universities as a result of information technology. Mario Morino told the audience of the dramatic changes coming to higher education, including a significant downsizing and redefining the role of higher education. Mr. Morino challenged the audience to envision the potential of technology in higher education.

The Andrew W. Mellon Foundation's Program in the Economics of Information

William Bowen, President of The Andrew W. Mellon Foundation, presented information on the JSTOR project. The JSTOR project is an electronic database containing digitized images of all pre-1990 issues of ten core scholarly journals in the fields of economics and history. Dr. Bowen described the history of the JSTOR project along with the Mellon Foundation's interactions with publishers and the need for archival considerations of these journals. Archiving the past one-hundred years of ten core journals and developing a search engine that provides scholars with searchable access to the articles is an important development in scholarship. Dr. Bowen also described possible library and individual subscription policies of the JSTOR project, both of which may provide significant savings to subscribers in storage and access costs.

Economic Modeling of Investments in Information Resources at Academic Institutions

This session convened a panel of four distinguished economists. Professor Malcolm Getz, Vanderbilt University, moderated the presentations by Professor Roger Noll, Stanford University; Professor Hal Varian, University of California at Berkeley; and Professor Michael McPherson, Williams College.

Professor Noll gave an overview of the economics of information including the high rate of return on information in the United States, the value of university research in the United States, and the public good model of information. Dr. Noll also explained the economics of research journal publishing, in print and electronic format. He explained that while electronic journals may have some cost savings, quality enhancements may increase the costs.

Professor Varian examined the economics of the Internet and electronic publishing. Dr. Varian spoke on the history, financing, and future of the Internet. This included an explanation of the current traffic and increasing demand and congestion. Professor Varian explained the business model of the Internet and possible methods of financing Internet services and metering traffic. He discussed several models of scholarly communication over the Internet that may replace the current print journal model. Dr. Varian also examined the problems of ownership of intellectual property, pricing, payment, refereeing, publishing, valuing, and the costs of scholarly communication in electronic format.

Professor McPherson described the economics of journal pricing and interlibrary loan. Dr. McPherson spoke on the value of electronic journals, journal reputation, and the future of scholarly communications. He also explained the interdependency within the academic community for access to scholarly journals and books.

Case Studies in Transforming the Scholarly Process: Costs and Benefits of Cooperation

In this session, the speakers provided examples of the transformation taking place in research as a result of electronic access. Speakers presented examples from their organizations and described the benefits and costs of projects using electronic access. Duane Webster, Executive Director of the Association of Research Libraries, served as moderator.

Richard E. Lucier, Assistant Vice Chancellor for Academic Information Management at the University of California, San Francisco, presented several examples of electronic resources available at his library. Shrinking library budgets, increasing paper based journal prices, and increasing demand for electronic resources required Dr. Lucier to downsize the library resources spent on the paper based library and increase the resources spent on the electronic library. Dr. Lucier presented the Knowledge Management Model of paper based and electronic resources. Dr. Lucier also talked about the costs and financing of the Red Sage Project which provides electronic access to 100 medical journals.

Richard Rockwell, Executive Director of the Inter-university Consortium for Political and Social Research, presented the history and present status of the ICPSR collection of databases. Dr. Rockwell talked about the ability of the Internet and networked campuses to provide access by researchers to the database, where previously access was provided via a campus representative. He also spoke of the present funding and membership fees for ICPSR and the budget difficulties they faced. New funding strategies and new services offered by ICPSR were explored.

Rush Miller, Director of Libraries at the University of Pittsburgh, presented a paper by Burkart Holzner, Director of the University Center for International Studies at the University of Pittsburgh. Dr. Holzner's paper described the Research Libraries Project Task Force on Acquisition and Distribution of Foreign Language and Area Studies Materials, conducted by the Association of American Universities in collaboration with the Association of Research Libraries, and supported by The Andrew W. Mellon Foundation. He recommends and discusses three methods of funding for strategies proposed by the project; funding from library acquisitions budgets for those participating in the project, cost recovery for document delivery, and grants from foundations and governments.

Alternatives to Current Access Models in Research Libraries—The Economics of Resource Sharing, Consortia, and Document Delivery

Meredith Butler, Dean and Director of Libraries at the University at Albany, and Bruce R. Kingma, Assistant Professor at the University at Albany, presented the results of a Council on Library Resources sponsored study on the economics of access versus ownership. James F. Williams II, Director of Libraries at the University of Colorado, served as moderator for this session.

Meredith Butler reviewed the results of several previously funded studies on the use of academic journal subscriptions. Dean Butler spoke of the value in providing cost per use statistics to faculty who had to participate in the difficult task of cutting journal subscriptions.

Bruce Kingma reviewed the methodology and results of the cost-benefit analysis on providing access to journal articles via a library subscription versus interlibrary loan. This study included the opportunity cost or value of the inconvenience to patrons of waiting for access to a journal article delivered by interlibrary loan. Dr. Kingma showed that at the State University of New York, University Center Libraries, savings could be achieved by a more extensive use of interlibrary loan and a decrease in journal subscriptions.

Can E-Journals Save Us?

Ann Okerson, Director of the Office of Scientific and Academic Publishing at the Association of Research Libraries, served as moderator of this session on the costs and benefits of electronic journals.

Lorrin Garson, Chief Technology Officer, American Chemical Society, described the dramatic increase in the costs in recent years of publishing print journals, particularly the costs of paper and color printing. Dr. Garson spoke of the Society's plans to start an electronic version of the *Journal of the American Chemical Society* and the potential savings and increased quality that might result.

James O'Donnell, Professor, Department of Classical Studies, University of Pennsylvania, spoke on the problems, solutions, costs, and benefits of the electronic journal the *Bryn Mawr Classical Review* which provides timely reviews of books in the classics. Dr. O'Donnell described the low-cost, high value method of producing an electronic journal in the humanities.

Economic Considerations for Digital Libraries

Thomas Galvin, Professor, School of Information Science and Policy, University at Albany, SUNY, moderated this session which explored the experiences of the speakers with digital libraries.

Hiram Davis, Deputy Librarian, Library of Congress, spoke about the experiences at the Library of Congress. Dr. Davis outlined the Library of Congress digital library initiative, its strategic plan, and its plan for financing from the public and private sector sources.

Paul Evan Peters, Executive Director, Coalition for Networked Information, reported on CNI's "Cost Centers and Measures in the Networked Information Value-Chain" initiative. The Coalition for Networked Information convened three panels of experts from libraries, publishers, and intermediaries to help identify the cost changes in the new networked information value-chain.

Ann P. Bishop, Assistant Professor, Department of Library Science, University of Illinois at Urbana, provided examples of the economics of digital libraries for users and non-users. Dr. Bishop provided examples of users and nonusers of the University at Illinois Digital Library including faculty and students, artists on the Internet, and Prarienet, a free-net in the Champaign area. Professor Bishop spoke on how income, race, and the wealth of the public library influenced access to the digital library.

The Economics of Information Access in Higher Education—Measuring Costs and Benefits of Distance Learning

James H. Ryan, Vice President for Continuing Education, Pennsylvania State University, spoke on the costs and benefits of using information technology for distance learning. Dr. Ryan discussed the experiences of Pennsylvania State University, Stanford University, and Washington State University in distance education. He outlined the value of providing distance education, the lowering cost of providing and accessing information, and the growing demand for distance learning.

Thomas Shaughnessy, University Librarian, University of Minnesota Libraries, and Chair of NASULGC's Commission on Information Technologies Library Board, served as moderator. Jeanne Simon, Chairperson, National Commission on Libraries and Information Science, spoke briefly about her interests in the outcome of the conference.

The Limits of Marketplace Solutions and the Need for Collaboration to Build the Knowledge Infrastructure

Richard West, Vice Chancellor, Business and Finance, California State University System, spoke on the changes he envisioned as a result of the information technology revolution. Dr. West also spoke on the need for further investments in technology at universities. He spoke on the different pricing models that may result, changes in copyright, fair use, and the method of promotion and tenure at universities. Dr. West challenged the audience to examine several of the assumptions on how the information technology revolution may or may not impact university budgets.

Barbara von Wahlde, Associate Vice President for University Libraries, University at Buffalo, SUNY, served as the moderator for this session.

The Economics of Information and the Need for Collaboration—Creating a Research Agenda

The final session brought together eight distinguished speakers to summarize the conference and give their vision of what research was needed. Each of the speakers agreed that major changes may lie ahead, but significant decreases in costs or the price of information were unlikely. The speakers included Deanna Marcum, President, Council on Library Resources; Richard Ekman, Secretary, The Andrew W. Mellon Foundation; Karen R. Hitchcock, Interim President, University at Albany, State University of New York; Duane Webster, Executive Director, Association of Research Libraries; Malcolm Getz, Professor of Economics, Vanderbilt University; Colin Day, Director, University of Michigan Press; Clifford Lynch, Director, Library Automation, University of California; and Timothy Ingoldsby, Director of New Product Development, American Institute of Physics. The panel was moderated by Meredith Butler, Dean and Director of Libraries, University at Albany, SUNY.

Welcome and Introductory Remarks

Meredith A. Butler
Dean and Director of Libraries
University at Albany, SUNY

It is my distinct pleasure to welcome you to this conference this morning for three reasons: first, because the idea for this conference started with a problem and the need to find answers to it. It began with a conversation in my office between Dr. Kingma and myself as we discussed how we might find solutions to some of our own problems in the economics of information. As an administrator, I rarely have the opportunity to develop an idea fully, to see a project through to completion, and then to find uninterrupted time to enjoy the fruits of my labor, so I am looking forward to doing just that over the next two days. The second reason for my pleasure is that this conference brings together a rich and provocative array of speakers and panelists and a wonderfully varied group of participants to examine and discuss complex and compelling issues raised by the development of the knowledge infrastructure and the transformation of scholarship. I am looking forward to interesting conversations, to looking at familiar ideas in unfamiliar ways, to making new connections, and to learning much that will be new to me.

The third reason for my pleasure is that planning this conference has allowed me the opportunity to work with an exceptional group of individuals who went to considerable lengths to make this conference happen. I would like to acknowledge my SUNY Colleagues: Christine Haile from SUNY Central Administration's Office of Education Technology, Barbara von Wahlde, John B. Smith, and Eleanor Heishman of the SUNY Center Libraries, and Albany's Interim President, Karen Hitchcock, for their support, cooperation and encouragement. From the Council on Library Resources, I would like to acknowledge Board President, Martin Cummings, Program Officer, Julia Blixrud, former President, David Penniman, and current President, Deanna Marcum. Their interest in our nascent ideas encouraged us to persevere with them. They not only believed our ideas were important, they funded them.

It has also been a great pleasure to work on this project and conference with my colleague Bruce Kingma. I can't stress enough how important it is that faculty, librarians, and computing professionals work together to examine issues of mutual interest and benefit. Paul Peters and Joan Lippincott, of the Coalition for Networked Information, and John Hamilton, of the National Association of State Universities and Land-Grant Colleges, offered wise counsel and many hours of their time to help shape and plan this conference.

And finally, I would like to acknowledge the generosity of Duane Webster and the staff of the Association of Research Libraries for believing in the importance of this conference and working so hard to make it happen. I owe a special debt of gratitude to Jaia Barrett, Deputy Executive Director of ARL, for her unfailing wise counsel and good ideas, hard work, and general optimism and good humor. Two other ARL staff members deserve special recognition. Mary Jane Brooks orchestrated the logistics and arrangement of this conference, in addition to her usual demanding job at ARL and her additional responsibilities as a new mother. Her extraordinary organizational skills and quiet can-do attitude were very reassuring. When Mary Jane took maternity leave, Allyn Fitzgerald stepped in with perfect ease and great efficiency. Both Mary Jane and Allyn are here this morning and I would like to acknowledge them and point them out to you in case you need any staff assistance during the next two days.

I will now turn the podium over to someone who is very familiar to many people in this room. **Deanna Marcum** is President of two foundations, the Council on Library Resources and the Commission on Preservation and Access. Dr. Marcum has enjoyed a varied career as Program Officer at the Council, as an educator and Dean of the School of Library and Information Science at the Catholic University of America, and most recently as the Director of Public Service and Collection Management at the Library of Congress. Dr. Marcum holds a Ph.D. in American Studies from the University of Maryland and a Master's in Library Science from the University of Kentucky. She is a widely published author with a keen interest in the transformation of scholarship and the economic issues with which we are struggling. We are very fortunate that she could join us today.

Deanna Marcum
President
Council on Library Resources

The Council on Library Resources is very pleased to be a sponsor of this conference. The topics that will be discussed over the next two days are at the heart of the greatest challenges facing higher education.

We are in the early stages of a revolution. Many of us in this room have sown the seeds, promising great results to be derived from technology. We have asserted that digital technology will bring a democratization of information and knowledge; that treasures of our libraries, archives, and museums will finally be available to all, not just the privileged. We have promised that each student will be able to learn in his/her own way, and will be freed from the rigid constraints of the classroom lecture. But in our enthusiasm for the new methods of teaching and learning, and the new possibilities for scholarly communication, we have said remarkably little about cost. This is in part due to our genuinely limited knowledge of the economics of information, but it also reflects our general lack of desire to face the truth.

Libraries and computing centers have been considered bottomless pits for absorbing money for years. We have not appreciated this label given to us by other campus community members, and we keep hoping to produce an information system that is so helpful, so easy to use, so magically efficient that everyone will realize these information resources are worth the cost.

The situation we find ourselves in, however, is that just as the technology is developed enough to make a real difference in how scholars and researchers do their work, universities and colleges have encountered unparalleled financial difficulties. Also, in our more reflective moments, library leaders have to acknowledge that our ability to effect genuine cost reductions are far from assured.

Inherent characteristics of digital technology make cost predictions very difficult. We know, for example, that there will be a rapid, predictable, and continuing change of hardware. We can calculate the schedule and the cost for new computers. Much harder to predict is the need to change software. We know that Windows 95 costs $89.95 per copy, but we can only imagine how many other software packages will have to be changed or upgraded to use in connection with Windows 95, and will we have to go through the whole thing again for Windows 96 or 97?

We are also painfully aware of being in a hybrid environment. It is the worst of times, in financial terms, for we must continue with the traditional costs of building the campus infrastructure, decentralizing computing resources on the campus, providing technology in the classroom, and buying books and journals for the library, while adding the new capabilities of digital technology. We are relatively certain that digital information can be a substitute for some of the print-based information we are now trying to preserve, store, and retrieve, but we know far too little about how quickly that substitution can be realized, and what the cost implications will be.

We also know that digital technology has erased national boundaries of scholarship, and it is now possible, even for the faculty member in a small, isolated, and resource-poor institution to have unprecedented access to information world-wide and to develop professional connections to colleagues everywhere. We do not know how these new capabilities and relationships will affect the institution in which the faculty member resides. Institutions of higher education without boundaries may find themselves facing boundless bills to pay.

For all of these reasons, the Council on Library Resources selected the economics of information as one of its three central program concerns for the next few years. We are not concerned simply with costs and how to reduce them. We are interested in how digital technology influences the cost of higher education, in general, and the economics of scholarly communication, in particular. We want to describe, ultimately, the relationship between costs and benefits for the users.

We believe this conference is an excellent launching point for our economics of information program. This conference evolved from a research project funded by the Council on Library Resources at SUNY, Albany. Meredith Butler and Bruce Kingma deserve great credit for identifying the topics that need further exploration, and we greatly appreciate the work they have done to make this conference possible. We gratefully acknowledge The Andrew W. Mellon Foundation's support of the Council's and many other institutions' efforts to expand the knowledge about economic issues. The Foundation's leadership in this area has been exemplary.

We are delighted that so many of you responded to what we believe is a critical topic. The next two days should be most stimulating, and I look forward to learning from each of you. Librarians and other information professionals have a responsibility to become managerial partners with their universities and find ways to contain costs. As much as we enjoy talking about new capabilities, we are now obligated to take a hard look at benefits as well as costs and to make some hard choices. These discussions will go far to prepare us to make informed choices and to assure that the information revolution improves information transfer and scholarly communications for society as a whole.

We are also very fortunate that **Duane Webster**, the Executive Director of the Association of Research Libraries, could join us this morning. The Association of Research Libraries is an organization of 119 major research libraries in the U.S. and Canada whose mission is to shape and influence forces affecting the future of research libraries in the process of scholarly communication. Duane was the founder of the ARL Office of Management Services and it was his extraordinary record of accomplishments that led to his appointment as Executive Director in 1988. Duane is a widely published lecturer and consultant and serves in a leadership role in many library and education associations. He is also a member of the Board of the National Humanities Alliance.

Duane E. Webster
Executive Director
Association of Research Libraries

It is my pleasure to add another welcome to the Economics of Information Conference. I am pleased the conference has attracted so many participants from every sector that contributes to the system of scholarly communication. I am also pleased to be able to partner with such a distinguished group of conference sponsors.

Planning and orchestrating this event has provided a useful occasion to work closely with the people from the State University of New York, especially Meredith Butler and the University at Albany, the Council on Library Resources under the leadership of Deanna Marcum, the National Association of State Universities and Land-Grant Colleges with John Hamilton, and the Coalition for Networked Information led by Paul Peters.

We hope this inclusion of diverse partners and perspectives will result in a stimulating and productive set of discussions for you. The idea behind these discussions is to assess our current understanding of the economics of information especially in the light of the growing public policy debates around market-based solutions. The current system of scholarly communication has demonstrated extreme strain due to an increase in quantity and formats of publications as well as the dramatic increase in the cost of information. You are familiar with the statistics ARL publishes showing how the explosive growth in the cost of information clashes with the stable budgets provided to libraries. (See Figures 1-5.)

Research libraries provide the cornerstone of an extraordinary system of access to information in North America. But pricing and funding issues are strangling the traditional means of providing this access.

The pressures on scholarly communication may be viewed as characteristics of a healthy process: knowledge and ideas are expanding, scientists and scholars are active and creative, new disciplines and subdisciplines are emerging, traditional library structures are embracing and deploying new tools and information. But, the stresses and strains are apparent. Scholarly communication is changing and it seems to be more than simply a modernization process. It appears to be transformational in character.

At the same time the current North American political environment is focusing on greater privatization and marketplace solutions as promising avenues for action. As recently as July 24, Bruce Lehman, U.S. Commissioner of Patents and Trademarks, met with the ARL Board of Directors and reaffirmed that the U.S. Government looks to the private sector to take the primary role in building the national information infrastructure. And, in order to guarantee continued investment from the private sector, the government is developing policies that maximize economic security for copyright owners in the marketplace.

When confronted with the concern that higher education is already struggling with dramatic increases in the cost of providing access to knowledge and that in the short-term, a commercialized NII will add to those costs, Commissioner Lehman's response was that marketplace solutions will have to be applied and only if these fail, will it be appropriate for the government to intervene.

Research libraries and higher education have been exploited by the marketplace in the past. Individual library-based responses to the pricing practices of some commercial journal publishers, for example, have over time proven ineffective in moderating price increases or in ensuring ready access to the growing volume of global information. This conference is an opportunity to identify what steps are needed to position higher education to succeed in this political and economic reality. How can higher education be a shrewd participant in the commercialized NII? How can we develop a better understanding of the marketplace as it affects scholarly communication? How can higher education work within the current market-place to be a more effective participant?

How should we act to redesign the marketplace to make it a more hospitable environment for education and research? What milestones could/should be set to measure the health and progress of scholarly communication?

There is a need for new and imaginative national and global strategies to address the information challenges facing research universities and society as a whole. ARL and the other conference sponsors are looking to this conference to generate ideas and insights that will contribute to collective responses that make the marketplace work to the advantage of the educational communities.

Figure 1

**ARL Library and U.S. ARL University Expenditures, 1982-1992
In Constant (1982) Dollars**

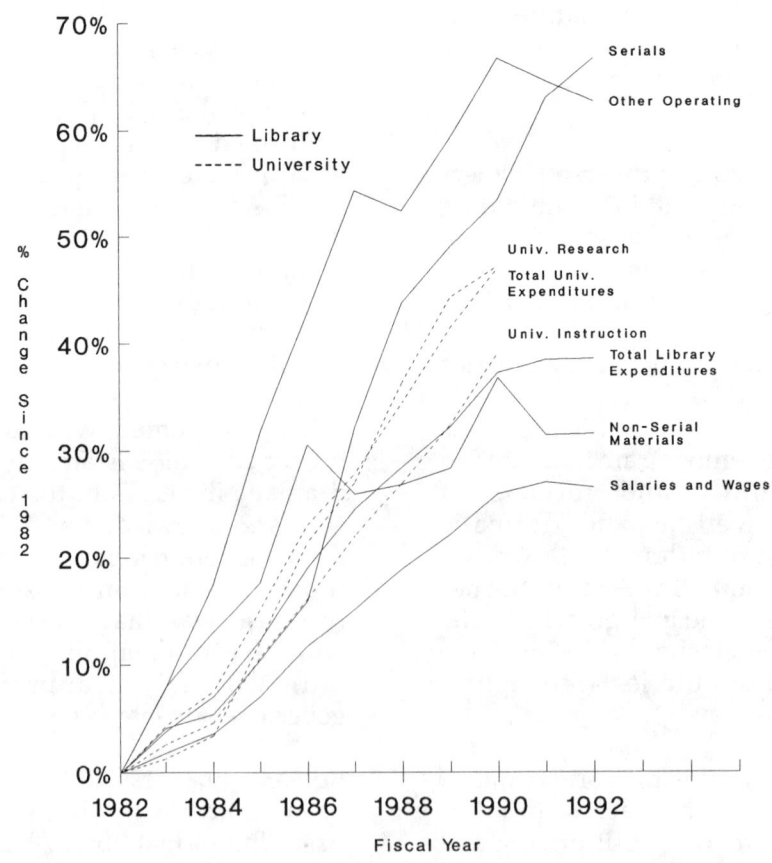

Source: *ARL Statistics* 1991-92.
(Prepared by Kendon Stubbs)

Figures 2-3

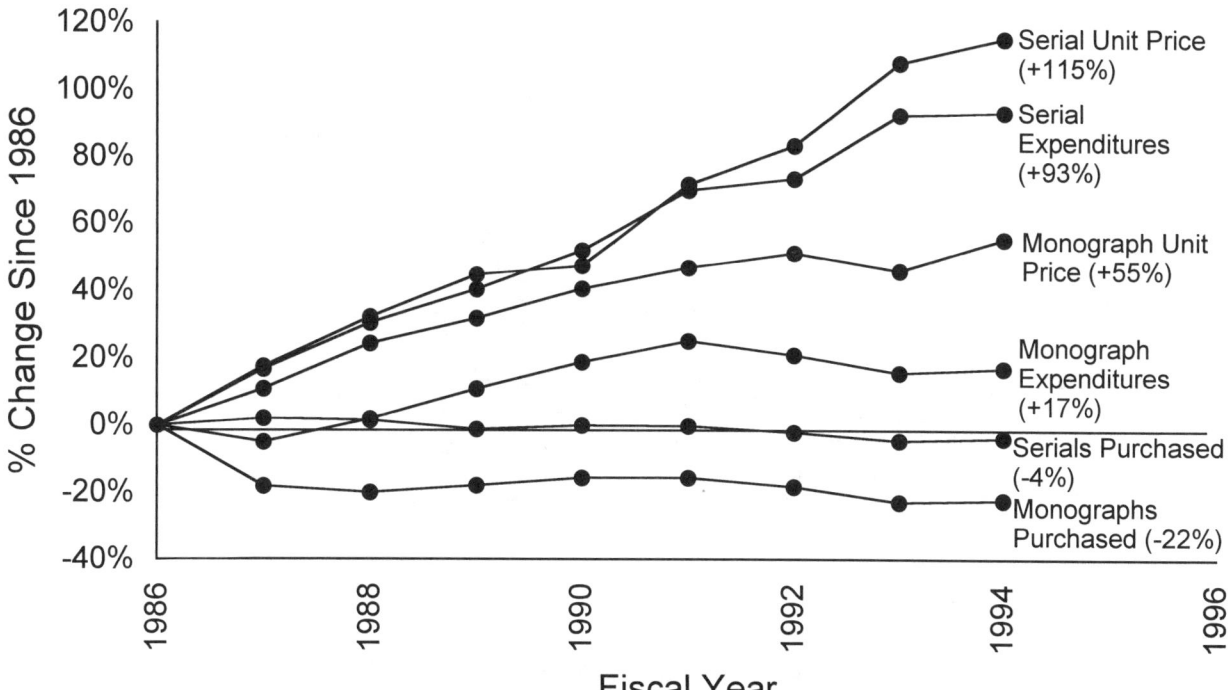

Monograph and Serial Costs in ARL Libraries, 1986-1994
Median Values for Time-Series Trends

Year (No. of Libraries)	Serial Unit Price (45)	Serial Expenditures (103)	Monograph Unit Price (64)	Monograph Expenditures (99)	Serials Purchased (45)	Monographs Purchased (64)
1986	$88.81	$1,517,724	$28.65	$1,120,645	16,198	33,210
1987	$104.30	$1,770,567	$31.76	$1,064,484	16,518	27,214
1988	$117.25	$1,979,604	$35.63	$1,141,226	16,443	26,541
1989	$128.47	$2,130,162	$37.74	$1,241,133	16,015	27,268
1990	$130.81	$2,304,744	$40.26	$1,330,747	16,182	27,999
1991	$152.43	$2,578,309	$42.04	$1,400,738	16,149	28,027
1992	$162.72	$2,630,827	$43.31	$1,353,865	15,846	27,158
1993	$184.71	$2,919,756	$41.78	$1,295,807	15,463	25,583
1994	$191.13	$2,932,091	$44.51	$1,309,807	15,583	25,803
Annual average percent change	10.1%	8.6%	5.7%	2.0%	-0.5%	-3.1%

Source: *ARL Statistics* 1991-92.
(Prepared by Kendon Stubbs)

Figures 4-5

Resources per Student in ARL Libraries, 1986-1994

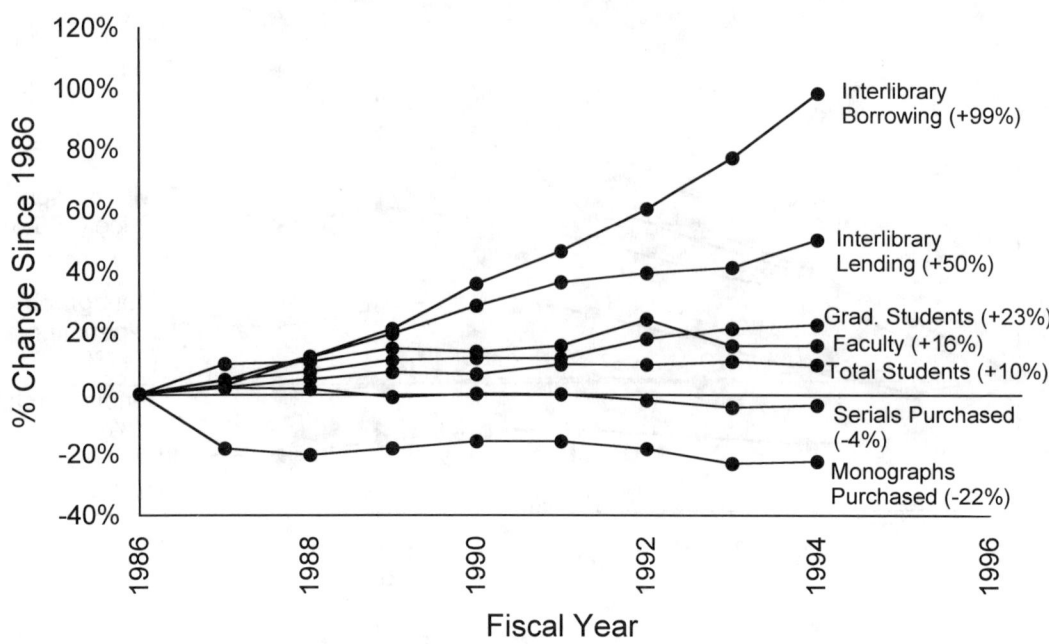

Supply and Demand in ARL Libraries, 1986-1994

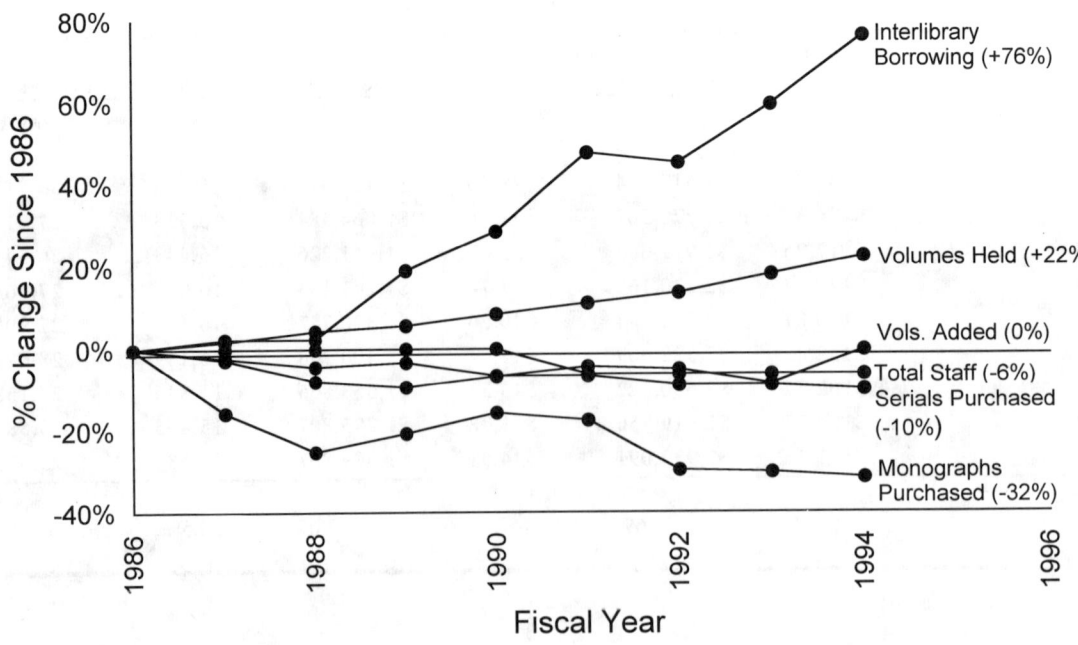

Source: *ARL Statistics* 1991-92.
(Prepared by Kendon Stubbs)

Information Technology and the Transformation of the University
Keynote Address
David P. Roselle
President
University of Delaware

David P. Roselle is currently President of the University of Delaware. He received his doctorate from Duke University and is a mathematician. Prior to coming to the University of Delaware, Dr. Roselle served on the faculties of the University of Maryland, Louisiana State University, Virginia Tech and the University of Kentucky. He served in the administration of Virginia Tech and the University of Kentucky as Provost and President, respectively.

Keynote speaker David P. Roselle described the several problems he faced when he took over the presidency of the University of Delaware in 1990. The University was in an economic downturn with many priorities competing for limited fiscal resources. Dr. Roselle presented a case study in the technological and economic transformation of his institution. He discussed the process of priority setting and decision making to determine the University's strategic choices and guiding principles, including the decision to "weave electronic resources into the fabric of campus life." He then used the example of student services to detail the steps involved in reengineering all aspects of these critical functions to take advantage of technological investments, make life easier for students, and allow the university to provide more service with fewer staff.

Dr. Roselle did not make his presentation available for the conference proceedings. Instead, he encourages use of the resources posted to the network by the University of Delaware <URL:http://www.udel.edu/>. (See Figure 1.)

Figure 1

Blue Hen Welcome Center
First Stop | Admissions | Alumni | The Electronic Campus | Conference Centers |

Learning and Research
Colleges | Libraries | Honors Program | Research Centers | Special Programs | Handbooks | Continuing Education | *More*

Campus Life
Campus Events | Athletics | Faculty and Staff | Students | Dining | Housing | Fitness | UD News | *More*

Offices and Services
Career Services | Technology | Employee Information | Central Stores | Student Services | Budget | Registrar | *More*

Adding Information to U-Discover!

University of Delaware WWW Style Guide

Please direct questions to www@udel.edu
URL of this document: http://www.udel.edu/
Last updated: May 20, 1996

Copyright © University of Delaware, 1996.

The University of Delaware is an Equal Opportunity Institution

Costs and Benefits of Investments in Technology: How Can Technology Serve the Public Interest?
Keynote Address
Mario Morino
President
The Morino Institute

Mario Morino is Chairman of the Morino Foundation and the Morino Institute, both not-for-profit organizations he founded to help people and communities find and cultivate ways in which the tools of the communication age can be used to benefit society, empower individuals, and create opportunity. He serves on the Board of Trustees of Case Western Reserve University and the National Learning Center, is a member of the Advisory Council to the National Infrastructure Campaign, the University of Virginia Institute for Advanced Technology in the Humanities, and the Medical Care for Children's Partnership.

Mr. Morino's career spans some 30 years as a business leader, entrepreneur, educator, and philanthropist. He is one of the leading experts on information technology. Following tenures with General Motors, Eaton Manufacturing, and the Bureau of Naval Personnel, Mr. Morino conceived and developed a suite of systems management software products that would become the foundation for Morino Associates, the company he founded in 1973. He led that company through many years of expansion, two successful mergers, a host of acquisitions, and one name change to become the Legent Corporation. When he retired in 1992, Legent had become one of the world's largest software companies and now enjoys revenues in excess of $500 million with worldwide presence. Mr. Morino remains active in the commercial sector as an investor and advisor to emerging information technology businesses.

Mario Morino challenged participants to think that the "unimaginable not only can happen, but will happen." He believes that higher education has priced itself out of the marketplace, and is now undergoing the wrenching and painful change that has been transforming banking and many corporations for the past twenty years. Mr. Morino feels that the sociological changes we are experiencing may be the most interesting aspect of the communications revolution, because the relationship between individuals and institutions are changing dramatically. Network communications have shifted the locus of information control from organizations to individuals.

Mr. Morino asked the audience to think about revenue recomposition and about where the revenue of our organizations will be coming from in ten years. Who will our customers be and what will they be willing to pay for? How can we create a culture that is adaptive to change and flexible enough to take advantage of opportunities in a rapidly changing environment? We must change our organizations and institutions into value-added, rather than transition pass-through organizations and institutions. And we must do this at a time when competition from the corporate sector challenges the very survival of many research universities and their libraries. Mr. Morino cautioned: "We will never again control information. We will have to think." He left the audience with much to think about.

Mr. Morino made the following overheads from his presentation available for the conference proceedings.

Figures 1-6

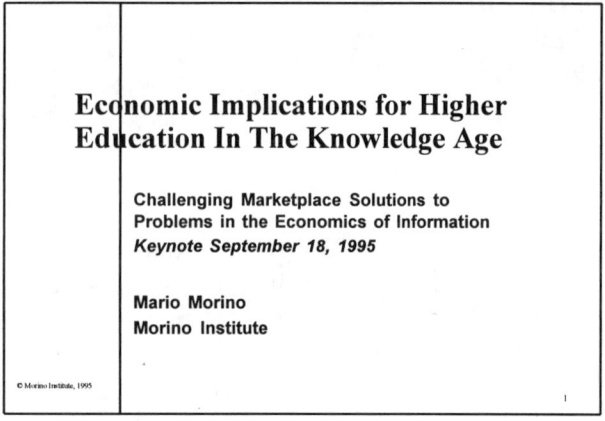

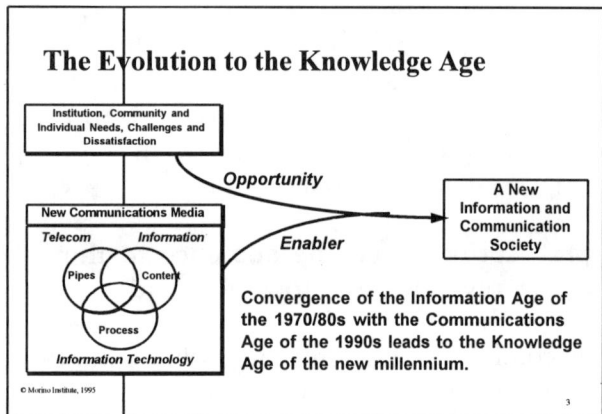

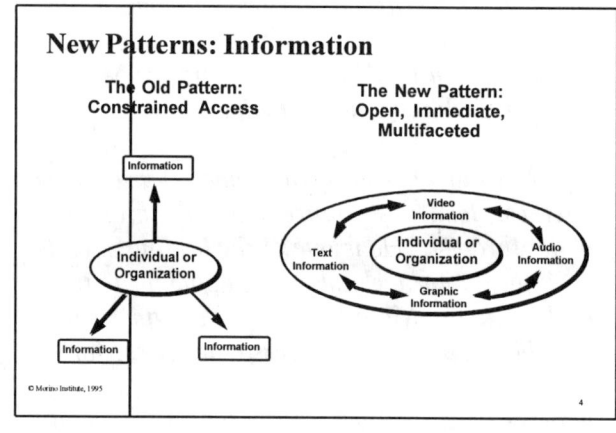

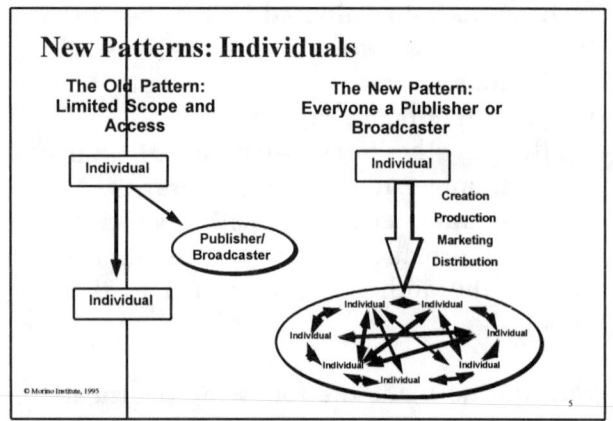

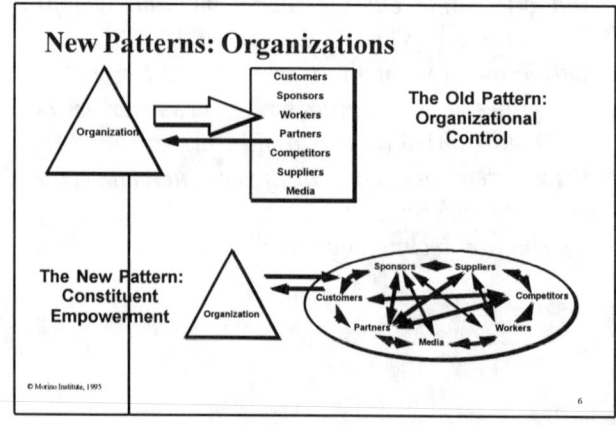

Figures 7-12

Higher Education's Changing Stakeholders

- Suppliers > Faculty and Staff
- Customers > Students, Alumni, Neighbors
- Competitors > Other education providers
- Shareholders > Boards, Alumni, Government

Dramatic Change for People, Organizations and Society

- Economic shifts
- Disintermediation
- Leveling of hierarchies
- Blurring of authority
- Revitalized learning
- Redefinition of core competencies
- Individual empowerment

The Most Profound Change: Opening the Doors of Knowledge and Opportunity

"The knowledge society will inevitably become far more competitive than any society we have yet known—for the simple reason that with knowledge being universally accessible, there will be no excuses for nonperformance."

Peter F. Drucker

The Future of Knowledge Institutions in the Knowledge Age

- Opportunity or threat?
- Evolution or transformation?
- Intellectual asset ownership or pass through?

Change comes hardest to those who have the deepest traditions.

The Transforming Effects On Institutions

- Institutional communication truly becomes a strategic imperative
- Recognition of knowledge as an asset, information as the raw materials
- A redefinition of distribution
- Managing a wired organization
- New potential for collaborative process
- New order of competitiveness

How to Respond?

- Innovate new ways to deliver education and advance research
- Continue to reduce costs
- Increase tuition, research funding
- Increase capital contributions
- Defray costs and increase opportunity through partnerships
- Seek alternative income sources
- Balance long and short term benefits

Figures 13-18

Production and Delivery

How will higher education move from low volume and high cost constructs to high volume and low cost?

A Changing Culture

How will higher education develop a culture that is adaptive to change and more competitive with external forces?

The Mortar or the Network

Where will future investments in higher education have their greatest return and create the most value?

Institutional Independence

Will educational institutions become hubs of larger cooperatives as has happened in the healthcare industry?

A New Core Competency

Will demand-based learning redefine the role and need for certain sectors of higher education?

A New Research Environment

Will research become more directed, controlled and results-driven as the shift from government to private industry funding continues?

Figures 19-23

Global Competition

How will we transform our academic culture to compete against multinational education corporations and the tightly-linked academic/business partnerships more common in other parts of the world?

The Unimaginable

Which corporation will be the first to acquire a university and all of its inherent intellectual capital?

Change Is No Longer a Debate

- Non-participation is not an option
- Each day on the sideline is one more day of obsolescence
- The cost of falling behind is too severe
- Keeping up is difficult, even for the pacesetters

Prepare Your Institutions

- Recognize that this change is occurring now
- Focus on the issues and applications, not the technology
- Recognize the new competitive landscape
- Assess the implications for your institutions
- Establish an adaptive, learning, collaborative culture
- Create incentives for innovation
- Imagine new possibilities

Seize The Opportunity

"I was struck by what a remarkable time 1890 must have been for the new institutions that were being founded and for the colleges that suddenly found themselves being turned into universities. But I also thought—and I believe it more strongly now—that 100 years later we may be experiencing the beginning of another revolution."

Donald Kennedy
President Emeritus
Stanford University

Part II
The Andrew W. Mellon Foundation's Program in the Economics of Information

JSTOR and the Economics of Scholarly Communication[1]

William G. Bowen
President
The Andrew W. Mellon Foundation

I am delighted to have this opportunity to describe "JSTOR" (our acronym for "journal storage"). This denizen of the world of electronic databases began life as one of several demonstration projects funded by The Andrew W. Mellon Foundation, moved rapidly from infancy to adolescence, and now enjoys an independent existence, having been incorporated as a separate nonprofit entity within the last few months.

Background: A Brief History and A Summary of Objectives

In its original incarnation, JSTOR was conceived to be an electronic database containing "faithful replications" of all pre-1990 issues of ten core scholarly journals in the fields of economics and history (including the *American Economic Review* and the *American Historical Review*). While the Foundation's long-term interests in the field of scholarly communications are broad, in this instance we wanted very much to be practical and to test concepts and general approaches by working with a manageable set of well-defined materials within a circumscribed terrain. Hence, the narrow definition of the initial content of JSTOR.

In creating JSTOR, we set out to serve three objectives simultaneously: (1) to improve dramatically access to journal literature for faculty, students, and other scholars by linking bitmapped images of journal pages to a powerful search engine; (2) to mitigate some of the vexing economic problems of libraries by easing storage problems (thereby saving prospective capital costs involved in building more shelf space), and also by reducing operating costs associated with retrieving back issues and reshelving them; and (3) to address issues of conservation and preservation such as broken runs, mutilated pages, and long-term deterioration of paper copy.

I will not take time to explain why we chose to start with the fields of economics and history (or the ten specific journals with which we are working), but I will anticipate another frequently asked question: why did JSTOR initially include in its database only issues of journals published before 1990? Why were current issues excluded? In making the decision to focus on back issues, we knew that we were swimming against the proverbial tide and "challenging marketplace solutions" (or at least assumptions). Consistent with Willy Sutton's explanation of why it was banks that he chose to rob, most publishers and other vendors have been interested primarily in current issues because "that's where the money is." Current issues generate revenue streams; back issues rarely do.

Since it is "contrarian," our emphasis on back issues has surprised many people. Early on, we explained our plans to the head of one widely known commercial enterprise, who was quick to comment: "No sane person would do what you propose." We were undeterred. We thought that we had an opportunity, and perhaps even an obligation, to make upfront investments that could have long-term social value for the scholarly community at large. Unlike commercial entities, the test of success for us is not any "bottom line," but how well we facilitate teaching and scholarship by improving the mechanisms of scholarly communication.

At the same time, we recognize that such broad statements of good intentions often mean little—as one of my friends likes to put it, "good intentions randomize behavior."[2] Fiscal discipline is needed, and we have always believed that JSTOR would have to be self-sustaining eventually. Perpetual subsidy is both unrealistic and unwise: projects of this kind must make economic sense once they are up and running. If users and beneficiaries, broadly defined, are unwilling to cover the costs, one should wonder about the utility of the enterprise. In this important respect, we *are* strong believers in "market-place solutions"—provided that what the economist calls "externalities" can be captured.

Given our objectives, there were strong pragmatic reasons for focusing on back issues. After all, they comprise that part of the journal literature that is: (a) least readily accessible; (b) most in need of preservation; and (c) most avaricious in its consumption of stack space (our ten journals run to some 750,000 pages). Also, from our perspective, the fact that back files do not generate much revenue for publishers has been a plus, not a minus. To launch this project, we needed to obtain copyright permissions, and we knew that this would be much easier if the project offered no threat to basic revenue streams. We wanted to work in concert with publishers as well as with libraries, to advance the common interests of both. It is only by adopting what might be called a "system-wide" perspective, which recognizes the legitimate needs of *both* the providers of scholarly materials and their users, that socially optimal arrangements can be put in place.

Let me now summarize a great many intervening developments in relatively few words. First, following much discussion, we were able to obtain copyright permissions from all ten journals to bitmap their back issues. Second, we arranged for colleagues at the University of Michigan (working closely with Ira Fuchs, Chief Scientist of JSTOR) to oversee the technical aspects of the project. Third, we selected several liberal arts colleges to serve as test sites, along with the University of Michigan. If all goes according to plan (almost too much to hope!), the full back files of four of the ten journals will be accessible at these test sites very shortly, and the remaining journals will be available by the end of the year.

Characteristics of the Archival "Product" (or "Scholarly Tool")[3]

In getting to this point, we made several key decisions about the archival "product" that deserve to be highlighted.

• First, we elected to set a high bitmapping standard of 600 dots per inch. The objective was to produce images of exceptional clarity, with every shading, every subscript in every equation, and every figure or photograph clearly visible. In short, we wanted to create something of archival quality, with print-outs so good that readers would regard these copies as equivalent to the originals—and superior in many instances to yellowed or soiled pages. This objective is being achieved, and we have sample pages for those of you interested in seeing them.

• Second, we decided to create and include in the electronic file a searchable Table-of-Contents Index. This feature permits readers to obtain bibliographic references to all articles, book reviews, and other components of the database by a specified author, containing a key word or words in their title (such as "Council of Economic Advisors" or "human capital"), or published in a certain journal or in some particular set of years—and then to call up the articles themselves on the screen.

• Third, although the user will see only page images on the screen, this database is linked to a text file created using Optical Character Recognition (OCR) software that will enable users to search not only the Table-of-Contents Index but also the actual text pages of all the journals. Specifications provide that the OCR-version of the text will be accurate at the 99.95 percent level; in other words, it will contain no more than one error in 2,000 characters.

• Fourth, our colleagues at Michigan have joined these elements to a sophisticated search engine that allows the entire database to be accessed online, via Internet connections, by authorized users. This online feature has obvious advantages, including both ease of access and the minimization of storage problems for libraries (since the database is stored centrally). The software also includes Printer Applications for MACs and PCs which permit authorized users to print exceptionally high resolution copies of pages or entire articles at their terminals.

In seeking to translate these concepts into actual electronic files, progress has been slower than envisioned in our original schedule—which, we admit, was aggressive, to say the least. The firm responsible for the bitmapping and OCR work, and our friends at Michigan responsible for technical aspects of the project, have encountered all (it seems like *all*) of the inevitable problems associated with creating a new tool of this complexity. Still, we expect the back files of four of the ten journals to be up and running at the test sites very shortly. By now there has been enough preliminary experience with parts of the database, and enough "demos," to convince us that JSTOR is real, and to give solid grounds for believing that it will perform as advertised.

Linking Current Issues to the Archive

In the last few months, as work on the Archive of back issues has proceeded, we have given a great deal of thought to the place of current issues in this project. Here again we decided to start out with a highly specific application from which it might be possible to generalize. Fortunately, the Ecological Society of America (ESA) expressed strong interest in being our initial partner in this undertaking, and the Society and JSTOR have now signed an agreement that provides for linking electronic formats of current issues of the Society's publications (including their main journal, *Ecology*) to complete electronic archives of these same journals.[4]

In principle, such an approach has great appeal. From the standpoint of users, there are obvious advantages in being able to search simultaneously the entire run of a journal, from the most recent issues back to the earliest ones, using common software ("beach erosion on New Jersey coasts" is one searchable subject that comes immediately to mind!). For both users and libraries, this approach would solve the problem of how the historical archive is to be updated, since updating would occur annually and automatically if linking were achieved. Also, some libraries might conclude that it was unnecessary to retain hard copies of current issues at their main location (or even to receive them in the first place), thereby achieving considerable savings in binding and processing costs, as well as relieving them of the burdens of storing, preserving, and retrieving paper copies of these journals from what can be expensive stack space.

Attractive as the basic approach may be, seeking to achieve this kind of linkage raises issues that are both technical and economic. Putting the technical issues to one side (since, in any case, I am not competent to discuss them), the economic challenge is to forge a structure and a plan that will simultaneously: (a) provide faculty, students, and other interested readers with dramatically improved access to journal literature at fair prices; (b) protect the publisher's revenue streams and membership rolls; (c) help control the operating and capital costs of libraries; and (d) generate sufficient revenue to allow JSTOR to create, maintain, and update the database and the controlling software over the long run. The pricing and other issues implicit in this formulation would have to be faced even if we continued to work only with back issues; it is better, we are now persuaded, to confront them directly in the context of linking current issues to back issues, since the advantages of this approach are so manifest.

After much discussion, we decided to focus on creating and distributing two distinct but complementary products: an electronic version of "Current Issues" (say, those published within the last calendar or fiscal year, but the cut-off could be pushed back to encompass the last two or three years); and an electronic Archive of all other issues. Under the arrangements we have been considering, the ESA, as publisher, would continue to be responsible for editing and publishing Current Issues and for determining the subscription prices and other terms (including restrictions on access) associated with sales of subscriptions to libraries and individuals. The ESA would also provide JSTOR with electronic source materials for Current Issues. JSTOR, in turn, would: (a) cover many of the upfront costs of launching this venture; (b) create an historical Archive according to the specifications stated earlier, which JSTOR would make available at appropriate fees to libraries and individuals; and (c) develop an electronic mechanism for linking Current Issues to the Archive and updating it each year.

Pricing and Controls Over Access

No decisions have been made concerning pricing and controls over access, but I can outline our provisional thinking:

• The ESA might offer library and individual subscribers the electronic version of Current Issues at roughly the same price it now charges for the paper version (assuming that subscribers chose to take one or the other—there could be a substantial discount for subscribing to both). The ESA will have to decide whether it wishes to offer "site licenses" (which would permit the institution to make the database available on a campus network) or only "library licenses" (which would restrict access to locations within the library system and perhaps in departmental offices as well).

• With regard to the Archive, we anticipate that JSTOR would ask libraries to make two types of payment for access: (a) a one-time capital charge for acquisition of permanent rights to the base Archive; and (b) an annual fee to cover the recurring costs of maintaining and updating the database and associated software. The one-time charge would be related to the amount of material in the Archive and would be significantly lower than the costs associated with storing and maintaining the equivalent set of materials in paper. Hypothetically, this charge might be set at, say, a penny or two a page. The annual charge would probably also be related to the size of the base Archive and to whether the library wanted new material added each year. It might be in the $25-$35 range for a journal such as *Ecology* and would certainly be significantly less than the recurring costs of processing, binding, storing, and retrieving new as well as old issues. Alternatively, JSTOR might offer libraries the option of combining the capital and annual charges into a single stream of "lease payments."

- We anticipate that JSTOR would also offer individual subscribers direct access to the Archive (so that they would not have to depend on their home institution making access available on a campus network). Charges to individuals could be very modest (for example, perhaps $10/year in the case of *Ecology*). Every dollar contributed by individuals would represent additional revenues for "the system" and would lessen the financial burdens on publishers and libraries, thereby reducing the risk that electronic publication might lead to substantial cost-shifting from individual subscribers to institutions.[5]

I want to emphasize again that these are initial thoughts and purely illustrative numbers. No commitments or decisions have been made by anyone. But I thought it would be easier for you to think with us about the prospects for JSTOR if we gave you some hypothetical reference points that had dollar signs attached to them.

Could this kind of model work economically? What levels of charges would be required for JSTOR to break even? Since there are tremendous economies of scale involved in creating and distributing a new electronic tool of this kind, much depends on the interest demonstrated by libraries and individuals. Our *guess* (it is nothing more than that) is that at least half of the current subscribers—libraries and individuals—would elect to participate. Under that assumption, and making another set of guesses concerning costs, we think that the project is viable. But no one can know for sure. The proposed collaboration between JSTOR and ESA is avowedly an experiment—the first of its kind, we believe—and much fine-tuning will surely be required, along with a willingness by all parties to admit mistakes and make adjustments on the basis of experience.

As at least partial protection against the risks associated with ignorance, we have developed a mechanism that should provide reasonable safeguards for all concerned. Our starting point is the concept of a partnership. Since the proposed experiment is a novel one, and no one can predict with confidence either costs or revenue streams, we are contemplating an "upside" sharing of any "Net Funds Available" that remain after costs have been covered. Also, while experience is so limited (nonexistent, really), we plan to provide a "downside" protection for the ESA and perhaps a small number of other publishers that choose to cast their lot with JSTOR in its earliest days. JSTOR might guarantee a publisher such as ESA that, for a period of two years, its gross subscription revenue would not fall below an agreed base level because of any declines in individual subscriptions attributable to the experiment.

The "upside" sharing might involve a commitment by JSTOR to rebate half of any "Net Funds Available" to the publisher and another one-quarter to participating libraries. JSTOR might itself retain the remaining one-quarter for development purposes. By committing itself in advance to give rebates to both publishers and libraries out of any "Net Funds Available," JSTOR protects everyone against the risk that any one party would benefit disproportionately. At the same time, since it is understood that JSTOR must be self-sustaining, charges would have to be renegotiated if JSTOR's revenues were insufficient to cover its costs. We believe the partnership concept to be the best—and perhaps only—way of handling the uncertainties inherent in a new initiative of this kind.

As a nonprofit entity, JSTOR is not permitted by law to accumulate funds beyond its legitimate needs, and, in any case, would have no interest in doing so. Its sole purpose is to serve the scholarly community by increasing the availability of scholarly journals and enhancing their usefulness, while concurrently reducing library costs. For this reason, the posture of JSTOR differs fundamentally from that of commercial vendors. In creating the "founding" board of Trustees of JSTOR, care was taken to assemble a group of individuals who would be known and trusted by the scholarly community—in part to assure credibility from the outset.[6]

Institutional Subscribers: Libraries and Campus Networks

Let us now consider in more detail how the economics of JSTOR might work for institutional subscribers. Conversations with a number of presidents, provosts, and librarians have persuaded us that there is considerable interest in the historical Archive (setting aside, for the moment, the question of linkages to Current Issues). We anticipate that, as one person put it, faculty and students will find JSTOR "irresistible" and will urge their institutions to acquire this resource. In addition to creating new search capacities, JSTOR solves one of the most vexing problems faced by readers and librarians alike—the unavailability of a particular volume because someone else is using it, it has been misfiled, the library is closed, and so on. JSTOR provides predictable access to multiple users at every hour of every day (assuming the continuing cooperation of the gods of cyberspace).

The positive case for acquiring this valuable new scholarly resource will be convincing across a broad spectrum of institutions, including:

(1) large research universities with faculty and graduate students who make considerable use of back issues and expect to have at their disposal the most up-to-date mode of access, even though their library may already have all of the back issues in paper format, available in open stacks;

(2) libraries using a closed-stack system that requires retrieving and reshelving large numbers of journals by staff members; and

(3) the many colleges and universities, in this country and abroad, that lack complete files of back issues in paper format.

For this last set of institutions, JSTOR offers a unique opportunity to acquire complete runs of journals, in pristine condition, for a small fraction (perhaps 10 percent) of the cost of acquiring paper copies—and without having to incur all the associated costs of building and maintaining library space. To illustrate, if JSTOR were able to offer the Archive at a one-time capital charge of as little as one or two cents per page, an institution with limited library resources could obtain the entire back file of *Ecology*, from 1921 through 1994, for something like $750 to $1,500 (there are 77,000 pages). What a bargain!

In other situations, where the back issues of *Ecology* are already available in paper format, JSTOR allows the library to save valuable shelf space on the campus by moving the back issues off campus or, in some instances, by discarding the paper issues altogether. (The natural fear of "losing something" will be minimized if, as we expect, arrangements are made for regional collections of paper copies. As another "fail-safe" mechanism, JSTOR would be able to provide CD-ROMs.)

What are these savings in storage costs worth? Much depends, of course, on local circumstances. Utilizing a methodology devised by Malcolm Getz and cost data assembled by Michael Cooper, we estimate that the one-time capital costs for storing a single volume of a journal in open stacks, excluding the cost of land (hardly negligible for libraries in major metropolitan areas, such as New York), to be anywhere from $24 to $41.[7] It follows that the capital costs associated with storing the complete

76-volume run of *Ecology* could range from $1,800 to $3,100. This cost is roughly twice the hypothetical capital charge for *both acquisition and storage* of the JSTOR electronic Archive. One key reason for this large disparity is that JSTOR centralizes the storage function at off-site locations while retaining all the advantages of browsing and providing readers with more or less instant access.

There also appear to be large savings in operating costs associated with the "circulation" function—retrieving and then reshelving paper copies of journals. The New York Public Library (NYPL), which is a non-circulating closed-stack library, reports that it spends an average of $1.94 to retrieve and reshelve a journal volume. We recognize that costs in New York will be higher than average and that closed-stack libraries are more expensive to operate from this standpoint than open-stack libraries. Michael Cooper has estimated the staff-only costs of circulation from open stacks in the University of California-San Diego library to be roughly $.60 per volume.[8] Of course, as Cooper, Getz, and others who have written on this subject recognize, open-stack systems save operating costs by, in effect, relying on users to do much of the "leg work" involved in retrieving volumes. The time-costs for users are of course considerable, and dwarf staff-only costs.[9]

We cannot hope today to be at all precise in suggesting the right figures, and we certainly do not want to exaggerate the potential savings; but it seems reasonable (actually very conservative) to use $1.00/retrieval as a reference point—*half* the actual cost incurred by NYPL. The implications of using even this modest figure are staggering. As part of the research associated with the introduction of JSTOR, staff at the University of Michigan have tallied usage on their campus of the ten economics and history journals in their paper formats. Also, we have surveyed experiences at the five college test sites. Weighting each institution equally (and thus giving the much heavier usage at Michigan only one-sixth the overall weight), we find that library users request volumes from each of these core journals an average of 45 times per year (the comparable average at the University of Michigan considered separately is 180 times per year). Using the cost figure of $1 per volume, the annual cost of circulation is estimated to average $45 per journal for this set of six schools and $180 per journal at the University of Michigan. These estimates should probably be doubled for libraries which operate like The New York Public Library.

In addition, use of paper copies involves recurring costs of preservation and conservation. The way library patrons use this literature, often spreading bound volumes on copy machines, subjects the paper to substantial wear and tear. Older journals must be mended, deacidified, and sometimes rebound. While electronic archives are not subject to these "handling" costs, they do entail costs of other kinds—especially maintaining computer equipment and answering questions posed by users. We expect to estimate these expenditures at our test sites this fall, but we find it hard to imagine that they can be close to comparable to the operating costs associated with paper formats.

Libraries participating in JSTOR might be able to lower their on-going costs even more if the historical Archive were linked to an electronic version of Current Issues. Acquisition and processing costs, estimated by one university librarian to be more than $20 per journal, would be substantially reduced. Also, it would no longer be necessary to bind individual issues into volumes, a process that can cost anywhere from $15 to $30 depending upon how one allocates the staff costs associated with preparing the journals for the bindery.

We recognize that we are enthusiasts, and no doubt our excitement about "our child" should be discounted somewhat. Still, the purely economic case for JSTOR, seen from the perspective of the institution, seems overwhelming. The highly favorable economics are driven by powerful scale effects, since JSTOR permits tasks (especially storage and retrieval) that are now done repetitively at thousands of libraries to be done once—centrally—and to be done far more effectively, as well as at much lower cost. Combining capital and operating costs, and expressing both on an annual basis, we estimate that the continuing costs of storing, retrieving, conserving, processing, and binding one journal, such as *Ecology*, in paper format are at least twice (and perhaps three times) greater than what they would be if the library contracted with JSTOR to provide what we are convinced would be far superior access.[10]

Figure 1

The Costs of Storing, Retrieving, Conserving, Processing and Binding Paper Journals

Assumptions
Typical core journal: *Ecology*
First year of publication: 1921; Number of Volumes: 77

Cost Description	Annual Cost for *Ecology*
Costs associated with Back Issues:	
Storage (@$3.07 per volume)*	$236
Circulation (average usage of 45 requests per year)**	$ 45
Conservation and preservation***	$ 5
Annual costs for the archived journal literature	$286
Costs associated with Current Issues:	
Processing and check in***	$ 20
Binding***	$ 20
Circulation****	$ 45
Annual cost for current issues	$ 85
Total annual costs	**$371**

*Combining Getz's methodology and Cooper's construction costs from four different locations in California gives a range of storage costs of $21 to $41, an average of approximately $30. Using Getz's amortization assumptions of a 25-year life and a 7% discount rate yields an annual cost of $2.57. Adding Getz's annual maintenance and utilities costs of $5 per square foot adds $0.50 per volume, for a total of $3.07.

**For pre-1990 issues, from a survey of six libraries participating in JSTOR. The $1 per retrieval assumption is explained in the text.

***Figures for conservation, processing and binding are estimates based on informal discussions with librarians.

****This figure for the circulation costs for current issues is nothing more than a guess. Our assumption is that there are just as many requests for issues from the most recent five years as for the many years of issues prior to 1990.

Individual Subscribers

How would an individual subscriber gain access to either the electronic version of Current Issues or to the electronic Archive? Our presumption is that, in both instances, individual subscribers would be given PIN numbers which would entitle them to access the database from any location. "Personal" access would be restricted to those individuals who had PIN numbers. Of course, those individuals who work on campuses that have purchased site licenses for the Archive and/or for Current Issues might have a reduced incentive to take out individual subscriptions. They would no longer have to trek to the library to browse; they could use the campus network.

This "fact of life" in an electronic world is a legitimate source of concern to the publishers of journals with significant numbers of individual subscribers and to professional associations that link membership to the provision of journals. At the same time, it is easy to exaggerate the risks. Apart from the power of inertia (not to be underestimated), publishers need to recognize that by no means all individual subscribers will have ready access to JSTOR files by means of a campus network. Many will not. In addition, publishers could consider giving individual subscribers "something extra," and a number of creative ideas have already been proposed.

At present, of course, individual subscribers have no personal access to any historical Archive except in those situations in which they happen to have accumulated an entire back run of a journal in their office or home. (And, as one colleague observed, it should be easy to demonstrate that a full run of even a few core journals in a field such as economics or history could "bury someone alive in his/her office—perhaps even before the person got tenure.") Since, in almost all instances, individuals must go to the library to peruse back issues, we expect the availability of an electronic Archive to be exceedingly attractive to a number of individual faculty members, who might well be willing to pay a modest annual charge (say, $10) for personal access.

We also suspect that there will be strong synergies between purchase of electronic access to Current Issues and purchase of electronic access to the Archive—which would be regularly updated if the individual subscribed to both. For this reason, demand for individual subscriptions might actually increase, rather than decrease, as a result of JSTOR. If it proves possible to include several core journals from a field (or sub-field) in JSTOR, the appeal of electronic access to a "collection" might be greater yet. We just do not know anything, at this stage, about the elasticity of demand for what would be a totally new scholarly tool. This is an important subject for future research, as experience begins to accumulate. Also to repeat the presence of such large unknowns is strong justification for the "partnership" concept, whereby the interests of publishers, libraries, and JSTOR are aligned.

Broader Considerations

The behavioral consequences of JSTOR (and other initiatives of a similar kind) also deserve careful thought. One question of great interest is how JSTOR will affect patterns of research and teaching. Our assumption is that dramatic improvements in ease of access, combined with the advantages of a powerful search engine, will cause students and faculty alike to make more use of back issues than they do today. We are told, and anecdotes abound, that students sometimes fill papers with what they perceive to be their quota of citations by relying heavily on recent literature, since current issues of journals are easier to find and use than back issues. Yet it would surely be better if all of us—students, faculty and research staff alike—were able to mine the full range of scholarly literature with less difficulty than present arrangements impose. For instance, one would hope that students writing about the end of World War II would consult articles written by scholars in the immediate postwar years to gain a sense of how the world looked then, rather than relying on more recent compilations of opinion. Similarly, current discussions of welfare reform might be helped by more study of writings in the 1930s about the New Deal.

Thinking about JSTOR also causes this observer to consider a number of aspects of budgeting and decision-making in higher education:

• First, JSTOR emphasizes the importance of considering various budget categories together when making allocation decisions. Specifically, capital costs, which are often neglected by colleges and universities,[11] must be taken into account in calculating the net effects of subscribing to JSTOR. For this reason, it is important that provosts and others with campus-wide budgetary responsibilities be involved in deciding whether an institution should (or should not) start down the JSTOR path. Compartmentalized decision-making, focused solely on acquisition budgets, for example, would not permit a proper assessment of the costs and benefits of JSTOR.

• Second, JSTOR reminds us that too narrow and compartmentalized a view of economic self-interest can be harmful in other ways. For example, if libraries refuse to worry about the effects of their subscription practices (such as purchasing site licenses through consortia) on the number of individual and library subscribers, they may inadvertently inflict considerable economic harm on publishers—who may in turn respond by raising the prices of library subscriptions.[12]

• Third, JSTOR also warns us that attempting to charge for journal literature "by the drink" can lead to results that are far from optimal socially. As the just-cited article by Lieberman, Noll, and Steinmueller emphasizes, the marginal costs of including another user are exceedingly modest, and this is one reason why it is so important that the product be offered on a subscription basis. It would be undesirable, from the standpoint of resource allocation, to discourage an impecunious student from using JSTOR because of a per-use pricing model.[13]

• Fourth and last, JSTOR is unusual in that it violates the usual axiom about the importance of forcing choices between "more" and "cheaper." Let me explain. When new technologies evolve, they offer benefits that can be enjoyed either in the form of more output (including opportunities for scholars to do new things or to do them better) or in the form of cost savings. It is my experience that in universities electronic technologies have almost always led to greater output, and rarely to reduced costs. Yet, it is imperative, if tight resource constraints are to be observed, as they must be, that technological gains lead to at least some cost savings. I make this speech regularly to my colleagues at the Foundation, as well as to my one-time colleagues in academia. In the case of JSTOR, however, it is hard to press for this version of the "discipline of choice" because JSTOR offers *both* great advantages to potential users *and* cost savings.

My puritanical tendencies cause me to worry about the potentially debilitating effects of such an unlikely product on the will to choose; but I will acknowledge that it is also nice, if only occasionally, to be confronted with an opportunity to argue on behalf of an innovation that is both better *and* cheaper. At least that is what I hope that our experimentation with JSTOR will demonstrate to be the case.

As a wise friend of mine said on another occasion (when contemplating the impeachment of Richard Nixon, to give the exact situation), "We'll know more later." So we will, and the JSTOR contingent will undertake to keep all interested parties posted on what we learn (including what mistakes we make). At the same time, we encourage you to give us your suggestions and best thinking as all of us contemplate the murky but exciting future of scholarly communication in an electronic age.

---

[1] In preparing this paper I have been helped by many people, including Kevin Guthrie and Ira Fuchs of JSTOR; Richard Ekman, Dennis Sullivan, and Harriet Zuckerman of The Andrew W. Mellon Foundation; Wendy Lougee and Sarah Turner of the University of Michigan; Hal Varian of the University of California-Berkeley, Elaine Sloan and Kristine Kavanaugh of Columbia University, and William Walker and Heike Kordish at The New York Public Library.

[2] Marion J. Levy, Jr., *Ten Laws of the Disillusionment of the True Liberal*, Princeton, NJ: M.J. Levy, 1981, Law 1.

[3] Terminology is a problem. The word "product" may seem too commercial to some, and it is certainly true that our objective is the development of more than just another "widget." JSTOR is intended to be a major "scholarly tool" with benefits that extend well beyond calculations of costs and revenues that may seem mundane to some. But it is also important that lofty ambitions and high hopes not distract us from the need to provide a "product" that is economically viable.

[4] We are also having preliminary talks with representatives of organizations in other fields, including the American Economic Association and the American Mathematical Society.

[5] I am reminded of analogous issues associated with charging students to attend college. In the United States, students customarily pay tuition to offset part of the cost of their education, at the same time that public and private sources also provide subsidies. In many European countries, direct payments by students are less common (though there are still opportunity costs to be borne), and much more of the burden of paying for education falls on the state. This is one reason, I have always suspected, why the United States has been able to channel larger total amounts of resources into higher education. Dividing the costs between direct beneficiaries (students) and society at large is, I believe, both fairer and more effective as a system of educational finance than a regime which relies much more heavily on state support alone. For similar reasons, I think it makes sense to seek ways whereby individual subscribers can make *some* contribution to the costs of JSTOR—provided that the effect is not to discourage access to the database by impecunious users. There are pricing and access mechanisms which can work to serve both objectives in a balanced way.

[6] The Founding Trustees of JSTOR include: Richard De Gennaro, Librarian of Harvard College; Mary Patterson McPherson, President of Bryn Mawr College; Cathleen Morawetz, Professor of Mathematics, New York University, and President of the American Mathematical Society; W. Taylor Reveley III, Partner, Hunton and Williams, and Trustee of The Andrew W. Mellon Foundation as well as of other nonprofits; Gilbert Whitaker, retired Provost of the University of Michigan and Professor of Business at Michigan; Elton White, former President of the NCR computer company and Trustee of Berea College. The author of this paper, William G. Bowen, also serves on the board of JSTOR (as its chairman) to ensure continuity.

[7] See Malcolm Getz, "Storing Information in Academic Libraries," mimeo, October 17, 1994; and Michael Cooper, "A Cost Comparison of Alternative Book Storage Strategies," *Library Quarterly*, vol. 59, no. 3 [1989], pp. 239-260. Getz postulates that shelving 10 volumes per square foot is typical for bound volumes of serials (as contrasted with 12 volumes per square foot for monographs). Since Cooper's data for construction costs pertain to the late 1980s, we have assumed (conservatively) that costs have risen 15 percent in the interim. As Getz, Cooper, and many others explain, construction costs are *much* lower for other types of shelving, but then browsing capabilities are sacrificed and circulation costs increase dramatically. Open stack shelving is most comparable to JSTOR, and even then JSTOR remains much more convenient to use.

[8] Cooper, 1989, pp. 251-252. Cooper's figures are for the late 1980s, and, again, we have raised his figure of $.53 to $.60 to adjust very roughly for inflation since then.

[9] Cooper estimates user costs at roughly three times staff-only costs, or about $1.80 per volume; Getz suggests a figure of $4 for the time-only costs to the user of retrieving a volume.

[10] Our calculations are summarized in Figure 1. The estimates are based in part on methodology suggested by Getz, including his assumptions for amortizing capital costs (25-year life, 7 percent discount rate). Some of the components of these estimates are rough (especially the figure for average circulation of journals from 1990 forward). Still, the overall level of costs seems reasonable and is, we believe, conservative.

For *Ecology*, these annual costs would appear to be in the range of $350 to $400 for our test-site libraries. (The comparable estimate for a large research library such as Michigan would be much higher because of greater circulation and thus greater retrieval costs.) In all likelihood, JSTOR would be able to provide the electronic database described here for one-third to one-half as much.

Richard Lemberg at St. Mary's College, Moraga, California has done a most elaborate and most impressive study of the potential cost savings nationally of digitizing "non-unique" materials already owned by libraries. See Lemberg's Ph.D. thesis, submitted to the University of California-Berkeley.

[11] See Gordon C. Winston's call for "global accounting" and his examination of the importance of capital costs in the setting of a liberal arts college. *The Capital Costs Conundrum*, NACUBO Business Officer, June 1993.

[12] See Lisa Lieberman, Roger Noll, and W. Edward Steinmueller, "The Sources of Scientific Journal Price Increase," mimeo, March 23, 1992, which lays out very well the basic economic characteristics of this unusual industry: high fixed costs (the importance of "first-copy cost" for journal publishers), the forces making for proliferation of journals, declining circulation, and its attendant impact on subscription rates. This pattern leads to a socially undesirable and economically inefficient widening of the spread between the marginal cost of a journal and its price.

[13] A recent article in *Investor's Business Daily* (August 29, 1995, p. A9) quotes the chairman of the Securities and Exchange Commission as saying that "a library that charges people by the page or by the minute is no longer a library." The comment was made in response to a proposal that would have provided 10 minutes free browsing time on "Edgar," the SEC's electronic database of corporate filings and other records, and then charged for downloading information.

Part III
*Economic Modeling of Investments
in Information Resources at Academic Institutions*

Moderator:
Malcolm Getz
Professor of Economics
Vanderbilt University

Speakers:
The Economics of Information
Roger Noll

The Economics of the Internet and Academia
Hal Varian

The Economics of University Investments in Information Resources
Michael McPherson

DR. GETZ: I'm delighted to be able to introduce to you our panel of economists. They are known for their insight and their breadth of imagination about economic phenomenon.

Roger Noll is the Morris Doyle Professor of Public Policy in the Economics Department at Stanford University, Director of the Policy Program, an expert on public policies regarding research and development, government regulation of business, economics, the business of professional sports, and various other issues in economics. His most recent book is entitled *The Technology Pork Barrel*, and he is an award winning teacher.

Hal Varian is the new Dean of the School of Information Management Systems at Berkeley, formerly the Reuben Kempf Professor of Economics at the University of Michigan. He is the author of very influential textbooks in economics, editor of prominent journals, and has an essay in the current issue of *Scientific American* on the information economy.

Michael McPherson is the W. van Alan Clark Third Century Professor of Economics and, Dean of the Faculty at Williams College. He is founding editor of the journal *Economics and Philosophy*, has authored several books on economics issues in higher education including *Playing the Piper: Productivity, Incentives and Financing in American Higher Education*, and was one of my son's favorite teachers.

The Economics of Information

Roger Noll
Professor
Department of Economics
Stanford University

This is a pleasure for me. I have on several occasions in the recent past engaged in communication with people interested in the management of library and information systems in universities. And I found it to be an extraordinarily interesting group, not at all like Marion the librarian in *The Music Man*. So I'm hoping that we can at least foment some interesting discussion. My title is vague and my duty here vaguely described. The progression through the three talks for this panel is supposed to be from the more general to the more specific about managing the information resources of universities and research institutions. I would like to start off by looking at the basic economics research that has been undertaken in the past ten years about the role of research and development in universities as well as the role basic research institutions play in American national growth.

I don't want to talk just about universities because that would be preaching to the converted. But there has been some very interesting work in the last decade or so about the mechanism by which the phenomenon of basic or undirected noncommercially oriented research that takes place in universities, national laboratories, or some of the less directed industrial basic research laboratories, leads to expansion of the economic base of the nation and the national welfare, not only in U.S., but worldwide.

Research that has taken place in the last few years has put some serious meat on an explanation of this phenomenon. If one does sophisticated statistical work about the relationship between research and economic growth, one has this peculiar result: the social returns in terms of economic growth and productivity enhancement from basic research are higher in the U.S. by a lot than anywhere else in the world. Since this was discovered about 15 years ago, it has created a puzzle that is only recently beginning to be solved by economics research. The core explanation that has begun to emerge is, first of all, that the research university, which is pretty much a unique American institution, is the key to understanding this phenomenon. And the mechanism of transmission from basic to applied research, from undirected to directed research, is essentially the student, in the first instance, and the consulting relationship, in the second instance.

There are great research universities in almost all advanced industrialized countries. But nowhere except in the United States does so much fundamental research go on in university environments in a way that involves students. That is the unique difference really between the United States and Japan and other OECD countries and EEC countries. In most of the rest of the world a disproportionately large fraction of fundamental research and science technology is being undertaken in either national laboratories or industrial facilities and students are not involved. There may be faculty involved but not students. In the United States, even the national laboratories are actually run by universities and overrun by students. And that is the interesting feature of the American research enterprise, the involvement of students.

This close integration between what goes on in a classroom and what goes on in basic research is one place to look for the reason for higher productivity of basic research in the U.S. than elsewhere.

It is not because Americans per-buck-spent are doing better research, because they probably aren't. But it is the case that the American research university is unique. It also explains why the U.S. has a huge balance of payment surplus, if you will, in higher education, particularly graduate education in science and engineering. There are several disciplines in science and engineering where over half of the graduate students in the United States come from other countries. This not only indicates that a lot of interesting work goes on here, but that it's well recognized world-wide that the American research university is a unique institution, and certainly its scale and scope is huge compared to research universities in other countries.

The second idea in this research literature is the importance of propinquity. There has been a great debate going on in American universities for 25 or 30 years about the importance of universities in the larger community in which they operate, and a debate about whether some very extreme examples of this coalescence of research universities and high tech industries in places like Silicon Valley and on Route 128 in Boston, is an accident or whether it really works. The research in the last five years has found it remarkable that the productivity of private applied product development research is higher in areas which are near a university than in areas where it's not. In other words, detailed firm-specific, plant-specific data on industry R&D indicate that the productivity of expenditures on private, directed, patentable, copyrightable research that goes into slightly improving the design of this week's mousetrap is higher when the facility is located in easy access to a university.

This is important to our enterprise today because the mechanism by which universities communicate through their students indirectly, and directly with collaborators, colleagues, disinterested bystanders, and industry is crucial to understanding the role of universities and the economic life of the nation. And, in particular, it's crucial that we take into account the mechanism by which our faculty communicate their new results to the outside world. We have to understand that mechanism before we can confidently state that a new method of dissemination is going to make things better or worse. This is the key to the basic economics of information, at least as far as research is concerned.

In some ways scholarly information, the products of research and development in universities, is like all information. The *National Enquirer*, patents, T.V. programs, or books on theoretical physics all have certain similar functions. And interestingly enough, all kinds of information, whether it's the *National Enquirer* or the product of a research project in the university, have what we economists call a public goods feature. That is, once you have produced this new and novel information, whether it's about some new ideas in electrical engineering that might reformulate computers, or some new information about aliens invading the heads of people in the *National Enquirer*, you don't have to reproduce it again for each subsequent reader or consumer. This public goods feature is what drives all the problems we face in trying to solve the dilemma that Bill Bowen referred to in his talk.

First, given that once you have solved the problem of generating information for the first person, because it's so cheap to have the information spill over to the second, the third, and the fourth person, you don't want to produce arbitrary or institutional barriers or pricing barriers to that widespread dissemination. Indeed, that constitutes the economic rationale for having public support for universities and basic research in general. Once this information is provided, having it made available in an open fashion that allows widespread dissemination is an extraordinarily valuable thing from the point of view of the nation. Putting barriers between potential users and the creator of the information is to limit the degree to which economic value will be derived from it. The other side of this dilemma is that, if no mechanism is in place for the inventors, or producers, or publishers, or disseminators of the new information to recapture their costs, then people will not produce as much information as is socially desirable.

So therein lies the dilemma. On the one hand you don't want to charge for things because you'd like to promote the dissemination. But on the other hand, if you don't charge for things, you have got to worry about how the person producing the new information is going to recover the costs for it and, particularly if it's in the private sector, have some additional incentive to be in the business of trying to find useful new information and disseminate it. Well, to summarize how this works, we need to worry about both the cost side and the demand or consumption side of this production mechanism to fully understand it. Then we can apply our concepts of what kinds of changes electronic media will bring to this equation on both the cost side and the demand side, so that we can anticipate the problems we have to solve, in order to make optimal use of this new technology.

On the cost side, essentially the costs have three components. There is the generation of the new information which takes place in somebody's research laboratory or maybe just the pad and pencil and head that are sitting in an office. There is the publication aspect of it, which means producing information in some transmittable form.

Then there is the access component of it, which is what libraries normally do, and which some individuals do themselves by subscribing to journals and buying books. I want to again ignore the production side, although that's perilous. Even two years ago I would have said we can safely ignore the production side because both state and federal governments have been willing to support research universities. Now I'm not so sure with what's happening both in Congress and in state legislators. I am currently engaged in a research project on the future of the American research university. And frankly, right now it's dismal. It's very likely that in five to ten years we'll have half as many research universities as we have now, if present financial trends continue. But that's a different topic and a different lecture. Let me proceed and assume for the sake of argument, that we now indeed have the research product and we are interested in publication and access.

Putting barriers between potential users and the creator of the information is to limit the degree to which economic value will be derived from it. The other side of this dilemma is that, if no mechanism is in place for the inventors, or producers, or publishers, or disseminators of the new information to recapture their costs, then people will not produce as much information as is socially desirable.

The key point that Bill Bowen referred to is, like the research itself which is a public good, there is also a public good aspect to publication. A very large fraction of the costs of publishing journals and books are what is called first copy costs, that includes everything that goes into preparing the rough manuscript until the final product is published in some form. These costs have to do with editing, refereeing, composing, getting the work to the point where the printing press or the electronic distribution system is ready to start making the work accessible or distribute it to a large number of users. Indeed, in my work, we have found that for the vast majority of scientific and technical journals, the first copy costs account for on the order of 80 to 85 percent or more of the total cost of production and dissemination. And the reason for this is quite simple. The median number of subscribers to all scientific journals that are published and are subscribed to by American university research laboratories is under 300. So that dissemination, in the sense of actually producing multiple copies and shipping them around the country, is actually a relatively small fraction of total cost.

For the vast majority of scientific and technical journals, the first copy costs account for on the order of 80 to 85 percent or more of the total cost of production and dissemination.

What's happening in the journal industry is that very large fixed costs are being spread through average cost pricing among universities. And if you look at the data collected and published by ARL, you will see that the prices of journals are going up substantially more rapidly than the budgets of research libraries. The reason for this differential is obviously on the one hand, as libraries cut back on the number of journals they subscribe to, there are fewer libraries over which to spread this fixed cost, so the prices go up more rapidly. This phenomenon is very similarly to the phenomenon we observed 20 to 30 years ago in public mass transportation systems where, if you try to deal with declining ridership by raising the price to spread the fixed costs over fewer people, you cause further declines in ridership. That exact same phenomenon is going on in the publication business.

Likewise, on access costs, essentially, once you subscribe to the journal, you have a component of it that's a fixed cost, which is cataloging it and storing it, and a component of it that's distribution, which has to do with how much does it cost you every time somebody comes in, pulls it off the shelf and reads it? Unless it's a very popular journal, these access costs are actually very small compared to the fixed costs of cataloging and storing.

So libraries have much the same phenomenon working for them: a high fixed cost, low marginal cost of use for what they have. And, indeed, for most of these journals, there isn't very much use. There is a handful of users per year. So the marginal cost of usage is very small compared to the average cost.

On the demand side, why do we have this demand to subscribe to all these journals given, as Hal Varian has pointed out, that, if we are measuring the journal business in terms of impact, and we have reasonably good ways of trying to measure impact, in all disciplines the top few journals account for a very large fraction of the impact? Of course, the reason is that, as time has progressed and more research scholars have come along, two things have happened. The first important thing is that researchers become more specialized, so that lots of secondary results simply can't get published in these main-line important journals. This does not mean that this research isn't important. Nor does it mean, as many have said, that if you're publishing a second- or third-tier journal, there is very little or no economic value added to that research. That's just not right. What gets published in the main-line journals, of course, is that stuff which has the most widespread appeal to other scholars. It is not necessarily the research that is least commercially valuable from the point of view of impact on the research enterprise in industry. Industries tend to be more and more specialized. You will find, if you go to industrial research laboratories, there is a great deal of interest in some of the more specialized journals. And it is not obvious at all, since we don't have any information on this point, precisely what would happen to the dissemination of information if these journals stopped existing.

Of course there is another side to the demand for journals besides the dissemination process to other institutions, which is that journals also serve two other functions. One is the mechanics of how they deal with the educational process. The more advanced the graduate class, the more likely it is that it's going to use readings from these more specialized journals. So they do play a role in most graduate education. But in addition to that, there is the status conferral aspect of journals, a function that journals provide even if they are never read. And, indeed, for many journals, the median number of references to the articles published in those journals is zero. One of the problems we face in doing our own research is trying to rank order journals. It's very hard to rank order all the journals where none of the articles ever get cited. And there are quite a few of them, I might add. But here the process that's being served is the refereeing process. Well, these are all functions that somehow you have to worry about performing in the electronic media. How does one cope?

There are just a few points I want to make about how the electronic media affect all these basic supply and demand characteristics. The first point is that most of the first copy costs in doing the research and producing a first publication are independent of the media. Now, that's not strictly true. There are some exemptions to that. But in the end, whether it's going to be stuck on a home page in the World Wide Web or printed in the *American Economic Review*, first copy costs are not very much different if you're going to try to produce something of high quality. One of the interesting features, of course, is that certain kinds of distribution are easier electronically and other kinds of distribution are easier in hard copy. For example, suppose that what you want to do is distribute extraordinarily detailed photos from electron microscopes. Obviously the degree to which you can do it is dependent upon the medium. Extraordinarily high resolution pictures require an extraordinarily high quality electronic reception device, which most faculty don't have in their office as yet.

By the same token, other kinds of electronic fancy publication possibilities vastly reduce the cost compared to print. So one can anticipate that journals, in competing for authors to submit their articles, will tend to accentuate some of the more fancy things that you can do relatively cheaply electronically. What this means of course is that not all of the cost savings that you might imagine through distribution from electronic media will take the form of cost savings. Some of them will be offset by quality enhancements. So that one shouldn't imagine that the costs of distributing a particular journal with a particular format electronically will be passed on completely as cost savings for libraries. In fact, some of it will be quality enhancements so that there will not be one-to-one trade-offs.

Likewise with regard to dissemination to students, students sitting in a dormitory with a computer and accessing publications is definitely going to vastly increase the degree to which professors use large numbers of journal articles and the mechanism by which they provide readings in classes, as contrasted to buying textbooks and readers. One expectation is that as time progresses, electronic access would actually be beneficial to educational productively with more specific readings tailored to courses. It will, at the same time, vastly increase the demands that many universities have on their electronic networks. I don't know what it's like at the institutions you come from. But I know that if you try to log on to the Stanford University network at two to four o'clock in the afternoon, it's not very much fun. All the wonders of the speed and ease and accessibility of the electronic network don't appear quite so real to you when 6,000 undergraduates and 4,000 graduate students are all simultaneously interconnected to each other playing bridge or chess or some other kind of game. So there is a spillover effect because of this accessibility, first because people are going to take advantage of it, and there is going to be an effect on the computer networks of universities. And even Stanford, which has one of the largest and most sophisticated computer networks of all the universities, is definitely under capacity. Neither the hardware nor the software is capable of dealing with the usage we now have, let alone the kind of usage demands we are going to place upon it, when we have substantially more extensive electronic distribution.

The last point I want to make is to refer again to the recovery of the cost of publications. I can easily imagine that, if we could ever solve the coordination problem, and if the major economics journals were online, I can just see hundreds of economists getting together and saying: "Well, Hal, you can be the guy who subscribes to *Econometrica*, and, Roger, you can be the guy who subscribes to the *Journal of Political Economy*, etc. And then of course we will immediately put it on my World Wide Web site or just put it in my own computer and you guys all know how to access and download anything you want."

This would, of course, drive the number of individual subscribers of all the major journals down to one. And, needless to say, to cover all the fixed costs the subscriber would have to pay a hundred thousand dollars a year for that particular journal, which probably isn't likely. How do we solve this problem? Now, there are ways to cope with it. I hope Hal Varian will talk about some of them. But one of the ways is the Microsoft way, which is basically the Internet cop snooper looking into everyone's computer to see what kind of software is loaded there.

That is what a lot of people really fear, that the mechanism of enforcement of paying a fair share of the costs of electronic publication will have to be giving up privacy rights for what's in your computer. I might add that where I'm currently on leave this year at the Brookings Institution, that is what Brookings uses to assure itself that individual Brookings staff members do not have unauthorized software on their computer. I find that frightening. It's not so bad at my home institution to have that being done, but something else to have it done ubiquitously. In particular I refer to the belief that the Microsoft Internet service will have that feature built into it. I don't know whether that's an apocryphal story or a real story.

But nonetheless, the notion that, to take advantage of the capabilities and cost reductions of electronic distribution, we will have to abandon privacy rights in personal computers strikes me as a trade-off that most people would not be willing to make. I doubt that I would be willing to make it in a very large community environment. I would only be willing to make it in a small community environment. Well, with these basic thoughts in mind I will let Hal Varian talk to you about academia and the Internet.

The Economics of the Internet and Academia

Hal Varian
Dean
School of Information Management and Systems
University of California at Berkeley

If you look on my Web page (see Figure 1), I have compiled a list of resources having to do with economics on the Internet and the information economy in general.

I want to start by reviewing with you a little bit of the history of the Internet. I know this may be old hat for several of you, but it's probably good to start from the same position. It started with ARPANET at the Advanced Research Projects Administration, a part of the U.S. Department of Defense. This unit funded the initial research for developing the Internet protocols. Legend has it the original motivation was to try to build a communications system that would work in the event of a nuclear disaster. They wanted something that was very robust, that was decentralized and couldn't be knocked out by just a few key hits, and would work even if there were great chaos in the system. As we all know, there is great chaos in the system, so they managed to get that part right.

Later on, by the mid-'80s, the U.S. National Science Foundation funded the development of the 12 regional supercomputer centers. Once the centers were built, the NSF needed a way to communicate with the centers. They decided to use the Internet protocol that was developed in the ARPANET project. In their design there was a backbone which basically connected together the supercomputer centers, and then there were regional network providers who were typically based at a major university in the region. For example, in the New England region it was MIT. In the bay area it was Stanford. In Michigan it was the University of Michigan and so on.

The NSF also had a connectivity program to try to help subsidize the connection of individual universities and colleges to their appropriate regional network, which was in turn connected to the backbone. There was also a foreign connectivity program. The foreign connectivity program was generally associated with scientific projects of one sort or another. For example, New Zealand originally gained access to the Internet through the Antarctica site which is in Christchurch, New Zealand. They needed to have a connection for their work. In fact a good trivia question is to ask "What is the continent with the highest per capita Internet connectivity?" The answer is "Antarctica." Everyone is connected.

One of the great beauties of the network is if each person is connected to the supercomputer centers, then of course everyone is connected to each other. From the very beginning the NSF decided to exploit that connectivity, so rather than going back and forth to the supercomputer center, one could send email and transfer files and do all those good things that we're familiar with in the Internet today.

The total cost to this program even at its height was about $20 million a year, which is peanuts when you think about the benefits that resulted. $11 million was funding for the backbone and about another $8 million was funding for the regionals. Of course, the regionals were only partially funded by the NSF, the universities also paid connect fees. So they were partially funded by the users and partially subsidized centrally. There was also a connectivity program to encourage universities to be connected to the Internet.

In April 1995 we said good-bye to the NSFNET. It's now history. The NSF decided that this was a mature technology and there was no reason to continue to subsidize the existence of it, when it could be provided very easily by the private sector. They did fund the creation of NAPS (network access points). The network access points are where the individual backbone providers can exchange traffic. So, they are an interchange point. The NSF is also funding research on the VBNS, which stands for very high bandwidth network system. It is not going to be a general use network, but will be used only for research in networks and very high tech science. It's going to be the network for the next decade. The VBNS is going to be for research that will allow very high bandwidth uses to be understood before they're made available to the general public. The VBNS will be irrelevant to you unless you do high energy physics or astronomy or something like that. But it should have great future payoffs. Its purpose is in line with the mission of the NSF, which is to fund basic research.

The current situation of the Internet is privatized backbones. There are six big ones, 14 or more if you count everything that is a T-3 backbone (T-3 means a high speed phone line). The regional networks are generally and gradually being privatized though not exclusively. While the regionals are being privatized, the independent service providers (ISP) are paying for connection to the regionals and then reselling it to the final consumers. So when you open *Computer Shopper* you see full advertisements that read: "Internet connectivity for $20 a month," those are the ISPs. Well, of course this transition leads to some problems.

Probably you haven't seen most of these problems as an end user, but they're still things that we have to worry about for the future; namely, there's a big difference between one network and six networks, and the big difference comes in coordination of the interconnection. All of these networks must interconnect. For example, the University of Michigan and the University of Texas use different backbone providers and so if they are going to communicate, that traffic has got to be passed from one to the other. The first problem was the technical model of how to do this, because all the technical protocols and procedures were designed with just one backbone in mind in the U.S. situation. The network engineers had to come up with new procedures which allow for multiple backbone networks. Even more importantly there has to be a business model. The technical model has been solved more or less. They had some glitches, of course, but things are working. The business model still hasn't been solved. The problem is figuring out what form of compensation have to be designed to enable one network to agree to carry the traffic of another.

It's a very tricky problem and is made more difficult by the fact that the accounting software, the metering software, and the other things that are necessary to support the business model are not part of the technical model of the Internet. There is a lot of interest now in models of accounting and economics and pricing that could support that kind of business model.

One of the reasons these models are increasingly necessary is the need to support quality service for real-time applications. For example, CU-SeeMe or some of these other video systems, put great demands on the network and they really can't be used without a relatively unloaded network. The question is how to have many different kinds of applications that place different demands on the network and still have it all peacefully coexist. That is probably going to require an economic model that means paying more for a higher quality service that supports use of many applications that demand different amounts of bandwidth. The work is already underway to make a business model for a network that can support many different applications.

Of course, because we now have a commercial environment the issue of developing standards has suddenly become much more difficult. Take, for example, this proliferation of standards in audio and visual services and applications; we have recently seen this with HTML. HTML is an instance of SGML developed at CERN. The NCSA adopted HTML from CERN to make the first popular Internet browser, Mosaic. Then came the commercial version, NETSCAPE, developed by the people who originally developed Mosaic. The first thing they did was change the specification of the language into this other kind of HTML that allowed for tables and other enhancements of the original design. Meanwhile there's an HTML3 group that's working at CERN trying to set reasonable standards (Now that group has apparently moved over to MIT.) There is a big issue of how HTML is going to be developed further. Meanwhile we have a clear public interest in having a uniform standard, but there is also a clear private advantage to having features your competition doesn't have. It will be rather interesting to see how it all shakes out.

I would suggest that a very nice model to look at is the Adobe model for PostScript. When Adobe developed PostScript, they realized it would be worthless unless it was a standard. So they released the specification of PostScript language into the public domain in the sense that they said, "Anybody can write a postscript interpreter. We're not claiming property rights to the language, per se." But Adobe built its own implementation of the language which had certain features that led to nicer looking fonts and that gave them the competitive advantage. The basic model is that you've got to give something away and then keep a little part for yourself in order to make a standard work. Finding that trade-off between what you give away and what you keep is the tricky part of the business model.

The other thing that people are very interested in these days is financial transactions on the Internet. Because everybody thinks that in order to become viable commercially you have got to be able to carry out financial transactions on the Internet as easily as you do, say, over the 800 number with the telephone and your Visa or Mastercard number, et cetera. There's much work going on in that area.

Let me suggest a bit of a heterodox view. I think that, rather than a software-only solution, we are going to see smart cards dominating this market. Smart cards are basically visa cards with chips in them. People are very used to using this card for transactions at the grocery, the gas station, and everywhere else. My guess is, in a few years, we will see credit card readers as a standard part of the computer, just like a disk drive. We will be able to just swipe the card through it and this will resolve a lot of problems very neatly. Of course, there are also all these issues about security and crypto. My feeling is that when we talk to our grandchildren, they're going to say things like "Gee, grandpa, is it really true that back in the old days everybody sent email that wasn't encrypted?" Right now the network is remarkably porous. The big problem with security is usually not the hardware or the software, but the user. The users just haven't developed the habits that are going to be appropriate for living in that electronic environment.

As academicians, we have a lot of concerns about this new privatized and commercialized Internet. Our biggest concern is that we want to maintain a system of scholarly communication, effectively, and cheaply. Let's look at an example organized by increasing bandwidth. Email is, of course, a very, very low bandwidth activity. Even at it's height, it was less than 15 percent of the total traffic on the backbone and it must be less than ten percent now. Nobody knows for sure, because one of the consequences of the privatization of the Internet is that we no longer have aggregate statistics on what the different types of traffic look like. However, email certainly has been going down as a proportion of total traffic. There are mail groups, E-prints and journals, FTP sites. As everybody here knows, people are expecting to see a proliferation of this sort of thing. Finally, there is realtime conferencing and collaboration. This is something that people are quite excited about, because it means we don't have to fly all over the country to have a meeting like this, but in the future we can have this kind of meeting online.

There's good news and bad news here. The good news is that the activities requiring low bandwidth is certainly going to remain cheap. Email uses so little of any kind of resource that you want to measure, that, no matter what kind of economic model you have for providing access to the Internet, it's got to end up having a very, very low cost. But the coordination of standards is going to be quite hard. This includes coming up with a good business model for academic publishing in this new environment. As an aside, one of my first jobs as dean last week was to explain to nonacademics how the academic publishing model worked. One of them said, "I must be misunderstanding something. Are you telling me that you give the work to the publisher and then they sell it back to you? Is that really it?" Yeah, that's it. So the current model is hard to explain. Let me say the new model is going to be at least as difficult.

I want now to talk a little bit about the cost of E-prints. I got some numbers from Paul Ginsparg, who runs the high energy physics server at LANL, which is one of the prime examples of an E-print server. The word was buzzing around the academic community a few months ago that he just got a million dollar grant to run this thing. It is quite interesting to look closely at that million dollars. It turns out it's a million dollars over three years. So that's $330,000 per year. The overheard rate at LANL is 50 percent, so now we're down to $170,000. It turns out this all goes for two postdocs and a system administrator. The hardware is a $5,000 work station. Of course the infrastructure is all in the network. There is some development time, his time and a few other people, in putting together the software to do this. So the hardware component is very small and the software component is basically "off the shelf" sorts of tools. So in terms of the actual resources it's very, very minimal. And, this is one of the prime communication sites for high energy physics these days.

When we try to extend this model to other fields we run into some problems. Somebody has observed that the high energy physics community has a unique feature; namely, in order to do high energy physics one has to have a lot of money. And, to have a lot of money you've got to be refereed. You have to have grants and since the grants are all refereed, it's a very self-selected group of people. If you're publishing anything at all in high energy physics, it's probably going to be reasonable quality work. They don't have the same problem with refereeing and quality control or filtering that you might have in some other community, where the entry costs are lower. So, maybe the journals really are irrelevant for that field. You've already got the quality imprint that you need just by the fact that you had the money, the millions of dollars, or at least hundreds of thousands of dollars needed, to get time on the particular collider that you were using.

In other fields there's always going to be a chicken and egg problem. Nobody is going to contribute to the electronic FTP site or E-journal site unless people read it, and people aren't going to bother to read it unless there are high quality contributions. So the question is how do we get things going? How do we exploit this network externality to get a critical mass in order for people to use the resource? One little model that I like is this FEN model. FEN is the Financial Economics Network which started with a current awareness, of—not E-print, but paper preprint abstracts. You subscribed to this mail group and each week they would send a list of the working papers with abstracts that were available in that particular subfield. They took financial economics and divided that up into six different subfields—derivative assets, corporate finance, and so on. If you had a working paper in that area, you sent the physical copy to the central site and they abstracted it. They listed the abstract and the title and they said "write to the author for a copy."

What was nice is people didn't have to change what they were doing before. It was just another way to advertise your work. It turns out that FEN got a hundred percent penetration of this particular subdiscipline in just a very few months. This shows that if you pick a little subfield of an area, you can get a hundred percent penetration. And it's much better to have a hundred percent penetration of a small area than it is to have a ten percent penetration of a big area, because once you've got complete penetration of a small area you can build on that. In fact, the Financial Economics Network is now branching into law, accounting, economic history and all sorts of other subfields.

Let me make some general observations about costs. Roger Noll has already alluded to the fact that in the publishing process there are large fixed costs and small marginal costs. The first-copy costs are significant, and the reproduction costs are minimal. If you ask an economist to predict what's going to happen to pricing in this industry, the first thing he'll say is we should expect to see price discrimination or product differentiation. In this environment, it makes sense to try to charge different people different prices for potentially different kinds of uses. We're familiar with this already in print publishing. There's usually a library rate and an individual rate—a form of price discrimination. People worry a lot about being exploited in this kind of environment. But the thing you've got to remember is that nobody has ever made money by pricing a product at more than people can afford. The trick is to price a product that people will buy. If different people have different willingness to pay, or can afford different things, or seek different services, then you're going to want to charge them different prices.

If you ask an economist to predict what's going to happen to pricing in this industry, the first thing he'll say is we should expect to see price discrimination or product differentiation.

Well, again alluding to what Roger was saying, how do you make sure that, when you're pricing a product for this segment of the market, it isn't bought by some other segment of the market and then transferred over; that is, how do you avoid arbitrage? The answer is to differentiate the product. You want to provide different products to different people. You target the product to that group, so that people buy the product which is most appropriate for them. For example, if you look at information goods— say journal articles—you can think of differentiating them along the line of immediacy. At one price you get it right away. For another price, you get last month's issue, and for a different price you get last year's issue. When we talked about the JSTOR model, the developers had explicitly looked at differential pricing for having access to the current issue versus the archival issues.

One can look at several examples of this phenomenon. A nice example is in financial data. If you want a feed of the prices on the New York Stock Exchange that's delayed by 30 seconds, it will cost you many thousands of dollars a month. But if you want something that's 20 minutes delayed, it turns out it costs you $9.95 a month over the Web. While if you want the historical data, you can get that for free. In this case, immediacy is a very nice example. Weather data is another good example. It is very valuable to have weather data for today's forecast if I'm worried about speculation or planting crops or some economic activity with a profit sort of payoff. But if I'm doing scientific research and I'm not so interested in the most up-to-date data, I can use nice, high quality archived data.

You can provide data or information to different users, but discriminate on the grounds of immediacy (how quickly does it arrive), format (is it marked up, is it ASCII), organization (does it come in a database with some software, is it a lower level organization), linking, etc. There are lots of different ways you can think about providing data or information that's the same, but is organized differently, or provided at a different time, or provided under different circumstances, that allows you to charge different prices. Many of us focus on the bad side of information. It's easy to copy, so they worry about information being stolen by someone else. But the good side of information is that you can sell the same product over and over again. You just sell it in a little different form. When you look at the companies who are going to be successful in this business, they're going to be people who manage to sell the same sort of information in a variety of formats to a variety of audiences at a variety of prices.

A nice example of this cost recovery issue can be seen in academic societies where you have two main purchasers of your product; namely, members of the society and libraries. The way these societies work is that they cover their cost of operation by selling subscriptions to their members and libraries. However, the big worry for societies is that if they make too successful a product for the library, they are going to lose their members. So it is necessary to make a difference between the product that is sold to the library and the product sold to the members. This can be done by either making the library copy not as useful— degrading the library version—or by enhancing the version that goes to the members. A society may want to do one or the other, or indeed they might do both. For example, they may say that library use of the electronic version would be on-site only. It could be mounted on the library network but not on the campus network. Certain limitations could be placed on the amount of access. Users could only access the product at certain times, like when the library was open, for example. Now, those are not popular options, because you'd like to have the product as useful as possible.

I tend to look at the positive side; namely, making membership more valuable. For example, a society might offer a current awareness service where the member lists the areas of interest and is automatically notified by email when articles are published in that area. This is a beautiful example because it's something that is inherently personalized. It is targeting individuals, so that the society can charge for providing a personalized service. This also gets us away from the public good problem. The whole point of how to deal with public goods is to turn them into private goods, something that is unique to the individual. Additionally extra features may be added like the linking feature that was mentioned earlier. It might be that certain features would be limited to members only, or to people who are paying a higher price in order to support the development of the product. Other services may be offered like data archives, E-print archives, and so on. As you offer the additional other services it is only reasonable to expect that people who are accessing them would pay a higher price.

For a lot of societies, their real objective is to have high penetration of members. In the American Economics Association for example, I would guess that if we had all the economists on campus subscribing to the journal, we'd be willing to provide it at a very low rate to the library. I think the same thing would work for political scientists or historians or whatever. Their prime interest is in having a high penetration among the professionals in their organization. That suggests thinking about schemes where the subscription rate to the campus network or the site license depended on how many individual memberships are at a given site for these enhanced memberships. In looking at the current model of publishing, there is one group, the publishers, who are responsible for the publication of current issues and another group, the libraries, who are responsible for the archiving. There is the question of whether these roles break down. Are the publishers going to allow this same division of labor to occur? That depends very much on what copyright law looks like, how those issues shake out in the future. I think there are going to be many, many interesting discussions about how to price archival use and its relationship to pricing for current documents.

There is also the issue of technical standards for preservation. Bill Bowen was talking about the size of the database for JSTOR—it seems very large. A recent article in the *New York Times* reported that Sony and Phillips have finally reached an agreement on a new CD that holds 4.7 gigabytes of data on one side, or nearly ten gigabytes of data on one CD if you use both sides. And all of a sudden a gigabyte isn't so much anymore. At this rate the whole run of a journal would fit on a half a dozen disks.

I also want to say a little about intellectual property. I think you have to think very differently about two kinds of issues with intellectual property. There is wholesale copying for commercial purposes, the kinds of thing that we used to see in Taiwan and we see today in China and some other countries where basically there is a competitive industry in providing copies of intellectual property. Economists are pretty familiar with competitive industries and we can model how that might work. The other kind of intellectual property issue is sharing, where people are sharing copies of a journal among a small circle of friends. Sharing isn't necessarily bad. After all, the whole model of libraries is sharing. You might think that the pricing of journals, the reason that it costs more for libraries than for an individual, is because the publishers know it's going to be shared among a number of users. If you look at video stores, which in a way are a form of library, it's absolutely clear, that the manufacturers will price some videos at $14.95, expecting people to buy them, and price other videos at $80, expecting people to share them; that is, expecting people to rent them. So you can look at products where sometimes people are going to buy and sometimes they're going to share. Some products are naturally better suited for one over model the other. One of the first things to understand about how intellectual property works is, where is the problem? Are you worried about wholesale copying, or small scale sharing?

There are more exotic solutions to the intellectual property problem. These are "information objects"—a copy of the journal which bundles its own special reader. The journal is encrypted and when you open the journal and looked at it, it automatically sends off a little bit of E-cash to the publisher. Some people are talking about models like that. They're also talking about secure hardware that will protect intellectual property but allow people to look at documents. There is work going on in this at Xerox PARC and other places. But I think we have to remember the lesson that we learned from the software industry; namely, if the price is low enough, copying just isn't a problem. Everyone worried about copying in the 1980s and created all sorts of copy protection schemes. Then there was a whole industry of breaking copy protection schemes. That's pretty much all disappeared because software has now become a ubiquitous mass market item.

I'd like to focus now on the really big economic issue in this whole area and that is the economics of attention. What is the value of journals for academic publishing? We all know that the real added value comes from the refereeing. Let me suggest now that, if we look at the changing cost of publishing in the electronic environment, we see a really dramatic change in how we might want to referee articles. Publishing used to be very expensive with big fixed costs for the editorial work, for typesetting, for fancy machines, certain kinds of skilled labor, et cetera. There were big costs to get the document from the manuscript into the publication stage. But now, those costs are dramatically lower, and it's easy to do desktop publication. What does that mean? When it was expensive to publish, it was important to filter before the item was published. And when it's cheap to publish, you might want to filter after the item is published; that is, make the item available to people and let them find what is worth looking at. So refereeing or filtering really has a different purpose when publishing is cheap versus when publishing is expensive.

I'll give two examples of software filters that I think are extremely promising and exciting: GroupLens and Ringo are both software projects coming out of MIT. GroupLens was designed as a filter for USENET News. USENET News is now about 90 megabytes of text per day, which is quite a lot for an individual to read, equivalent to about 90 books. Somewhere in that mess, there probably is something that's useful that the reader would like to know. The question is where? Here's how GroupLens works: I read an item and at the end of that item there are five little buttons where I rate it one through five on how interesting or useful the item was. Then when I go look at the titles of the articles, I'm presented with a rating of that article which is a weighted average of previous readers' scores. The rating is a weighted average—but more weight is given to people who have agreed with my assessments in the past. The idea is, that it's not just the unweighted average of past readership, but more weight is given to people whose opinions are correlated with mine. The possibilities are really very exciting, because you can use the group as a "lens" to focus on what's of real interest to you. It allows you to identify people with common interests. It does not necessarily have to be only people who were correlated with me in the past, but I could ask for example, how the article has been rated by people at the top 20 universities, or by the people who have been in the profession for 30 years. There are different opinions for sorting. If you sort by the characteristics of individuals whose opinions you might value, you can use the software to focus on things that are useful. Ringo is a similar system. With Ringo, the user sends in the list of music that he/she likes and it comes back with recommendations. It does this by looking for correlations. For example, if Roger and I have the same tastes in music,

90 percent of our choices might overlap, then Ringo would suggest the other ten percent to each of us as music we might like.

Paul Ginsparg, who is running the LANL server, made the observation that when we look at frequency of requests for the articles on the server, there will be 12 requests, 15 requests, and then boom, 120 requests. What are those articles that get 120 requests? It's not the ones by the Nobel Prize winners. It's the surveys. Because all of us are working in areas that are so specialized, there is a huge demand for knowing what's going on in general; what's the broad stream of discourse in my subject. Now when you look at surveys and you look at articles in general, there is this problem. Articles, I believe, are typically too long. When I was editor at the *American Economic Review*, the standard advice in the last line of every letter to the authors was "make it shorter." It wasn't because it was so costly to publish extra pages in the journal; it was because by making it shorter you tightened it up and made it easier for people to read. The economy wasn't the economy in the pages. It was the economy of attention of the readers. That's why the editors always say "make it shorter."

The other side of that is that you can make it too short. Look at *Physics Letters*. Lots of people read *Physics Letters* because the articles are short. So lots of people want to publish there because people read it. But they take an article and compress it so it's almost unrecognizable. The standard is to get rid of all the prepositions and conjunctions, and just put the equations in—then you can publish it in *Physics Letters*.

The neat thing about electronic publishing is you can have both worlds. You can have the short version, and you can have the long version, all in the same document. You can do this using expandable hypertext links. You can have a document that has a very flexible structure. It's going to be a challenge to learn how to create such documents.

Finally, I want to touch on the issue of format of communication. There is a lot of discussion about what is the unit of scholarly communication. Is it the article, is it the book, is it the conference, et cetera? Let me suggest it is the thread; that is, it's the literature. It's a whole list of things that point to each other and reference each other and carry out a discussion on some particular academic topic. Consider interactive journalism. Recently I was talking to one of the editors at *Time* magazine who was working on *Time On-Line*, which comes out on Sunday evening, while the print copy doesn't make it until Wednesday. When *Time On-Line* comes out on Sunday, the publisher gets lot of email response to the articles and some of this email is great stuff. A lot of it's garbage, but there's some really great material there, better than the article in many cases. The question is how they can use the readership to interact with the author of the article? Well, that's what we do in academia. We're both the readers and the authors. You read the article, you respond to it, you correct it, you enhance it, you enlarge it, et cetera. That kind of interaction is something that we have learned how to do to one degree or another. In the new electronic environment this is going to be even more important. So you see, there's a certain convergence between what's going on in that "threaded" communication in the academic world and the kinds of trends that we see in the commercial world. Look at talk radio, talk shows on T.V., and at the ways they can use letters to the editor at *Time* magazine. What we're doing here isn't really so different than what's going on Oprah right now. On Oprah they have this panel of people sitting up there talking about things that are of interest to them and the audience is cheering or laughing or siding in with their own comments. Maybe this is a good model for both forms of communication.

Figure 1

The Information Economy

by Hal R. Varian

The Economics of the Internet, Information Goods, Intellectual Property and Related Issues

Tools For Viewing Downloadable Files

- Accounting & Measuring Traffic
- Announcements
- Background and Reference
- Commerce
- Electronic Publishing
- Government
- Intellectual Property
- International
- Miscellaneous Resources
- Network Economies
- Pricing
- Slides and Notes from Talks

The Information Economy is part of the School of Information Management and Systems at the University of California Berkeley

Send feedback regarding The Information Economy to: infoecon@sims.berkeley.edu
Last Modified:

Copyright © 1994, 1995, 1996 Hal R. Varian. All rights reserved.

http://www.sims.berkeley.edu/resources/infoecon/

The Economics of University Investments in Information Resources

Michael McPherson
Professor, Department of Economics
Dean of Faculty
Williams College

My aim is to offer you a somewhat different perspective from earlier speakers by burrowing in on one aspect of the economics of information and offering a perspective that is, in some ways, a little more concrete and a little bit more directly tied to institution-level issues. Specifically, I will focus on one matter that Bill Bowen mentioned earlier: the *system* aspect of this whole business, the tremendous interdependency of the different parts of the U.S. academic system that are involved with scholarly publication.

I'll begin with an illustration, a rather specific illustration that I think is familiar in all of our lives: the institution of interlibrary loan. I want to talk to you about interlibrary loan of books or monographs. Journals raise somewhat different issues. It's apparent to everybody that there's increasing reliance on interlibrary loan and increasing interest in extending that reliance still further as a way for libraries to economize on cost. Book prices are going up. And the idea of being able to efficiently share books across institutions is highly attractive to librarians trying to balance their budgets.

Interlibrary loan is not inexpensive, especially for books, where the physical objects generally have to travel across space as part of the sharing operation. There are many elements of cost. You have to verify the reference, you've got to identify a library, you have to place a request, arrange shipment, receive the book, provide it to the borrower, recover the book, get it back to the library, make sure it got back to the library. The Association of Research Libraries did a study in which they estimated the average cost of such a transaction, counting both borrower and lender, at about $30. Although the cost varies apparently tremendously across universities, it would be worth understanding better what the components of those costs are and why some universities do it so much cheaper than others. Even if ILL is or can be made cheaper than $30 per transaction, it's still a clumsy system. It's inconvenient for the borrower who has to wait. There are all kinds of opportunities for error and uncertainty. Yet even at $30 a pop, it's clearly cheaper if you have very little use for a book in your library to borrow it than it is to buy it with what the cost of hardbound scholarly monographs has gotten to be these days.

So this is a familiar phenomenon. And I think there are three interesting kind of ironies to notice about it. One was again anticipated in Bill Bowen's remarks. This strategy is a collectively self-defeating strategy for libraries because most of the costs of the books are first copy costs. Book prices are rising in important measure because the number of copies sold of any one scholarly monograph has fallen from about 700 to about 500 copies. And that reduction in volume pushes up costs. As the numbers sold fall further, the costs will rise further. So you can sell 600 copies of a monograph at $40 each or 60 copies at $300 each. Or one copy which will fly around the country on Federal Express for $15,000. For the system as a whole, there is no big saving involved in accomplishing an interlibrary loan, at least for new publications. That's one fundamental feature.

> *You have got academic libraries and academic presses locked in struggle to balance their budgets and the provost is overseeing both of them. And then, of course, the people who are both the customers and the producers of the stuff that is being shipped around the country by Federal Express work for the same universities. It's hard to deny that there really is something bizarre about this situation. And one suspects that it is fundamentally unsustainable as technologies change.*

The second related feature is that libraries are treating books like they're expensive. We ship these items around the country like they are scarce gems. The idea that you would actually have to take the same copy of this book and get it from Dubuque to Iowa City, and then up to Madison and so on, implies that it is precious. But books are cheap. To print one more copy of a book costs certainly well under $10. One suggests that these specialized books often are being shipped around the country on interlibrary loan, while unsold copies are sitting in a warehouse somewhere. These could be mailed out at very little cost, perhaps on condition that the library receiving them agrees to send $15 per copy and promises to throw each book away after they read them. So the interlibrary loan system treats books like they're scarce, but they're not in some fundamental sense scarce. That's the second irony.

The third irony is perhaps the richest. Libraries are turning to interlibrary loans to balance their budgets by buying fewer books. Presses are raising their prices to balance their budgets as they sell fewer books. And the *same people* own the presses and the libraries! You have got academic libraries and academic presses locked in struggle to balance their budgets and the provost is overseeing both of them. And then, of course, the people who are both the customers and the producers of the stuff that is being shipped around the country by Federal Express work for the same universities. It's hard to deny that there really is something bizarre about this situation. And one suspects that it is fundamentally unsustainable as technologies change.

Yet clearly there is a logic behind all this. It's the phenomenon of copyright that makes these books scarce. And (a point that Roger Noll made well) copyright here functions as a device by which to generate a revenue stream to cover those first copy costs. But the combination of that requirement with the increasing attempts by libraries and other users to minimize the number of copies produced means that we currently have an increasingly precarious institutional fix for the real problem of finding a way to generate a revenue stream that will finance these publications.

Now, that's one illustration. The larger lesson, Bill Bowen's lesson, that I want to underline is that this enterprise of scholarly publication is a highly interdependent system which is worked deeply in the way the U.S. academy functions.[1] There are three main components: libraries who buy and store publications, presses who print and sell publications, and faculty who write and occasionally read publications. So in the larger sense we could ask, what is this highly self-referential system for? And you can quickly get to ultimate questions, which the first part of Roger Noll's talk addressed. What is the value to humanity of all this scholarly activity? One of my favorite quotations about this activity is from a philosopher at Harvard named Burton

Drebin. This has to be offered with a European accent. Drebin once said, "Junk is junk. But the *history* of junk is scholarship." Or modernized, junk is junk, but *digitized* junk is the Internet.

It's clear that the social and human contributions of different parts of the scholarly enterprise must be in very different categories. Roger talked about science and technology. But there is also a lot of humanistic publication. However we value literary theory, it's got to be quite different from the way we value nuclear physics or molecular biology. Bracketing these ultimate value questions, though, thinking about the internal workings of this as a system we come to the obvious point that academic publishing is central to the academic employment system. And that's something that has to be thought about in any attempt to examine how this system is going to evolve. Publication is central to promotion and tenure. It's central to the competition for prestige among individuals and universities. And it's central to the incentives that make people want to do good work, get it published, get it out there. Now this can be sneered at as publish or perish. But it is clear that an academic system at all resembling the one we have needs some reasonably objective and impersonal way to appraise peoples' scholarly potential and achievements.

The system of refereeing journals and scholarly books plays quite a critical role in this appraisal process, maybe an increasingly critical role. Clearly the system needs some external check on departmental appraisals which are going to be influenced by all kinds of personal interaction that are valuable but need to be balanced by other inputs as well. Speaking as a dean I can guarantee you that we can't simply rely on deans to make those judgments because it's impossible to know all the subjects well enough that various faculty are involved in. And outside letters written for tenure evaluations are increasingly prevalent and increasingly worth less—not worthless but worth less—because people are very cautious in their comments and there's very little incentive for them to be frank in those contexts. The kind of decentralization and distancing that happens with the refereeing process is therefore very valuable to assembling a sense of somebody's achievements. Now again, the ability of the traditional system to serve this function actually traces back in part to intellectual property and copyright.

Presses and journals have reputations to maintain. It's a kind of brand name phenomenon. And part of that flow of revenues to the publishers is needed to sustain these really quite effortful processes of screening and evaluation and editing that are key to performing that function. There are lots of reasons to think that this system is going to undergo fairly dramatic change. And I think Hal Varian talked very well about some of what's on the horizon. I would urge that any proposals for radical change must in some sense get the deans and the provosts in on the action to think about how this affects the system we have all grown to know and feel ambivalent about of evaluating candidates for tenure and evaluating the academic performance of scholars. If the system as we know it starts to fall apart, then one way or another we are going to have to figure out some other way to perform those functions.

---

[1] Meetings and conversations with Colin Day, University of Michigan Press, have helped me appreciate this point.

Questions and Discussion

DR. GETZ: I think we should take time for some questions. So we will open the floor.

QUESTION #1 from COLIN DAY: Could I ask for a clarification of one point in Hal's talk. He reported on Paul Ginsparg's figures. And I confess I should have read more carefully the message that I got that also had those figures in it. As I'm hearing it, the two postdocs, et cetera, costing about $160,000 a year was something of an ongoing cost rather than the development cost. I think for any of my colleague publishers, $160,000 a year to run a journal is a very handsome amount of money. And on 300 median subscriptions it also is an extraordinarily high subscription cost. This isn't a zero cost activity is the point I wanted to make.

DR. VARIAN: Yes, I would agree with that. But the proper comparison would be all the journals in high energy physics. Because if you believe Ginsparg and the people you talk to, they think they can handle all communication on this subject using very little in the way of resources. Of course, as we all know with postdocs, is that they probably aren't devoting a hundred percent of their time to this activity either. So, I think you should look at those cost figures as being an upper bound rather than a lower bound.

QUESTION #2 from DON KING: I'd like to make a comment on Roger Noll's paper. I think there is one regular tool that you left off and that is the site of use. Because users spend, if you put a dollar value on their time, over ten times as much in reading articles as the cost of producing them and making them accessible through the libraries. Second, as far as academically produced scholarly materials are concerned, at least in science and technology, there is far more reading of that outside of the academic communities than within the academic communities. And the third thing, you made a comment about there not being very many citations to journals. But in fact there are roughly 50 to 100 times as much reading as there are citations for an article.

DR. NOLL: To the extent that your point was that secondary journals are more important than one would infer by looking at how many people subscribe to them and how many citations they get, I agree. That was the whole point. In other words, if the current death spiral of library budgets, subscriptions and journal prices has the effect of eliminating the bottom half of all the science and technology journals, it may well be the case that, if we had a broader measure of usefulness and value, it would have a significant effect on the ability to disseminate academic research to industry and other groups. And I agree with you that there are a few ways to get alternative measures of value. I think that with an 80 percent probability, we can say that most scholarly dissemination is in the heads of students who would then go to work for industry and that the rest is in journals and publications of various sorts and seminars. But even if it's the case that it's through students, it still has a journal element to it and a publication element to it. So even if we found that we could find areas where some journals are not read by industry, they may well be read by the graduate students who go to work in those industries.

I think I would take exception to my good friend and the former president of Stanford who used to complain about too much scholarly publication. And we hear this a lot, that a lot of scholarly publication is essentially thumb sucking by academics to justify their existence. I think there is something to be said for that. But I would be very wary of applying that model ubiquitously. Particularly in applied physics, fields of engineering and biomedicine.

DR. VARIAN: Actually, let me follow up on that comment. This issue of how people use articles is extremely important. And I alluded to this quite briefly in my talk. I think one of the great promises of electronic journals is that you don't have to have the one-size-fits-all model, that you can have the abstract. The first two pages are a little bit bigger and you can go a little bit bigger, more in detail, click here for the regressions, click here for the original data. So you can have a whole documentation of the research at all sorts of different levels for all sorts of different readers right down from the lay person or the granting agency to the person who's trying to reproduce your results. One of the great features of this new world is that we can have a much more flexible article structure that will be then much more useful to the progress of scientific research.

QUESTION #3 from SUE MARTIN: I find it interesting that we seem to be talking about journals in electronic form. And as I listen to everybody who has spoken today--and correct me if I'm wrong--that tends to be the theme that comes through. We are talking about journal titles and articles underneath it. In the past decade or even longer, as I think about our own professional literature, there has been an awful lot of speculation that suggests that with electronic information the journal as an entity will of necessity disappear and we will be looking at articles or pieces of work that are the articles that we now know today, but they will be in different formats, or they will become different entities. And I wonder if anybody could respond to that.

DR. VARIAN: Yes, I have thought about that issue a little bit. I think I have been using journals as a shorthand. But your point is very well taken. When you look at why we have journals as the form of scholarly communication, obviously part of it has to do with the technology. There are economies of scale and scope in producing a bunch of articles at once and mailing it out. When you move to an electronic environment those are no longer there. I think that's really the start of this whole set of discussions. But there is a revenue side. Economists have this phenomenon known as bundling. It says when you've got an item, where there are widely dispersed evaluations for the components, you've got a group of components and they're dispersed evaluations among the potential purchasers of that. So in economics there might be articles in microeconomics, in macroeconomics. I'm mostly interested in micro and he's mostly interested in macro, but I want to know a little bit of what's going on in that area and he wants to know a little bit about what's going on in mine. So you come up with a situation where people are willing to pay more for the bundle than for those individual components. It may well be that this kind of demand side phenomenon still leads to the existence of journals, not just for the economic reason that I described a moment ago but also for this attention side. I still want somebody to tell me what is it that I should be reading? What are people doing in this field that's outside my narrow specialty. So there is still going to be room for editorial innovation or editorial filtering or at least some sort of addressing of this problem of the economics of attention, of what should I really be paying attention to.

DR. McPHERSON: Another way I think of the same point is that the journal as a glued together physical object is not necessary in an electronic situation. But the fact of a list of articles certified by Hal Varian, which is one way of interpreting what the *American Economic Review* might have been at one point, is still going to be a article of value. You need some kind of organized judgment about what's worth reading. And also for the reasons I mentioned, some kind of objective judgment to appeal to about what's good.

DR. NOLL: I'd just like to make one observation on the same point. First of all, we economists are well known for using fancy econometric models to forecast the future. And I've just brought my computer and I've plugged in, and with probability one there will still be journals 50 years from now. The really interesting question, of course, has to do with the distribution of survivability and mutation by kinds of journals, both with respect to fields and disciplines and with respect to degree of specialization. It strikes me that the forecast of the demise of the journal is highly contingent upon the community that it is targeted for. The point that was just made about to what extent the subscriber is gaining access in a very targeted and focused way to the detailed informational content of the article as contrasted to keeping abreast is important. If you are a member of a department of economics at a leading research university and you are going to have to cast four or five votes a year on whom to hire, whom to grant tenure, whom to promote, you have to have a degree of knowledge about what people in the various fields of the discipline believe is important, because you have to apply that in your own judgment to make these decisions. For that reason there is always going to be a market among academics, among almost all universities, since some degree of research competence is now required for promotion and tenure everywhere.

There's always going to be some market for the general purpose journal. It's true that the economies of scope, economies of scale reason for journals diminishes in a pure, technological production side of journals but it doesn't disappear in this cognitive side. There really is value in having a handful of peak journals in a discipline which are general purpose and which represent the judgments of the best people in the profession about what the best work is. That can be done electronically, but I suspect that in 50 years from now, even if the *American Economic Review* or other fields, in chemistry, in physics, in whatever, those journals, if they don't exist in hard copy they will still exist electronically as journals for that reason.

COMMENT from DON KING: Could I comment to that, too? If an individual has a journal where they read say 80 articles from it a year, the cost per reading of those articles is very, very inexpensive even though you don't read all of them. For that reason there still is merit in bundling those journal articles together. Another aspect is that the frequently read articles within a particular journal title subsidize the infrequently read articles that may have high quality but are not be frequently read. And I think that Roger alluded to that earlier.

Part IV
Case Studies in Transforming the Scholarly Process:
Costs and Benefits of Cooperation

Moderator:
Duane Webster
Executive Director
Association of Research Libraries

Speakers:
**Knowledge Management:
The Co-Existence of Multiple Models of Scientific Communication**[1]
Richard E. Lucier

Funding Social Science Data Archiving and Services in the Networked Environment
Richard Rockwell

Building the Distributed North American Collection for Foreign Languages
Rush Miller, substituting for Burkart Holzner

MR. WEBSTER: Our panelists have been asked to focus on specific efforts to transform the scholarly information process. During the turbulent transition from mainly print-based to mainly electronic forms of publication, it is apparent that experiments, pilot projects, and fresh thinking can serve to profoundly influence evolving practice. The current electronic environment is at an open and fluid stage. Much of the innovation in electronic dissemination of research and educational materials is coming from university- and government-based initiatives. We are hoping in turn, that the lessons from these initiatives can provide insight, contribute to a strengthened understanding of new roles, and identify strategies for cost effectiveness for the university. In the current climate of increased demand and economic constraints, the solutions to the problems of access to scholarly information necessitate shrewd thinking and determined action.

What is the experience of these projects that relate to cost containment, improved access, or more effective management of knowledge for the benefit of the student, researcher, and society as a whole? Three projects will be reported on during the course of this session.

Richard Rockwell has three titles. He is the Executive Director of the Inter-university Consortium for Political and Social Research. He's a research scientist at the Institute for Social Research Center for Political Studies, and he's also an adjunct professor of sociology at the University of Michigan. His current research interests lie in three areas: archiving and dissemination of quantitative data, national statistical systems, and the human dimensions of global environmental change. Richard will address the topic of funding for social science data archiving and services in the networked environment.

Rush Miller will present **Burkart Holzner's** paper. Dr. Holzner could not be with us today because of unexpected, but required travel to the Far East. Apparently he was scheduled to go to China a week or so ago and the International Conference on Women's Issues created a political situation that required China to reschedule his trip for this week.

I appreciate Rush's willingness to fill in for Dr. Holzner. Rush hails from the University of Pittsburgh where he is the Director of Libraries.

As you know, Dr. Holzner is also from the University of Pittsburgh where he is the Director of the University Center for International Studies and Professor of Sociology and Public and International Affairs. The presentation will focus on Dr. Holzner's involvement with building a distributed North American library collection for foreign language and area studies.

---

[1]Richard E. Lucier, Assistant Vice Chancellor for Academic Information Management at the University of California, San Francisco, presented several examples of electronic resources available at his library. Shrinking library budgets, increasing paper based journal prices, and increasing demand for electronic resources required Dr. Lucier to downsize the library resources spent on the paper based library and increase the resources spent on the electronic library. Dr. Lucier presented the Knowledge Management Model of paper based and electronic resources. Dr. Lucier also talked about the costs and financing of the Red Sage Project which provides electronic access to 100 medical journals.

Dr. Lucier chose not to include his paper in the conference proceedings.

Funding Social Science Data Archiving and Services in the Networked Environment

Richard C. Rockwell[1]
Executive Director
Inter-university Consortium for Political and Social Research

Knowledge is a peculiar thing. You can give it away any number of times without ever giving it up. The more knowledge that you give away, the greater the likelihood that someone will give you back new knowledge. If you horde knowledge, its value may decline; if you do not refresh your learning with contributions from others, its value will certainly decline. These peculiarities apply strongly to a special kind of knowledge: factual information that is organized for analysis, otherwise known as "data."

Data is conceptually unlike any other known resource. It is inexhaustible, non-renewable, and non-substitutable. Data cannot be exhausted no matter how much it is used; one person's use of data does not diminish the data in any way for the next user. However, despite being inexhaustible, data is also a non-renewable resource. Once the chance to collect data has passed, the potential data is lost forever. It cannot be recovered like a burned forest can be replanted. The only recourse is speculation or reconstruction, and neither is ever fully satisfactory. Finally, data is not a substitutable resource. Unlike the 1980s substitution of silicon for copper in telecommunications, there is nothing other than data that can serve the function of data.

Today's network environment makes it possible to distribute data and other kinds of information (and knowledge generally) at little or no marginal cost. Virtually all of the expenditures are in the background: acquiring information, digitizing and processing it for ease of use, validating its content, providing index and search tools, archiving it for future generations, and making it available on the World Wide Web. Most of these expenditures must be incurred in order to service just one user. The actual distribution process itself is highly automated. Assuming that personal user support is not required, the entire transaction is handled without human intervention in the course of routine computing activities. With the cost of computing cycles approaching zero, with sharply declining costs of storage media, and with (presently) minimal communications charges, the marginal cost of servicing a request for information from the n_{th} user is almost zero.

However, Nothing Is Free

If data and other kinds of information can be given away repeatedly on the networks without any loss of its value and at very little cost, does it then follow that information provided on the networks should be free? Knowledge, broadly construed, is typically not free: encyclopedias are for sale, authors earn royalties for books, magazines charge subscription fees, and college professors prefer to be paid. Is information on the network to be treated differently?

There is widespread a tenacious but shallow belief that information should be free on the Web. Such an imperative to make information available free or nearly free—whether mandated by regulation or subtly enforced by an "Internet culture"—would effectively prevent many major suppliers of information from making their services available on the Web. Information providers are not in business for their health. Some of them are in business to make money, and others are in not-for-profit businesses that must cover their costs. These costs are routinely so large relative to the direct costs of Web distribution of information that the costs simply could not be covered by a pricing algorithm based upon the marginal cost of servicing a request from the n$_{th}$ user. If user fees are to be imposed, they will have to be substantially above marginal cost.

And the current model, voluntarism, will carry us not much further into the task of equipping the Web with information providers.

Apart from imposing much steeper user fees, are there alternatives for financing information providers? Most service providers do not have the power to levy taxes, but for governmental agencies that do, taxes can provide the needed support. It should be clearly acknowledged that these agencies are not providing "free" services; they are simply charging differently and without regard to use. Few information providers can expect largess from either private foundations or the Federal Government, given the large number of claimants for such funding. It seems highly doubtful that free-will donations will finance large information operations as they do churches. Host institutions—which now are often the real supporters of information services, through their subsidies of personnel, equipment, and communications access—will probably decide that they do not want to support a "free" information service for the whole world in perpetuity. And the current model, voluntarism, will carry us not much further into the task of equipping the Web with information providers.

There are sectors of the Web that are already economically quite viable. Many organizations are now establishing professional Web services as a routine aspect of their outreach, such as publicizing the resources of a university, advertising a piece of software, or getting feedback from television audiences. The cost of such services is presumably covered by diversion of funding from other marketing programs or by an expectation of increased business. Some organizations are substituting network services for labor-intensive clerical operations such as student registration, presumably saving money. Entertainment on the Web will surely carry a subscription fee or per-use fee and may well end up subsidizing most of the telecommunications infrastructure.

However, these marketing, administrative, and entertainment services little resemble the information services of a great library or a data archive. At my own organization, the Inter-university Consortium for Political and Social Research (ICPSR), those costs total more than $2 million annually at a minimum, ignoring support from targeted grants and contracts that add another $2 million to the base. It would take rather a lot of transactions priced at the marginal cost of data distribution to replace that $2 million. Division by zero remains undefined even at Ethernet speeds. At a price of $25 per transaction, some 80,000 transactions would be required to replace that $2 million—and I have been told there would be considerable price resistance even at that low level.

Talk of user fees raises hackles in parts of the Internet community. The preferred economic model for network information services is apparently the model of the cooperative volunteer: "I provide information for free, and you provide information for free, and thus everything is fair." This ethos reflects either a dramatically new vision of an unprecedented level of altruism and cooperation, or a wonderful naïveté. To be sure, it works to some degree: today many information services are ostensibly provided for "free" by Web home pages, gophers, and anonymous FTP. But the appearance of being free is mostly false, because many of these services have invisible but hefty external subsidies behind them.

Nothing is free; the only question is "who pays and how?" Exchanging information in payment for information will not long work. The present quasi-barter economy can hardly apply when paychecks have to be written and vendors have to be paid, and it does not in fact apply even today. That is why, despite many requests to pay by barter over the years, ICPSR is unable to extend membership privileges to organizations because they donate data— the bills still have to be paid. Somebody is already paying for every service offered on the Web—and paying not just for the cost of putting the information up on the Web but also for the background costs that far exceed the Web-related costs. The question is, of course, whether those somebodies will pay forever.

This is the dilemma faced by ICPSR, an organization established in 1962 that has become the world's largest archive of quantitative social science data. ICPSR's "somebodies who pay" are colleges, universities, and research institutes in North America and national archives elsewhere, which pay annual institutional dues so that their faculty, students, and staff may have access to ICPSR's data archive and other services. What would be their motivation to continue to pay membership dues if ICPSR were to make all of its services available "for free" on the Web? It would be irrational for them to do so.

This article focuses on ICPSR because that organization and its dilemma are most familiar to the author, but the analysis and the tentative funding strategy probably have much wider application. This is not intended to be a sales tract for ICPSR, but at times it will necessarily read like that. This is because I have to make a point: a professional information provider does something qualitatively different from most of the services now being offered voluntarily on the Web. This point needs to be made clearly and firmly, and without any sense of shame that the laborer expects to be paid, and paid adequately.

The data that could be provided on the Web by ICPSR dwarfs the social science information resources presently available there. The Web still contains relatively little information; it mostly contains information about information (meta-information)[2] and a wealth of opinion pieces and responses to random questions. Provision of meta-information is a considerable improvement over the situation as recently as 1993. In its birth pangs the Web was the epitome of reflexivity: what was available on the Web was mostly about the Web.

The early Web was an anarchistic blossoming of amateurs, rich, complex, and exciting but basically not to be looked to or relied upon as a provider of information.[3] Today, information providers such as ICPSR are making tentative moves towards the Web, often under the guise of free trials and marketing efforts. It is great to be able to search the *Encyclopedia Britannica* on the Web in a way that I could not conceivably search with the printed form. However, once my free trial expires, will I be willing to pay the substantial per-use charges that the *Britannica* can justifiably impose? Perhaps, but then I do have financial resources not available to most of the population. Analogously, would some graduate student be willing to pay $500 for access to one of the EuroBarometer survey data sets in which ICPSR has invested at least $20,000 of its members funding?

It costs real money to do what professional organizations do. The difference between a professional provider and (the worst of) non-professional information service providers is approximately the difference between, on the one hand, a well-catalogued library with an aggressive acquisition program, a strong preservation program, and a professional reference staff, and on the other hand, a used book store, with a sloppy proprietor, where there is no shelf list, no systematic acquisitions program, the roof leaks, and the rent has been overdue for two months. One can admire the pluckiness of that proprietor and wish him well without setting him up as a model for the new information age. The problem is that there are social forces in action that may make it difficult for the library or the data archive to survive and prosper as we have known it, while encouraging the sloppy proprietor to expand his shelf space, acquire more out-of-date books, and advertise internationally. The use of outstanding software by this proprietor—art work, fast response, user-friendly interface—would do absolutely nothing to improve the quality of his collection.

What is required to do it right is not technical expertise in use of the Web; computer scientists are generally not the experts who know how to do this right. Instead, good information products are the work of people who understand scholarship and how people use information resources. They are in the tradition of those professionals who have thought about cataloguing, indexing, preservation, and acquisitions policies for hundreds of years. Their skills and their wisdom are still pertinent today; what has changed is the technology with which they must work. I find it rather saddening that some of today's leaders of information technology consider the traditional work of librarians to be irrelevant to their aims and plans.

Imagine a world in which *King Lear* disappeared from the stage upon the death of Shakespeare in 1616. In which the Ninth Symphony vanished from the orchestral repertoire upon Beethoven's death in 1827. And in which *The Division of Labor in Society* disappeared from the sociological literature when Durkheim died in 1917. None of these events occurred because the authors of these works were not solely responsible for their preservation: each had a publisher, and the publisher (or the publisher's archive) took responsibility for ensuring that the work remained intact and usable.

Had there been a World Wide Web on which Beethoven distributed his sheet music, who would have run his file server in 1828? Who would have ensured that even if the file server burned up, there would have been a backup copy of the music somewhere else? Who would have answered questions from musicians who thought something had gone wrong in the transcription? And who would have adapted Beethoven's network service to the new TCP/IP protocol when it displaced the old one?

It has turned out to be very useful to have publishers, great libraries, and scrupulous archivists. The same is true in the social sciences. ICPSR is among the handful of organizations for which the cliché is true: if it did not exist, someone would have to invent it. The question of the day, however, is how such information providers and archives will be able to survive and prosper in the new age of the Web.

Support of the traditional, background work of the library and the archive is what concerns me today. For more than 30 years, ICPSR has been supported by annual dues, and by special-purpose grants and contracts. ICPSR has provided services to institutions as a whole, usually to their libraries or computation centers, and those facilities have provided direct user services on their campuses. Institutions got visible products of their memberships: printed codebooks, bulky guidebooks, racks of tapes. Campuses all over the world have parts of rooms set aside for "the ICPSR collection."

In the near future when data services are provided by ICPSR directly to individuals, and when the products of those services are bytes that float invisibly over the network, will institutions still be willing to continue to pick up the tab for usage of ICPSR services by their faculty, staff, and students? They will, under most models, have essentially no control of that usage. ICPSR can provide voluminous reports to institutions of services provided to them, but will a report have the same impact as does a room of delivered products?

The problem of funding services inside the ICPSR membership is trivial in comparison to the problem of funding services outside the membership. Who will pay for services provided to those individuals? To be sure, most of the expense will already have been incurred in order to serve the membership. Will members therefore be willing to pick up everyone else's tab for acquiring, processing, and preserving data, and for associated user support services? Why in the world should they do so?

These questions may be cast in a form peculiar to the membership situation in which ICPSR now finds itself, but the broader questions pervade many current discussions about the Internet. A strategy is here proposed in which institutions are asked to make a firm commitment to support of an integral part of the infrastructure of social science, in which foundations and government agencies are asked to recognize the costs of archiving, and in which individuals pay modest user and/or annual fees. At the same time, ICPSR will improve its services to the membership. An analogous strategy might work for other information service providers.

A Brief History and Description of ICPSR

Thirty years ago a group of leading social scientists established a consortium of universities and colleges through which they could share electronic data and the training to use that data. To ICPSR they gave responsibility for acquiring social science data from all over the world. Recognizing that the data was often in poor shape for use by anyone other than the people who collected and therefore knew the data, they also assigned to ICPSR the tasks of processing and documenting the data so that many different kinds of persons, with different levels of expertise, could effectively undertake research now and well into the future. ICPSR was further given the responsibility for distributing the data in forms that are compatible with current and future computing technology in all its varieties, no matter how that technology changes, and for providing technical assistance to social scientists in using the data in their home environments. This technical assistance has been provided through both personal consultation and a Summer Program that annually attracts more than 500 faculty and graduate students to ICPSR from many disciplines and from all over the world.

Moreover, the founders of ICPSR mandated a fundamental responsibility that has been virtually invisible to most social scientists because the task has been flawlessly performed and is usually under-appreciated wherever it is performed: they gave ICPSR responsibility for archiving the data for posterity. By taking data preservation seriously, they sought to ensure that the empirical observations of the social sciences will forever be available. ICPSR has, to my knowledge, never lost a data set. It takes extraordinary steps to ensure that this continues to be the case, including renting space in two off-campus warehouses for duplicate data storage in the event the central facilities are destroyed. ICPSR has, in fact, served as the archive that provides government agencies such as the U.S. Bureau of the Census with their past data products. In the current fiscal year ICPSR expects to spend $65,000 just for the purpose of migrating from one archival medium to another.

ICPSR has become an integral part of the infrastructure of social science. This is *not* primarily due to its distribution of data, although that is clearly the most obvious product of ICPSR. Less than 20% of ICPSR's expenditures are for activities even remotely connected to data distribution— and that is with the expensive medium of magnetic tape. However, data distribution is much less of a big deal these days. It has increasingly become easy and cheap to disseminate data over the Internet. In addition, the standards by which principal investigators prepare data sets for use by others have risen to the point that data sets in the form in which they are turned over to ICPSR are occasionally ready for use by others. Electronic documentation is now much more commonly produced by the data collectors, although, curiously, not especially so by federal statistical agencies. Some of the more obvious and public services of ICPSR are thus declining in salience for the research community.

That does not, or should not, matter. The reason for ICPSR's centrality to social science is and has always been its proactive program for acquisition of data and its firm commitment to archiving those data. Virtually each day ICPSR adds to the archive a new study, ready for use in this generation or the next. The social sciences now do not misplace their past surveys, censuses, and data bases, although data from some of the classic studies of the 40s and 50s is apparently lost forever. It has become routine—even expected by granting agencies—for data collectors to share their data with the entire social science community through deposit in a data archive, an ethic just now emerging in some disciplines outside social science.

Access to data is a deeply important prerequisite for the advance of any field of science. Without the data archiving and data access provided by ICPSR, the social sciences in the U.S. would be markedly thinner and weaker than they have actually been. ICPSR has made it possible for social scientists to ask diverse research questions that go well beyond those posed by the original data collectors, to address new questions to old data, to ask old questions in powerful new ways, to construct time series and repeated cross-sections, and to perform meta-analyses. ICPSR-provided data sets have been the foundation for thousands of monographs, research articles, theses, dissertations, and reports. The agencies that support research have saved much money because ICPSR has been there to capitalize on the potential of data-sharing in the social sciences. Many social scientists have been enabled to do research that would otherwise have been beyond their financial capacity. Training in the social sciences has increasingly come to resemble the laboratory-oriented training of the natural sciences. All of this potential and promise will still be there in the future. The social sciences of the next century would be malnourished without an ICPSR.

Those social scientists who follow us would

find considerable fault with our generation if we failed to build and maintain this data collection. Although the scale of data gathering in the social sciences is dwarfed by similar projects in the natural sciences, the sum spent during the last thirty years on collecting social science data must be beyond half a billion dollars—and many times that if the decennial U.S. Census and other Federal statistical agency data products are included. Those investments are preserved at ICPSR. Those resources will make possible a future for the social sciences in which they are based on empirical observations that have been sustained over a considerable period of time, something that the social sciences, being young disciplines in their present empirical form, have never had. Astronomy in its first fifty years of observation by the Maya and Egyptians probably had a richer data collection than the social sciences have so far had. It is organizations such as ICPSR that are changing this for the social sciences.

The resources of ICPSR are being accumulated for the use of today's faculty, staff, and students, and for the use of those who follow them. This holds whether or not an institution even obtains a single data set in a given year. ICPSR is one of the resources that make it possible for institutions to have faculty who do research and graduate students who write empirical theses. In this regard ICPSR is rather like a great library that buys a book because a librarian expects that in 15 years some professor or graduate student will come looking for it. Not all libraries can adopt such policies, and even the greatest must make judgments—but without a few such libraries nationally, scholarship would be impoverished.[4]

ICPSR is a public good in a pure sense, for its goods and services cannot be provided through a private market, only collective action could have created and sustained ICPSR. The costs are such that no one social scientist could finance it, nor could one institution. However, once ICPSR came into existence as the result of a pact between 21 U.S. universities and the University of Michigan it began to serve *all* social scientists—those who are now alive and those to be born, at member institutions and not at member institutions—by performing a service that it could withhold from *all* social scientists no more than a lighthouse could withhold its beam from a passing ship: ICPSR preserves social science's sole inexhaustible, non-renewable, and non-substitutable resource, its data. The data collection is preserved for all of social science. Social scientists and their heirs thus benefit from ICPSR whether or not their institutions are members. And their institutions can take full advantage of ICPSR's resources by the simple expedient of joining ICPSR sometime in the next century, even though other institutions have invested heavily for years. This all makes ICPSR a pure public good. Taxation is the ordinary method of supporting public goods, and the one used everywhere but in the U.S. for the support of data archives. In the peculiar way of Americans, voluntary memberships support ICPSR.

ICPSR is a public good in a pure sense, for its goods and services cannot be provided through a private market, only collective action could have created and sustained ICPSR.

In recent years when an institution's membership was challenged by a dean or business officer, ICPSR has produced a special report detailing the amount of data that had been provided to that member institution and the cost of obtaining those data sets were the institution not a member. The comparison of the two sets of costs—annual dues and sums of non-member fees for the same data—was usually convincing.

It was also inadequate as a rationale for membership in ICPSR, for that tabulation was always only a weak measure of ICPSR's value to the institution. The true measure of ICPSR's value is the fact that the institution's faculty, staff, and students have access to a continually-growing and diverse resource of guaranteed permanence.

From the viewpoint of libraries at member institutions, however, providing data resources to their institutions is what ICPSR is there for. To libraries, we are somewhat like a publisher from which they order materials, having paid in advance, or perhaps like a buying cooperative in which libraries pool funds to reduce the cost of a resource to each participant. If individuals have drawing rights on ICPSR, would the same arguments for membership be persuasive for libraries? Could an assistant director of libraries defend the annual ICPSR membership dues when, after being asked how much data the library had acquired, answered "None for the library— but faculty and students acquired a gigabyte directly from ICPSR as a privilege of the membership"?

However inadequate as a measure, the distribution of data is far more easily quantifiable than is the building of a resource. It can be understood by people who understand nothing about social science, particularly if distribution statistics are accompanied by non-member cost estimates that are several multiples of the annual dues. ICPSR does indeed quantify its acquisition of studies and publicize that number, but this measure says little to a business manager who has little basis for knowing that ICPSR's acquiring and archiving data is useful to the local institution's pursuit of its own goals. Further, the business manager may figure that the institution can rejoin ICPSR at any time if some faculty member wants a particular study.[5] The base of institutional support has thus always been somewhat shifting, with some members leaving each year and (generally more) new members joining.

Today ICPSR has more than 325 member colleges and universities in the U.S. and Canada, and national members in Europe, Latin America, and elsewhere (collectively serving hundreds of additional institutions). In 1995, a research university will pay annual dues of $9,500; larger undergraduate institutions, $5,950; and smaller undergraduate institutions, $3,000. These dues are substantially under-priced in comparison to data base services commonly purchased by libraries, but after 20-30 years of under-pricing, it is probably too late to change. National members—typically, the national archive for the social sciences in a country—pay annual dues ranging from $2,000 to more than $10,000. These fees are intended to depend upon the country's economic resources and the size of its social science community. ICPSR's annual budget currently totals $4.7 million.

The institutional memberships provide the backbone of ICPSR support, leveraging grants and contracts for special-purpose projects. They provide the only general support that ICPSR has. The rest of the ICPSR budget is targeted to specific areas of social science through contracts or grants restricted to such projects as crime and justice data, and data on aging and the aged. These are important areas of research, but most of social science is left out of these targeted programs—meaning that the annual member dues must be drawn upon for activities in most of political science, economics, sociology, history, etc. The ICPSR infrastructure is also largely provided by member dues: they have historically provided most of the support for the costs of servicing requests for data and documentation even in the areas in which special-purpose grants have been obtained. The commitment to archive in perpetuity the data resulting from such special projects still rests squarely upon the ICPSR membership.

Implications of Internet Methods of Data Delivery for Institutional Memberships

For most of its history, the magnetic tape was the principal means by which ICPSR distributed data. Today tapes are slowly being displaced by FTP service as social scientists acquire the equipment and skills to use FTP. Use of CD-ROMs is also growing. ICPSR is investing $45,000 this year in a project to move the core of the archive to magnetic disks so that FTP service can be generally provided. Client-server facilities will soon come on line at ICPSR, largely obviating the need for importing copies of data sets to the desktop. These new methods of data access hold much promise for returning the researcher to the world of immediate hands-on contact with data that was known, in primitive form, in the days of rotary calculators and card sorters. They also pose a significant organizational problem for ICPSR as well as a pricing problem for services to non-members.

ICPSR has historically provided its services through a designated individual on each member campus known as the Official Representative. On many campuses, the Official Representative is a trained Data Librarian (often with a small staff). The membership is often financially located in the university library or a computer center, although there are remnants of the original departmental form of ICPSR representation (typically a junior professor in the political science department). This arrangement provided for maximum efficiency in the provision of data for use on mainframes; for non-duplication of services by ICPSR to people on the same campus; for the ability to share data and documentation among all faculty, staff, and students on a campus; for a local level of expert service, for backstopping ICPSR's headquarters staff in technical assistance; and for a local point of contact on all things concerning ICPSR and social science data in general. The arrangement has, in effect, resulted in more people "working for" ICPSR outside Ann Arbor than at the organization's headquarters.

When FTP becomes the dominant mode of distribution of data, it will make little sense for ICPSR to transmit data solely to a campus's Official Representative. While the Official Representative might today place the data on a file server, rather than in a tape rack at the mainframe as before, this would still be a highly centralized mode of operation. It would rather resemble the department stores of the 1950's that were laced by pneumatic tubes, with every transaction involving someone in a central, distant office where the web of pneumatic tubes converged.

The question arises: why not eliminate the middleman? Would not services be delivered more effectively if individual users had, if they wished, direct, personal access to ICPSR? That is the clear preference of many social scientists. To be sure, there are still arguments in favor of ICPSR's dealing with a single point on campus, essentially the same arguments that held in the days of the mainframe. But solely providing centralized service seems archaic and is clearly not the wave of the future.

However, providing services directly to individuals poses real problems for ICPSR. There may be increased demands for personal technical assistance, particularly in the first few months or years in which people are learning new technologies. There is a high likelihood of serial retransmittal of identical data from ICPSR to multiple users on a single campus, resulting in network congestion at the ICPSR end and a need for heftier servers. Had such a system been in place when the 1994 National Election Study was released by ICPSR, it is likely that five or six scholars on the campuses of each research university would have tried to obtain the data set within a couple of days. For the institution, at a minimum there will be a sharp reduction of the ability of people on a campus to share data and documentation. The researcher might suffer directly because the expert services that had been locally provided are no longer available, or because the Official Representative is unfamiliar with a data set that he or she has never seen and for which he or she cannot take responsibility. Even locating the right data could become more difficult despite the use of various catalog services and searching tools; the Official Representative has typically been quite expert at locating data at ICPSR or elsewhere.

There is even an authentication problem: how can ICPSR be certain that a person with an email address at a member institution is actually affiliated with that institution? The University of Michigan alone maintains an estimated 10,000 "umich.edu" email addresses for people who have no employment or student affiliation with the University. Universities are increasingly giving their alumni email addresses; would this mean that ICPSR eventually is at risk of being expected to provide services to the nearly 400,000 living graduates of the University of Michigan?[6] Among other things, this would mean that General Motors, Ford, and Chrysler would suddenly have access to the ICPSR archive at no cost to them.

An Alternative to Institutional Memberships: Adequate User Fees?

If the justification for institutional memberships is difficult to communicate to institutional officers who pay the bills, perhaps user fees set at an adequate level to pay for the whole enterprise are worth considering. If ICPSR's acquisition, processing, and archival activities were funded entirely through user fees, the resulting price would probably put data out of reach of many of those whom ICPSR presently serves. Based upon the current structure of usage and expenses, these fees would be about 400% greater than the actual cost of data delivery on the expensive medium of tape. This would probably price most data sets at something around $300-$500, given that we would not expect to distribute 64,000 data sets a year (as we do now) if people had to pay for each one. Such a price would put ICPSR data out of the reach of most undergraduates, many graduate students, and some faculty members. Nevertheless, that price reflects what the operation actually costs. This has basically been the price structure that ICPSR has used for years when delivering data to non-members. Sales have been very low, probably because the price is so steep by the standards of the social sciences.

Imposition of such a price throughout the social sciences would be extremely destructive. It would, in effect, terminate much research, particularly outside the elite research institutions. As difficult as it might be for someone at an elite university to believe, there are faculty members who— despite never having had a grant or contract in their lives—nevertheless occasionally contribute empirical articles to the professional literature. One reason that they can do this is that their institutions provide them the resource of a membership in ICPSR. Removal of that membership would seriously undercut research and teaching at many institutions. An analogy might be found in what would happen to academic libraries circulation if readers had to pay for each book checked out, with the price including not only a part of the purchase cost but also cataloguing, shelving, space, and preservation costs.

On this argument, access to data resources, as well as to books, is one of the things that colleges and universities should provide at no direct cost to the user. The argument partly rests on a sense of what constitutes democratic access to data and partly on a fear of the power differentials that would be accentuated if only the economically privileged could obtain access to data. In this era of the Newt, such an argument may be labeled paternalistic or socialistic.

The Imperative to Provide Access for All, Not Just the Privileged Few

The argument for democratic access to data can turn around and bite the idea of the ICPSR membership structure. Most postsecondary institutions in the U.S. are not members of ICPSR. There are no businesses and few government agencies with memberships in ICPSR. Ordinary citizens cannot become members, yet the U.S. public paid for the collection of most of the data in the ICPSR archive.

We recognize the imperative of moving beyond providing services to skilled people at the leading academic institutions. That imperative is consistent with ICPSR's fundamental mission: to advance social science research. However, we do not know how to price those services in a manner that truly opens our archives to every faculty member, much less every citizen, and at the same time protects the financial resources that a membership structure has provided. We do not know how to preserve the integrity of the collection if we are providing data at the marginal cost of reproduction. Our situation is somewhat like that of a university library that cannot or will not charge much for use of its services but is about to lose core support from the university while simultaneously being mandated to expand its services to the entire nation. How do you support a public good without taxation or voluntary contributions?

One solution would be to enroll every institution of higher education in the U.S. as a member. That seems improbable, and it fails to solve the problem of providing services to journalists, government employees, and high school students. Another solution is to obtain a sustaining NSF grant to replace the members' contributions. This would involve the same sort of commitment to ICPSR as an integral part of the social science infrastructure as NSF has made to institutions like NCAR and the Arecibo radio telescope. At more than $2 million per year just to replace current member dues,[7] this seems an impractical objective given the scale of general funding of social science at NSF, although it is precisely such a system that funds most national data archives in Europe.

If these two solutions are impractical, what is left but charging users adequate fees for access to ICPSR data? A concrete example can provide a basis for addressing the complex dimensions of this issue. The example that I have chosen is that of the American National Election Studies.

The Example of the American National Election Studies

The American National Election Studies (ANES) are the core data resource for the large branch of political science that studies political behavior in the United States. Initiated in 1948, the ANES now provides a rich time series of information on diverse changes in national politics during a turbulent period in the nation's life: the Civil Rights Movement, the Vietnam War era, and repeated recessions are among the events that have been tracked since 1948. Political scientists are not the only users of ANES data; for example, it has extensive use within sociology because it provides detailed socioeconomic, cultural, and demographic information that cannot be obtained from data products of the Federal Government. Because of its importance to social science, ANES was designated a "National Resource Data Set" by the National Science Foundation, one of only three so designated.

As a National Resource Data Set, the ANES must be available to social scientists (and others) throughout the country without regard to whether the social scientist is located at an institution that maintains an ICPSR membership. However, NSF long provided no support to ICPSR for processing, archiving, and distributing the data set. Until the advent of FTP, the ANES staff had no enthusiasm for setting up a data distribution operation themselves. Therefore, the need for universal access has been accommodated by distributing two forms of the data. The first-issued data was the version turned over to ICPSR by the ANES study staff, along with the documentation as prepared by them. This was made available to people at non-member institutions at a price of $200. While high by current Web standards, this price just recovered the actual personnel and computer costs that ICPSR incurred in acquiring these data, doing minimal processing, and writing a tape for a non-member institution according to its technical specifications. Magnetic tapes were always an expensive storage medium. The U.S. Bureau of the Census, employing similar calculations of marginal cost of reproduction, typically prices a reel of tape at $175 or more.

After receiving and distributing the study staff version of the data, ICPSR worked intensively with the data set, adding derived variables, doing various sorts of checks on the data, and preparing documentation. The costs of this operation were substantial. For example, just the documentation for the 1992 ANES cost ICPSR some $15,000 in payments to outside printers. The personnel cost of producing that documentation was additional. These investments in the ANES are made out of the funding base supplied by member dues.

When a non-member wanted to acquire the ICPSR version of the data, ICPSR sought to recover a portion of these investments. Under present prices for delivery of data sets on magnetic tape, ICPSR would currently charge an individual at a non-member institution $1,425 for the 1992 ANES.

But today if the data is provided by FTP, the marginal cost to ICPSR of making data available to an individual at a non-member institution is virtually zero. A reasonable charge for the data set—ignoring the work done by ICPSR on it—might then be $5 or even $25. However, ignoring the acquisition and processing costs is unfair to the members who supported the work. Therefore, charging such a low fee has always been felt to endanger the basis of membership—"if they can get all that they want for less money than the annual member dues, why would they pay member dues?"

Despite this deep concern about undercutting our own membership rationale, ICPSR is undertaking an experiment in cheap pricing of data sets. In May 1995 ICPSR released a CD-ROM containing all of the ANES studies conducted since 1948. This CD-ROM also contains a cumulative file of repeated questions, SAS and SPSS data definition statements for every data set, and full electronic documentation of every data set. Further, it provides an interface for three of the more complex data sets, which assists users in drawing extract files that are ready for use with SPSS or SAS. Were we to price this CD-ROM to non-members at our current prices for single data sets, it would carry a price tag in excess of $37,000.

The actual price to individuals at non-member institutions is $65. This is partly justified by the fact that the ANES study staff made both a substantial personnel investment in assisting ICPSR in preparing this product and a direct transfer of funds from the ANES to ICPSR. But the justification also involves the fact that this is an experiment. It is a risky experiment, in that investments in the ANES that must total at least half a million dollars have been made by ICPSR members in making it possible for this CD-ROM to exist—and we are letting that investment go for a price of $65.

What does this pricing model do to ICPSR's funding base? Clearly, ICPSR would have had little success in selling even one copy of the $37,000 CD-ROM, and our income from sales of $65 CD-ROMs could conceivably be greater than $37,000. In fact, the initial pressing of 2,000 copies is virtually exhausted. This does not mean that ICPSR has obtained a gross income from sales of almost $130,000. Most of the 2,000 were given to member institutions as a service of their memberships, and faculty on member campuses can order personal copies at only $30. It is likely that the commercial sector would price such a product in the range of $2,000, if prices for data bases are a predictor, but they expect sales primarily to institutions, while ICPSR hopes to put a copy of this CD-ROM on the desk of every political science graduate student in the country. Had Hershey priced its chocolate bars at $10 apiece, it would have had an excellent profit margin and few sales. At $0.50 apiece, the company makes a great deal of money and brings to the world the wonderful benefits of Hershey's chocolate.

But it is actually not the amount of income from the product that worries us; it is instead what such prices will do to the motivation of an institution to remain a member. We might earn $60,000 from sales of this one CD-ROM and simultaneously lose $200,000 as institutions drop their memberships. To be sure, obtaining one study or even one large set of studies, such as the ANES, cannot be the sole reason for an institution's membership. But if a noticeable portion of ICPSR's major studies could be obtained by non-members at such prices, membership might well be endangered. Providing free or nearly-free access to the data by FTP would only add insult to injury.

There are considerable pressures to set such prices for most of our "best-sellers," including pressures from funding agencies. There are pressures on principal investigators to provide free access to the data they collect, using funds provided by the grant that paid for the data collection. This acceptance of responsibility for disseminating their own data is well and good, but who pays for archiving these data in 2010? Who pays for acquiring the little-used data set that nevertheless will be part of the foundation for a major book in 2020? Who pays for providing technical assistance in 2030 on the use of a data set from 1995? And who ensures that the data can be used on the spiffy computers that are sure to abound then, when nobody remembers precisely what those shiny little disks were used for, now that everyone uses molecular storage methods?

A Blended Strategy for Sustaining ICPSR

This is the dilemma facing ICPSR and probably facing many other information providers. Every solution that has been mentioned has been rejected as inadequate or as inappropriate given the aims of the organization. What, then, to do? Why not employ all of them at once? This is a lesson from ecology, which highlights the dangers of an organism being dependent upon a single food source; diversification of feeding habits is protective. The aim of this blended support strategy is to preserve all the benefits of a membership organization while permitting ICPSR to service its public on-ramp onto the Information Superhighway, thus extending its services beyond the institutional memberships.

(1) *Retain the foundation of institutional memberships*. Institutional memberships should remain the core support of ICPSR. In addition to all the benefits for ICPSR mentioned above (which sum up to providing stable and general funding), a membership structure carries several other benefits for the social sciences and for ICPSR. It would be difficult to replace these benefits given any other funding system. Through its members ICPSR is governed by and directly responsive to the social sciences, not to a governmental agency or foundation. The ongoing dialogue created by membership provides a "say" in future directions for ICPSR. Membership creates a partnership among scholars who cooperate in the creation and archiving of data for redistribution within the social science community, thereby realizing aspects of "the scientific method" such as replication, verification, and extension of findings. It networks the Official Representatives and offers them a means of upgrading and sharing their skills. Data finding is centralized and cost-effective, not requiring shopping at multiple providers.[8]

This part of the funding strategy depends upon the success of an argument: institutions such as colleges and universities have a vested interest in ICPSR, not just in terms of obtaining data and documentation but also—more so—in developing and maintaining an integral part of the infrastructure of social science. Therefore, they should be members of ICPSR. Beyond that, institutions receive concrete benefits from their memberships, including benefits that are not publicly available. If this argument is not successful, institutional memberships are not likely to be around very long. Given the success of the argument, institutional memberships should be retained as the foundation of ICPSR's support.

(2) *Offer individual subscriptions on member campuses and at non-member institutions.* ICPSR should be responsive to faculty and students at member institutions who wish direct access to ICPSR services, but it should not make those services automatically available at no fee. There are real costs to ICPSR of providing services outside of the Official Representative system. One solution is to establish individual subscriptions, which would be priced for basic services (receipt of a certain quantity of data by FTP) at (perhaps) $100 - $200 per year for individuals at member institutions. In addition, there could be a universal one-time charge of $25 to defray costs of establishing individual computer accounts.

Individual services on member campuses would be offered with fairly restrictive licenses. The volume of services that could be used by a subscriber in a year would be limited, and those services would be licensed solely to the individual subscriber, not to an institution. They could not be used to create an institution-wide resource; that would remain the task of the Official Representative, upon whom the institution should rely to "get it right."

An annual subscription fee for an individual at a non-member institution, or for a member of the public, might be 3-4 times the rate on member campuses. Additional restrictions are needed to squelch any tendency for member institutions to turn into non-members because four times the individual rate is still a bargain compared to their annual dues to ICPSR:

- The value-added services of ICPSR would not be available outside the membership except at a premium, if then.
- Only selected data sets—those publicly funded—would be eligible for this service.
- Obtaining a data set through non-

member arrangements could not create a campus-wide resource; the data set would be licensed for the exclusive use of the individual user and could not be deposited in a campus facility.
- The data would be on loan, not sold to the individual, and the license to use the data would expire after a period of time (two years?).
- The annual total transactions with all individuals at an institution would be capped, as well as the volume of transactions with any one individual.
- The only distribution method provided for by this non-member subscription would be FTP. The subscriber is in the predicament that Henry Ford once recommended for the American consumer: you can have any color car you want so long as it is black.
- User support by ICPSR would be provided only for a fee.

It is conceivable that annual subscriptions simply will not succeed except with users with very high demands for data. For that reason, ICPSR needs to consider a transaction price as well. With exactly the same restrictions imposed, a charge of $25-$50 per data set to persons at non-member institutions might be sensible.

However, none of these prices—subscriptions or transaction fees—has a basis in market research. They have essentially been pulled out of thin air. There is no sense of the potential size of the market; therefore, there is no way to calculate a price so that costs can be recovered. ICPSR's first test of the size of the individual market is that provided by the ANES CD-ROM, and from that test it appears that market sizes are likely to be in the hundreds rather than in the thousands. However, no one knows. This is a serious lacking of this aspect of the blended strategy. We have no real way of knowing whether we are under-pricing our services (as might be the case with the ANES CD-ROM) or over-pricing them so high that we will have few takers. If the price is set too high, the motivation for cheating by reselling ICPSR data at a lower price might become overpowering. Even at a very low price, the barter ideology might lead some people to copy ICPSR data sets to their hundred closest friends and relatives. At almost any price, professors are likely to "share" their ICPSR subscriptions with their graduate students.

There is very little guidance to be had in pricing from the cost of servicing the n_{th} user, unlike in the pricing of automobiles or toasters. The literature has little to say on pricing strategy for information products. Discussions of pricing rapidly turn into discussions of paying and how the security of transactions can be assured. This is an area ripe for experimentation and research. Among the data that is needed is a measure of the size of the potential market.

(3) *Opening membership beyond colleges and universities.* ICPSR already has some members that are not colleges and universities, such as the Library of Congress Congressional Research Service, the Consortium for International Earth Science Information Network, and the Brookings Institution. However, there has never been a systematic effort to recruit such members. Such an effort should be mounted, at a scale of about $15,000-$25,000 annual dues for each membership. Federal agencies—but not the Federal government as a whole—would be eligible for these memberships.

(4) *Ask NSF and other external funders to share developmental and equipment costs with ICPSR members.* ICPSR has undertaken a massive amount of developmental work over the years with resources provided by member dues. Allocation of those dues to developmental ends has precluded their allocation to the routine functioning of ICPSR, and the result is that the time to process data sets for release to members

has lengthened and some services are not offered at the scale we would wish (such as preparation of data definition statements for SAS and SPSS for all data sets). Developmental activities such as scanning of all documentation in the archive, SGML/HTML markup of that documentation, and programming of a user-friendly interface for the General Social Survey should be undertaken only if ICPSR can obtain the endorsement of the social science community through its allocation in peer review of funding for that purpose. This strategy has been successful, in the recent awards of more than $100,000 from NSF for the General Social Survey project and $60,000 to aid in equipment purchase.

Development is a continuing organizational need, and it is one from which the agencies making special-purpose grants and contracts to ICPSR have profited. Ideally, those grants and contracts should make an explicit allocation for developmental activities and equipment purchases every year as a condition of the continued acceptance by ICPSR of those projects. Realistically, ICPSR is likely to accept a grant or contract that barely covers its own costs, because the social science community benefits from our doing so.

(5) *Ask NSF to support what it requires be done.* ICPSR shares something with state and local governments: it is also the victim of an unfunded mandate. NSF expects each recipient of a grant that involves the collection of data to deposit the data in a public archive. ICPSR is not specifically mentioned as the public archive, but it is hard to imagine ICPSR not being the recipient of most of these data. The three National Resource data sets are thus special cases of a more general NSF requirement to make data publicly available. NSF is, in this manner, obtaining services from ICPSR without paying for them in any way. ICPSR, consistent with its mission, has been happy to assume those costs. It can no longer do so without cutting something else or beginning to refuse to accept data sets.

No model for NSF support of ICPSR's archiving costs is perfect. A flat annual grant makes little sense, in that it would not reflect variances in ICPSR's work load. But a per-deposit subsidy, either paid directly to ICPSR or to the data producer for transferal to the data archive of the PI's choice, might be an administrative nightmare. Despite that, it would recognize that NSF is imposing costs on the members of ICPSR when it requires the deposit of data in a public archive. A small amount of funding would remedy that situation. The amount of the subsidy would be about $15,000 on average for large studies such as the National Election Studies, and perhaps as low as $1,000 for studies that were much less complicated. The likelihood of ICPSR's receiving such a grant is probably low, because for more than 30 years ICPSR has done business without such support. The question will be asked by both program officers and peer reviewers: why should NSF provide this grant now, particularly at a time when NSF's own budget is being cut? However, the rationale for the grant is so strong that it would nearly be irresponsible to pursue it.

(6) *Permit ICPSR to expend some of this subsidy to assist principal investigators to prepare data to acceptable standards.* In many cases, the recipient of an NSF grant runs out of money at just the time it becomes necessary to deposit the data with a public archive. The result is that ICPSR receives a mess: poor documentation prepared according to no known standard, undocumented codes, exotic data formats that perfectly met the researcher's needs but would make it impossible for others to use the data, etc. And it is often the case that the graduate research assistant who can answer ICPSR's questions about the data has gone off the project by the time ICPSR receives the data. At the beginning of a

project, ICPSR ought to contact the grant recipient, providing information on the standards preferred for deposit of data with ICPSR and offering a subsidy (paid out of the NSF funds identified in [5] above) if the data is prepared according to those standards. ICPSR would reserve part of the subsidy that it has received from NSF for the costs of its own checking of the work of the researcher and for the costs of perpetually archiving the data, but a substantial portion of the subsidy might often be passed on to the researcher. This practice might achieve, among other things, much more rapid adoption by the community of archival standards than if those standards are purely voluntary. It might result in a slight decline in ICPSR's own expenditures on data processing but also in an increase in the flow of data through ICPSR.

(7) *Create a means for social scientists to put their money where their hearts are.* This idea is best explained through a specific kind of investment that some social scientists might be willing to make, particularly towards the ends of their careers. ICPSR has taken upon itself the responsibility for maintaining and updating a number of historical data series. This is not a trivial commitment; on average, ICPSR would expend about $10,000 per year to update a given data series. Because that money has not been available, many of these data series have not been updated for some time. If we were able to solicit contributions totaling $200,000, we could dedicate the interest on that money at 5% to the updating of a data series each year. Similar endowments might be created for other data collections. Raising such funds would not be easy, but we realized that it would be easier to start the ball rolling if we had an initial donor lined up. In 1994, Dr. Paul T. David established the first endowment for a data set at ICPSR.

A strategy in which ICPSR will prosper cannot consist solely of a funding strategy; it must also include plans for enhancing the value of ICPSR membership. A number of development programs are already underway at ICPSR to provide "value-added services." ICPSR was never simply a disseminator of data, despite that having been a widespread perception. Many of the value-added services now being offered around the world by data archives were developed first at ICPSR, from high-quality, standardized documentation, through desktop statistical programs, to electronic documentation.

Tomorrow's value-added services for individuals at member institutions will include: good documentation and better preparation of data sets for computer use, in line with ICPSR's long-standing practices; hypertext electronic documentation for use on the Web; user-friendly interfaces for complex data sets; access to client-server facilities that permit exploratory analysis and the customized drawing of extracts of data sets; delivery of data sets in media other than FTP and CD-ROM; preparation of integrated data bases containing several related data sets; intensive consultation with users; and enrollment in the Summer Program at reduced rates. These value-added services significantly extend ICPSR deliverables beyond the distribution of data sets. These services could be made available to individuals at non-member institutions at a premium. For more information on this aspect of the suggested strategy, see *Journey to the 21st Century: Towards a Strategic Plan for ICPSR*, by the author and available from ICPSR.

This "blended strategy" of multiple funding sources and improvements in services delivered is not, in fact, a particularly new strategy for ICPSR, because all of these funding sources have been employed in some way over ICPSR's 30-year history, and value-added services have always been available to some degree. What is new is the mix of funding and services, with far more emphasis being placed on funding sources other than traditional academic institutional memberships and on services directly provided to individuals. Whether this strategy will work to sustain an institution that is quite valuable for the social sciences is unknowable, but at least it constructs a good possibility of enabling ICPSR not only to survive but also to prosper. A similar strategy might work for other major information providers.

[1] This paper is more than ordinarily dependent on contributions from others. In particular, it is a direct result of a unique Retreat held by the ICPSR Senior Staff on May 25, 1994. That Retreat revolved around papers written by teams of members of the senior staff on which I have extensively and shamelessly drawn.

[2] Varian and Mackie-Mason, on their gopher server, state "There are vast troves of high-quality information (and probably equally large troves of dreck) currently available on the Internet, all available as free goods." If meta-information is counted as information, this is certainly true. However, my own searches have revealed surprisingly little true information in the social sciences. There are also problems of a lack of quality control (the "dreck"), preservation programs, and adequate indexing and search services. The accuracy of information is fragile: the student-run *Summer Michigan Daily* of August 9, 1995, records the site of testing of the first atomic bomb as Los Elmos, probably planting a false fact in the minds of a couple of thousand undergraduates. Various Elmos and Elmiras have probably given us lots of trouble over the years, but the atomic bomb was not among them.

[3] The Web's anarchy is also one of its most exciting qualities, because we may be seeing the birth of a new democratization of information. Of course, this promises a host of new problems. How, for example, will users of the Web sort out which page provides accurate projections of the growth of world population by 2050 and which represents incompetent demography? How will users discover that one copy of the U.S. Declaration of Independence is subtly edited for modern readability, while another is the genuine McCoy? This used to be the task of trained librarians; is it today in the hands of undergraduate computer scientists?

[4] Approximately $1 million more than is available at present is required to make this statement absolutely true, because ICPSR does not now have the resources to acquire and preserve absolutely everything done by social scientists. Perhaps it should not strive to do so, but over the years, ICPSR has learned the hazards of deciding that a data set was not worth preserving. That study of 73 nuns in Cedar Rapids could become very important to a 21st century scholar who is interested in the disappearance of monastic orders.

[5] There is a re-entry fee of 50% of the annual dues, plus a year's annual dues, but this does not fully dissuade institutions from coming in and then leaving the ICPSR membership.

[6] A day after I wrote this sentence, I received the following email message: "I am a UM grad & familiar with ICPSR; also, dues paying alum! Wife & I ... would appreciate access. Web site indicated existence of enhanced FTP service. Could you approve access and send information & 'how to'. Thanks in advance."

[7] More than $2 million would be needed; our estimate is that general support needs to be increased by approximately $1 million annually to permit ICPSR to meet the goals that social science has set for it.

[8] This section is lifted almost verbatim from the Retreat paper authored by Erik Austin, Peter Granda, and Mary Vardigan.

Building the Distributed North American Library Collection for Foreign Languages

Burkart Holzner
Director, University Center for International Studies
University of Pittsburgh

Introduction

The project on the future of North America's research libraries conducted by the ARL and the Association of American Universities (AAU) and the Mellon Foundation had been underway for some time before I became aware of it in the late fall and early winter of 1992, three years ago. I was asked to be a member of the *AAU Research Libraries Task Force on Acquisition and Distribution of Foreign Language and Area Studies Materials*. This was a distinguished and lively group of people, ably led by John H. D'Arms, Vice Provost at the University of Michigan. I had a lot to learn about libraries and their problems in a short time.

To overcome my ignorance of libraries at least a little, I asked the University of Pittsburgh librarians for help and they enthusiastically and generously provided it. Later on, we set up task forces on campus paralleling the national task forces. The complexity of the issues and their interrelations became readily apparent, as did their fearsome seriousness for scholarly work and communications.

In the spring of 1993 I became convinced that the work that had been done by ARL's staff, the Mellon Foundation, and the AAU Task Forces on defining the strategic choices that America's universities and research libraries have before them was so important that this knowledge and this challenge had to be brought home to our campus.

I was inspired by the example of Duke University—they had asked Davydd Greenwood and me to come and evaluate their international programs. Deborah Jakubs had at that time just held a campus-wide library conference: I thought that hers was a good example to follow.

With the help of colleagues from ARL, AAU, the Mellon Foundation, and other task force members we organized at the University of Pittsburgh an all day conference on February 16, 1994 to discuss the findings and recommendations of the national study in the light of our own University of Pittsburgh task force reports. It was a good and lively day with a little more than 300 faculty members participating. The university had been stirred up by the research library study. The issue of the transformation of research libraries and the need for a national, distributed collection of materials produced abroad had become an important item on the university's agenda. At the May 1994 annual meeting of the ARL I was able to give a brief report on these matters.

That is how I became drawn into the circle of people who worry about libraries.

Simultaneously, as a sociologist and director of a large center for international studies, I took and continue to take a strong interest in the changes in international scholarship occurring today as a consequence of historical shifts in the world and rapidly escalating changes in technology. Many projects have been conducted in this country and abroad to gain a better understanding of the changing nature of our national knowledge systems in the context of global change.

For example, the Social Science Research Council convened a *Workshop on International Research and Training in U.S. Social Science* in June of 1993 to focus attention on the institutional dimensions of the increasingly international agenda of social science. The themes raised included the relationship between area studies expertise and disciplinary frames of reference; the tension between theories claiming universality and culturally and institutionally specific forms of knowledge; the effect of "demand structures" on shaping the agenda of international social science and more. The workshop also considered the needs for a new research agenda on international social science.

In November of 1994 the American Council of Learned Societies convened a much more comprehensive conference (with help from the Mellon Foundation). It invited representatives of all its member societies to this conference. The summary report and the ACLS Occasional Paper No. 28 entitled *The Internationalization of Scholarship and Scholarly Societies* present a fascinating picture of the thorough internationalization of scholarly work and of the activities of the learned societies. The disciplines of scholarship are being transformed into international communities. Perspectives are changing dramatically in this process, "alternative perspectives that have grown up in different national scholarly communities are now confronting one another in fruitful exchange, the boundaries of disciplines are becoming more porous, and some entirely new fields of study are taking shape."[1]

Also in the early 90's OECD launched an ambitious study of the internationalization of higher education in all its member countries. There was a conference on this project in Washington in October 1994 and a major conference on the results is planned later this year in Monterrey, California. With Davydd Greenwood I wrote the paper on the internationalization of the universities in the United States.

The experience of working on this paper and participating in the discussion of the reports from other world regions was an eye opener for me. I have been an international education administrator and scholar for some time. Nevertheless, it was through this internationally collaborative project that I came to understand the full scope and depth of the change in store for United States universities along the international dimension. The transformation going on is truly awesome. Related transformations, sometimes using very different strategies, are occurring in all OECD countries and in all parts of the world.

Listed below are the major internationalization strategies of higher education institutions in the United States and their components and instruments of implementation.

- Institutional incentives to internationalize
- Institutional strategies: is there one?
- Components of strategies for international education
  - Development assistance and co-operation
  - Area and language studies
  - International studies and international affairs
  - Research and scholarly collaboration across international borders
  - International students and scholars on campus
  - Study-abroad and exchanges
  - Ethnic and cultural diversity
  - Internationalizing the professions
  - Public service and outreach
- Instrumentalization of strategies
  - Leadership and administrative arrangements
  - Faculty recruitment
  - Faculty development
  - Faculty rewards systems

- ♦ Curriculum development
- ♦ Inter-institutional linkages and co-operation agreements
- ♦ Public/private partnerships
- ♦ International studies and education consortia
- ♦ International fundraising
- Internationalizing Entire Institutions

Further, a research agenda on international higher education in the United States was the subject of a workshop convened in August here in Washington by the Association of International Education Administrators (AIEA) in cooperation with the American Council on Education (ACE). There is a broad concern with understanding the internationalization of scholarship, of higher education, and of learning.

The Problems

All these changes have a lot to do with libraries, and especially with research libraries. The period of history through which we are living is a "crisis" in the sense of Jacob Burckhardt (whom W.R. Connor, the Director of the National Humanities Centers at Research Triangle Park in North Carolina cites). A crisis in this sense is a period of history in which "the historical process is suddenly accelerated in terrifying fashion. Developments which otherwise take centuries seems to flit by like phantoms in months or weeks, and are fulfilled." Connor makes a very significant statement when he says "There is reason then to suspect that the current world situation constitutes an indeterminate system, one with close interconnections among the constituent parts, and recurrent patterns such as the tendency toward disintegration in the multi-ethnic state, but one not amenable to accurate predictions."[2] This situation is also an "epistemological crisis" in the sense of Alasdair MacIntyre in that we are confronted by the unprecedented and are bewildered by "what is going on here?"[3] I want us to keep these notions of "crisis" in a productive sense in mind as we think about how one produces planned, desired and beneficial reform in this context.

The research library challenge is only one part of the multidimensional changes in the world today that occur sometimes simultaneously, intersect and produce complex effects. We have vast increases in publications in all forms throughout the world. Rapid and successive changes in technology open up new forms of analysis and research, as well as new forms of scholarly communication and information storage. We are confronted by increasing costs and severely limited budgets in our research libraries. Let me illustrate the rise in library costs with Figure 1 from the Mellon Foundation study of research libraries.[4]

Multi-dimensional changes occur sometimes simultaneously, intersect, and interact with complex effects:

- structural change in the world;
- rapid changes in information and communications technology;
- rapid but in part lagging changes in information policy and economics;
- internationalization of scholarship and universities;
- escalating costs of acquisitions;
- limited budgets; and
- declining proportion of acquisition of materials published abroad.

The situation clearly imperils the adequacy of foreign acquisitions as Figure 2 from the AAU Task Force dramatically shows.

Figure 1

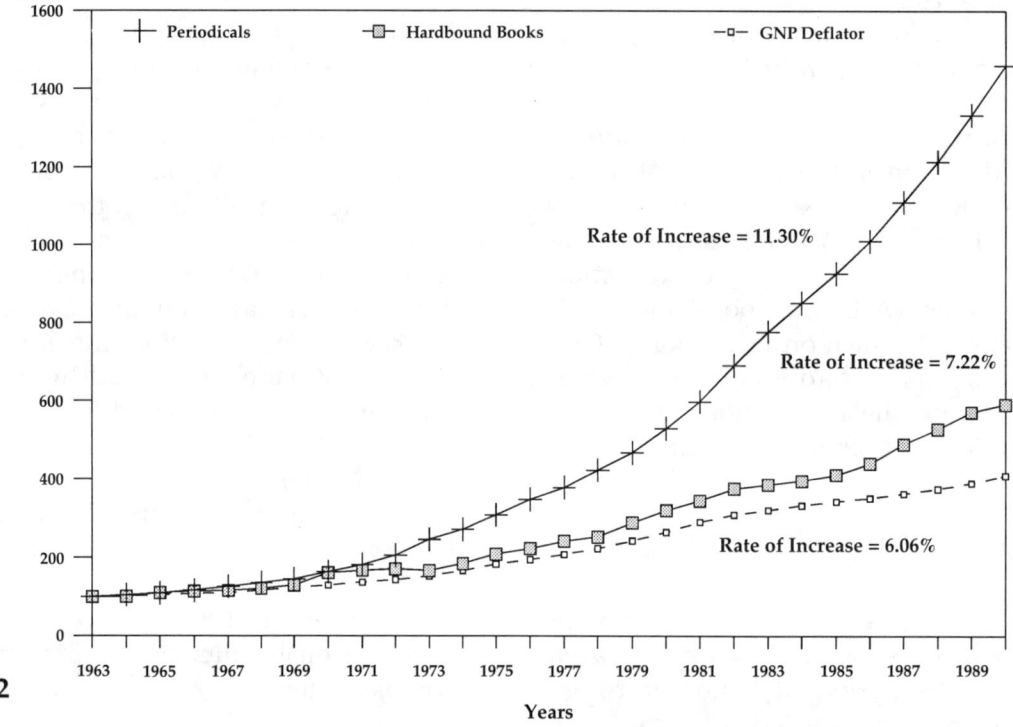

Increases in Average Price per Volume
Periodicals and Books, (1963 = 100)

Figure 2

Trends in Foreign Acquisitions

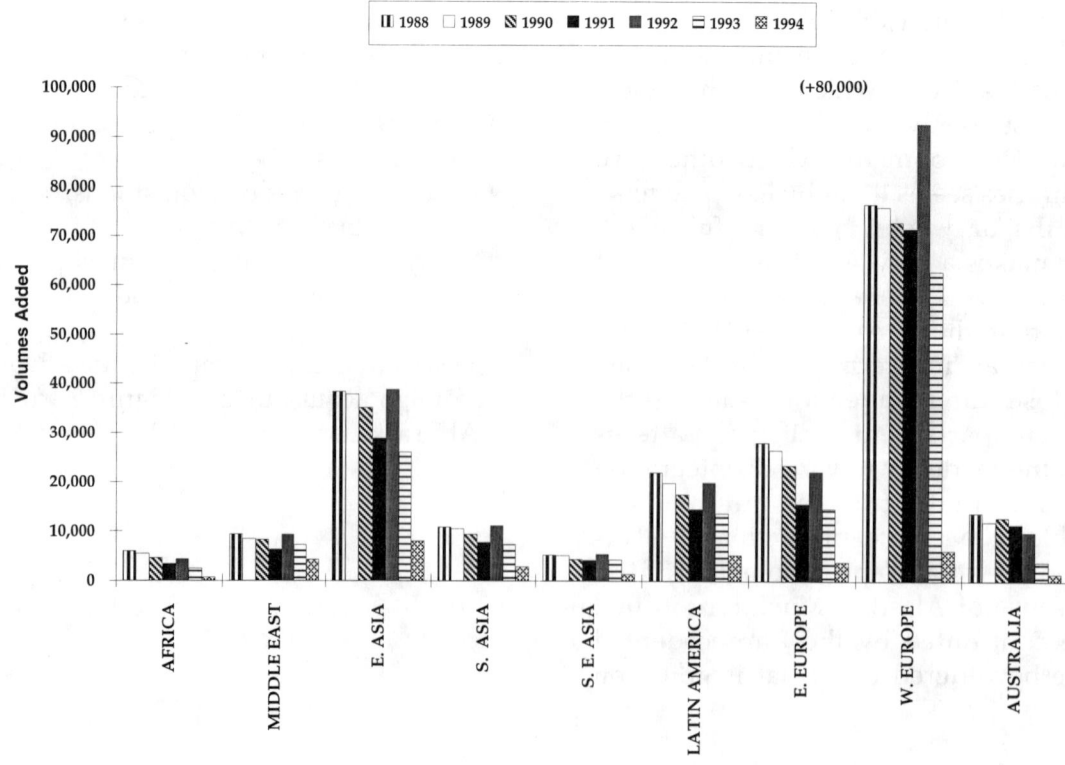

The Task Force recognized the complexity of the issues and realized that solutions will take time. Not all issues can be addressed at once. However, it certainly concluded that action must begin now. There were three major recommendations of the Task Force on acquisition and distribution of foreign language and area studies materials.

Summary of AAU Task Force Recommendations

The Task Force concluded that a trial collaborative program would provide the most effective strategy for improving access to global materials. At the same time, this program would also provide the needed information infrastructure that supports the transition to electronic resource sharing.

Recommendation I

The major North American research universities and libraries should organize a distributed program for access to foreign acquisitions. This program should include the Library of Congress and foreign national and research libraries working together to organize a cooperative program that shares the responsibility for acquiring, organizing, and facilitating access to foreign acquisitions.

The Task Force believes that such a program is the most effective way to provide access to foreign materials in research libraries. It builds on the current architecture of collaborative interdependence among research libraries. It also calls for the long-term development of a systematic program for coordinated collection development of foreign materials among U.S. and Canadian research libraries. Under this plan, participating institutions will share responsibility for collecting foreign imprint publications, and for distributing the "distributed North American collection of foreign materials." Implicit in the design of the program is the need to develop organizational structures and selection mechanisms to support the building of foreign language collections on a multi-institutional, cooperative basis. The Task Force recommends that the program be developed in an evolutionary manner, taking advantage of cooperative programs that already exist.

Recommendation II

The major North American research universities and libraries should implement the program through three demonstration projects.

The Task Force recommends that three demonstration projects be launched to show how different world areas can be incorporated into one successful program. The demonstration projects will aggressively test the barriers to distributed access and evaluate their impact on faculty. The initial projects will target Latin American acquisitions, German language acquisitions, and Japanese language scientific and technical resources.

Recommendation III

The Task Force identified several strategic objectives that must be addressed:

- **Universities should plan and fund the electronic infrastructure necessary to support the new avenues of access and delivery crucial to the success of a distributed North American collection.**
- **University leaders and their research librarians should articulate incentives to scholars and faculty for moving away from local and toward remote access, so that an individual institution's library may develop in-depth collections in a few selected areas, but provide remote access to many more in-depth collections.**
- **Planning and development of the distributed program should focus**

- special attention on meeting the needs of scholars and researchers and thereby build support among faculty; without such faculty support, the ultimate objectives will be difficult to achieve.
- **University leaders and their research libraries should recognize the need for addressing issues related to managing intellectual property rights, recognizing that copyright laws differ substantially throughout the world.**

These three recommendations encompass the core of the Task Force proposal, but thought was given to ways to reach these goals. The overall goal is to create "a network-based, distributed program for coordinated development of foreign acquisitions for U.S. and Canadian research libraries."

Participating institutions are expected to commit resources to the program. A high priority in implementing the plan will be placed on digitization of materials.

Obviously, such a large, cooperative undertaking will require attention to governance of a kind of confederation of research libraries. AAU and ARL are named in the recommendations as the organizations to work out a governance system.

The Task Force suggested a "layered" funding plan, involving a major shift in the way in which research libraries operate, emphasizing cooperative collection development and sharing.

Funding is obviously crucial for the entire effort. The Task Force suggested a "layered" funding plan, involving a major shift in the way in which research libraries operate, emphasizing cooperative collection development and sharing. Three "layers" of funding are recommended: the first is the utilization of existing acquisitions budgets which would be partially redeployed to increase acquisitions in target areas.

The second would be full cost recovery for document delivery. Libraries not participating in the program but using it for access will be asked to reallocate funds to pay for delivery of materials.

The third layer would be outside funds from foundations and from the federal government, "perhaps in conjunction with Title VI Centers."

Obviously, the implementation of this funding plan will be one of the most difficult aspects of this recommended strategy. The implementation of such measures may require a great deal of political sensitivity in building a continent-wide management and governance system.

The implementation of the cooperative, distributed, network-based collection of materials published abroad in the North American research libraries:

- Requires organizational efforts of a substantial scale;
- Will cost additional money not now in the system at least for a period of time as technology investments will contribute to a cost bulge while both print based and electronic information will be used;
- Will have a substantial impact on the functioning of universities and their faculty; and
- Will require legal resolution of copyright issues to become fully workable.

The Demonstration Projects

In order to get a better understanding of the needs of the implementation process, three relatively modest pilot projects were recommended which are now in progress, dealing with Latin American, Japanese, and German materials.

The Latin American project involves thirty one ARL libraries and institutional collecting responsibilities have been accepted for about three hundred serials published in Mexico and Argentina. A database has been designed to provide access to table-of-contents information for the project serials. Some further efforts at digitization are underway.

The Japanese project focuses on increasing network access to the scientific and technical journal literature published in Japanese.

The German project has its target on German politics and public life since 1945. It will encompass monographs, serials and federal government documents. A plan of work has been established that also includes improvement in the processing of German materials. Cooperation with German research libraries is emerging.

The demonstration projects were deliberately designed to tackle very different challenges in three very different world regions. Even as they are getting underway, they have already yielded more precise understandings of the nature of the critical issues that need to be addressed. At the ARL membership meeting in May 1995, a panel consisting of the chairs of the Working Groups in each of the three demonstration projects concluded that the emerging key issues were:

- Addressing the "scaleability" of the demonstration projects and developing plans to move beyond the relatively limited scope of the three projects to a comprehensive Foreign Acquisitions Program.
- Creating mechanisms to finance the add-on costs of project administration and participation.
- Reconsidering how research libraries are internally organized in the context of a linked digitized network of libraries and information resources.
- Committing to the technology investments on each campus to support transformed methods of scholarly access.
- Determining the best means to evaluate the three projects in terms of the impact on research libraries and their universities, especially financial; and the impact on users, especially the consequences of greater reliance on remote access to digitized materials.
- Resolving the issues of copyright in order to expand use of electronic storage and delivery mechanisms.

In short, it is becoming even more apparent that the fulfillment of the goal of a cooperative, distributed, network based collection of materials published abroad requires organizational efforts of a substantial scale, that it will cost additional money not now in the system at least for a period of time as technology investments will contribute to a cost bulge, that it will have a substantial impact on the functioning of universities and their faculty, and that it will require legal resolution of copyright issues to become fully workable.

University of Pittsburgh Perspectives

The University of Pittsburgh Task Forces of faculty and libraries discussed all three major components of the AAU/ARL Research Libraries Project before, during and after the February, 1994 conference on this topic. As you know, in addition to the international focus which we are talking about here, there were task forces on scientific and technological information and on intellectual property rights issues. The Pitt Task Force had some reservations on some points, which the National Task Force on Intellectual Property made, but certainly the overall thrust of the national project has the support of the University of Pittsburgh. This is especially true of the international component.

Yet, even in early 1994 my colleagues had some special points to make. The Pitt Library System is the major library resource for institutions of higher education in a large region encompassing Western Pennsylvania, some parts of Ohio and of West Virginia. Our interlibrary loan service is already overburdened. Progress in library technology has been made, but the reality is that American research libraries, our own included are still *far* away from the realization of a "fully digitized library". The problems of costs are serious.

Since early 1994 several things have happened on the Pitt campus that have caused us to take a careful and cautious stance on library planning. There have been changes in leadership: Rush Miller has become our Library System Director. James V. Maher is our new Provost. Mark Nordenberg is our new Interim Chancellor following the resignation of Dennis O'Connor. The fiscal situation is tight and very careful assessments of what is feasible have to be made.

In a detailed planning paper entitled "The University Library System and Information Technology: Past, Present and Future"[5] Rush Miller and his colleagues mapped the future of the library system. They demonstrate a commitment to technological advances, but they pursue a cautious "near leading edge strategy." It is instructive for our purposes here to list four of their nine planning assumptions:

University of Pittsburgh, University Library System (Selected) Planning Principles

- Libraries apply technology to serve the research needs of faculty and students, but not as extra or special services. Rather, electronic resources are increasingly part of the necessary core services of a library.
- The traditional role of librarians in acquiring, organizing and making available the products of scholarly communication positions them well for their emerging role as information managers.
- The print-based scholarly communication system will not be replaced by an electronically-based one for a long while, primarily because the acceptance of the new media for reporting scholarship lags behind the technology and the economical uncertainties for publishers in shifting to electronic products.
- The considerable cost associated with purchasing and licensing electronic information resources and developing technology-based services must be treated as add on costs for the University Library System. The need to build and maintain comprehensive, research/level print collections remains fundamental to the mission of ULS and will for many years ahead. The current library acquisitions budget is not sufficient to be a source for new electronic resources unless they directly replace existing commitments to print material. Replacing print with electronic equivalents does not always create a saving.

The same period that produced these sobering assessments of the issues to be resolved in library planning saw a very rapid expansion of the international activities of the institution. At the University of Pittsburgh the number of major centers that are part of the campus-wide federations of institutes in the University Center for International Studies grew dramatically through the revitalization of the Institute for International Studies in Education, and through the founding of the

International Technology Center and the International Law Center. In addition to four large area studies centers the University now has five very active profession specific centers and has vastly increased the participation of faculty and students in international work.

It is clear that the realization of the international vision of the AAU/ARL Task Force remains a necessity, but it also has become clear how difficult the path from here to there truly is.

One crucial dimension of the task is, I think, political and requires cooperation of leaders from diverse sectors to define cooperative goals and resources. I believe it will require more than discussions between librarians, university faculty and presidents: it will continue to require the participation of private foundations like the Mellon Foundation, but it will also need support by state governments and the federal government.

An Historical Precedent for a Distributed, National Collection of Materials from Abroad in Germany

Not being a library expert, I think I can be forgiven for not being very familiar with the history of the German library system. I learned about it, however, as I told friends at the **Deutsche Forschungsgemeinschaft** (DFG), loosely translated as the German Research Association, in Bonn, earlier this summer, about our American project. They generously prepared a collection of literature on the German experience in this field and sent it to me. It was quite a heavy parcel.

The fact is that Germany decided 75 years ago that it needed to create a national, distributed and interconnected system for the acquisition of scholarly literature abroad. This happened in the year 1920. That year was probably close to the nadir of German science support, soon after the defeat in World War I. The library issue, especially for the Humanities and Social Sciences, was one of the main driving forces creating this reform effort to link all the scholarly and scientific institutions of the country in one "emergency union" or "Notgemeinschaft."

The historical materials I have received gratefully acknowledge the constructive role played in this project by American foundations, mentioning Mr. Embree at the Rockefeller Foundation and a grant from the Laura Spelman Rockefeller Memorial of New York to improve the German collections in the Social Sciences.

The overall initiative was one of truly major significance. It led eventually to the establishment of the **Deutsche Forschungsgemeinschaft**. Most American scientists and scholars will know DFG as a functional equivalent of our National Science Foundation, the main national instrument for the support of science. However, DFG is not simply a federal institution. It is an autonomous organization representing all universities, libraries and research institutions in the country. It has a complex participatory governance structure including participation of the states as well as the universities themselves and it is funded by federal, state, and private sources, with a preponderance of governmental funding.

DFG has a history very different from NSF. Its predecessor was established in 1920 under the leadership of the former Prussian "Kultusminister" Schmidt-Ott as the **Notgemeinschaft der Deutschen Wissenschaft** which I have translated as the Emergency Union of German Science. The purpose of the creation was to avert the total collapse of Germany's scientific and scholarly institutions.

The Emergency Union became a federation

of all German academies of science, universities and other scientific or scholarly institutions who were its co-owners. The Emergency Union created a Library Committee under the chairmanship of the Director of the Prussian State Library, consisting of nine prominent library directors, later augmented by five faculty members including such illustrious names as Max Planck and Hans Spemann. I find it interesting that the establishment of special national collection efforts for materials from abroad was one of the high priorities of this organization and it emphasized especially the humanities and the social sciences.

The history of the Emergency Union of German Science and its successor organization became as turbulent as the history of Germany through the Nazi period of dictatorship, World War II and Holocaust. It was re-created in 1949 and became the current DFG, German Research Association in 1951.

Currently DFG is very active in the area of research libraries. It continues to maintain the system of special collection points. I have been sent among other literature the index to these collections by world area as well as by discipline. The system represents a truly national network. The agenda of the German research libraries are today not that different from our own: the convergence of budget limitations, internationalization of science and scholarship, the technological revolutions in the information field create pressures similar to those we face. The need to rebuild the libraries of the East German Institutions and to extend the network of special collection areas to them intensifies the pressure.

However, the severe emergencies through which German science and scholarship lived in the aftermath of two disastrous wars triggered the creation of a national, institutional framework for the support of scholarship comprehensively, but with a major focus on the research libraries.

Obviously, the American systems of higher education and research are different from the German ones, as are the political systems. However, there are similarities in the relative autonomy of the states within a federal political structure and in the reliance on self governance in the academic institutions. Another historical similarity is the constructive role played in the creation of this system by a private American foundation which then was the Rockefeller Foundation. I do not know enough about the Rockefeller Foundation's efforts. I do believe, however, that research libraries and their problems have become much more complex. I therefore suspect that the Mellon Foundation's effort towards reform is much more extensive and research based than what the Rockefeller Foundation did in Germany. In any case, the experience with shared governance in the library acquisitions, distribution and accessing policies in many institutional components may be of interest to us as we begin to think about how to move beyond research and recommendations to small demonstration projects and then on to the required actions in the research library system of continental scale, massive scope and great cost.

Conclusion: Reform in a Period of Transformation

The project on research libraries that AAU/ARL and the Mellon Foundation have started is an effort at reform in a period of crisis in the sense in which I have defined the term before. Such reforms are needed in many domains of American society, in our schools, in our system of justice, in our system of government. There will be some solutions to our vexing problems, but few perfect ones. We probably won't quite achieve the perfect solution for the research library problem either.

But it is clear that the experience to date shows that progress will depend on understanding and cooperation linking many different epistemic communities and multiple bodies of knowledge and mobilizing all relevant constituencies for action. I believe that librarians and area studies scholars may be very good at such a task: after all, knitting domains of knowledge together across cultures is one of their main professional tasks anyhow.

It seems obvious to me that we cannot attain a utopian vision in a few short steps. What we have to do is to create a momentum for change, while remaining flexible as unanticipated new developments either create new opportunities or difficulties. As in many other areas of reform (such as school improvement) we have not yet progressed to the scale of effort we need to make for real change. I hope that this conference will contribute to moving us along toward real and lasting change in the system.

---

[1] ACLS Occasional Paper No. 28, pp. vi - vii.

[2] W.R. Connor "Why Were We Surprised?" in *The American Scholar* spring 1991, pp 175-184, Volume 60 #2.

[3] Alasdair MacIntyre, "Epistemological Crises, Dramatic Narrative, and the Philosophy of Science".

[4] *University Libraries and Scholarly Communication*, 1992, ARL.

[5] University Library System, University of Pittsburgh, January 17, 1995.

Questions and Discussion

MR. WEBSTER: Are there questions for the panelists?

QUESTION #1: This is less a question than it is a comment. There seems to be such a plethora of digital activities going on these days. I don't know that there exists an inventory or summary. And I think it would be terribly useful if someone somehow could develop such a list or inventory. I think it would help all of us to see what we might be able to do to collaborate and find some cooperative way of bringing a lot of these efforts together.

MR. WEBSTER: Well, it's certainly a rapidly changing environment. The Coalition for Networked Information is often one of the best places to get a description of work in progress from a number of different projects. But Deanna would like to add to this.

DR. MARCUM: I just wanted to say that the Commission on Preservation and Access did try to gather such information and posted on the CNI-Announce list our request for information about scanning projects that are being done in this country. We got a lot of responses and we are going to make those available to all of you very soon. But what we did was gather information for only about two weeks. And there are obviously many more projects, but we would like to build this inventory and make it available to everyone.

MR. WEBSTER: I'd also like to mention that Richard Ekman and Richard Quandt at the Mellon Foundation have written a paper describing both the Mellon strategy and interest in the economics of information arena, but also describing a number of projects that they are watching and that are influencing their thinking. That paper is available both from Mellon, and on the ARL Server <URL:http://arl.cni.org>. I would also note, since Rush mentioned it, that the *ARL Newsletter* does attempt to capture progress on some of the projects. And for those of you who are not within ARL, that newsletter is widely available. ARL makes it available on a cost-recovery basis to any institution or individual.

Unfortunately, we must close to prepare for the reception this evening. Again, join me in acknowledging the contribution of our panelists.

Part V
Alternatives to Current Access Models in Research Libraries

Moderator:
James F. Williams II
Director of Libraries
University of Colorado

Speakers:
**The Economics of Resource Sharing,
Consortia, and Document Delivery**
Meredith Butler

**The Economics of Access versus Ownership:
The Costs and Benefits of Access to Scholarly Articles
via Interlibrary Loan and Journal Subscriptions**
Bruce Kingma

MR. WILLIAMS: Welcome to the session on **Alternatives to Current Access Models in Research Libraries.** For lack of a better phrase, I have also given this session a second subtitle, and that is Alternative Models to Enlightened Self-interest.

Our first speaker is **Meredith A. Butler,** Dean and Director of University Libraries at the University at Albany, SUNY. Prior to her appointment as dean she served as assistant vice president for academic planning and development in academic affairs at Albany. She holds a B.A., an M.A. from the Ohio State University and the M.L.S. from Syracuse University, where she began her professional career. She is currently the Chair of the New York State Board of Regents Advisory Council on Libraries and holds a joint faculty appointment in Albany's School of Information Science and Policy where she teaches a graduate course on the management of information agencies.

Bruce Kingma is an assistant professor in the School of Information Science and Policy and the Department of Economics at the University of Albany, SUNY. He's also a research associate at the Mandell Center for Non-Profit Organizations at Case Western Reserve University. His research interests include the economics of information, libraries, and non-profit organizations. He has a forthcoming book entitled, *The Economics of Information, a Guide to Economics and Cost Benefit Analysis for Information Professionals.* He holds a B.A. from the University of Chicago and a Ph.D. in Economics from the University of Rochester.

The Economics of Resource Sharing, Consortia, and Document Delivery

Meredith A. Butler
Dean and Director of Libraries
University at Albany

The SUNY University Center Libraries have a quite recent but active and successful history of cooperation and resource sharing. This activity has been fostered by their common identities as University Centers in the 64 campus SUNY system, by their directors recognition of the value of sharing resources and committed leadership, and by their common pursuit of several grant projects that have further interinstitutional cooperation.

Antecedents

The first cooperative project was a 1988 HEA Title IID demonstration grant to study the effectiveness of telefacsimile and scanning technologies as means of improving access to remotely held information resources. From that study, we found that:

- heavy reliance was placed on a fairly small common core of materials that was needed at each Center;
- academic program emphases at each Center were different and demanded local core collections of primary importance to each Center;
- journal titles that were considered mid-use titles by national standards were duplicated at all four Centers even though they received low use at some of them;
- an effective delivery system could be used to reduce the level of journal duplication; and
- fax did not routinely provide high quality copy in 1988.

A second grant funded by the Council on Library Resources for the period 1991-1993 led to more significant cooperative research and decision making. The goals of the CLR project were to develop policies and plans for the implementation of an active program of cooperative collection development and resource sharing among the four SUNY University Center libraries, and again the focus was on journals.

We worked to increase communication among librarians, faculty and administrators about the range of concerns and budgetary issues facing higher education and research libraries; to obtain advice about policies needed to foster greater cooperation on resource sharing and coordinated collection development and ways to move the University Center libraries toward greater interdependence.

We needed faculty to understand the advantages of cooperation in an increasingly constrained fiscal environment and to gain support for the "access model" as a likely future.

Recognizing that "policy must derive from data," we pursued four research studies during the two-year grant: a journal collection overlap study; a periodicals use study; and an interlibrary loan survey. A fourth study, a survey of faculty needs for and use of electronic resources, investigated the needs of faculty and researchers at each University Center. I will not go into the details of each study, but I have provided additional information. (See Figure 1.) Suffice to say, study results and recommendations were of great benefit as we sought to increase cooperation among the University Center libraries.

Several policy decisions grew out of our cooperative studies: the libraries committed themselves to coordination of their journal collections, to priority resource sharing, to the joint development of an electronic document delivery system, to exploration of the benefits of shared access to electronic resources, and to continuing cooperation and the development of shared applied research agendas and development opportunities.

- The results of the Faculty Electronic Access survey provided additional issues and topics for further cooperative endeavors—user and staff training, joint network development, in-depth analysis of the needs of humanities scholars, and the never-ending challenge of educating and involving faculty, administrators and students in the issues that shape our and their future.
- We agreed that each library would consider the users of the other three campuses as if they were its own users and endeavor to serve them as expeditiously as possible. Each of the University Center libraries would be libraries of first resort for those access requests that we judge can be filled most cost effectively within this group.
- Subscriptions to new journals and cancellations of lesser used or needed journals would be jointly negotiated and budgetary commitments made and honored. Service and budgetary commitments would be based on the principles of reciprocity and mutual advantage.
- Fundamental to the successful long-term implementation of cooperative programs among the University Center libraries was institutional support of a high-speed electronic document delivery system which could produce materials on demand. Although not all the necessary pieces are yet in place on the

four campuses, through a combination of Ariel software, Z39.50 protocols for our online systems, Internet and telefacsimile, and UPS, each of the four libraries have increased their overall responsiveness to faculty and students as they draw on a larger collection of pooled resources through the development of an electronic document delivery system called SUNY EXPRESS.

The data gathered in all of these studies provided the foundation for the current study on the economics of journal access. However, it was my experience in using the data obtained from our CLR studies to negotiate journal cancellations with academic departments that led to our plans for the present study. As we worked with faculty on the Albany campus, we found that the aggregate use data was not meaningful to faculty and caused them to question our data collection process or contradict our findings with anecdotal evidence. But the cost per use data in the form of spreadsheets prepared by our Assistant Director for Collection Development which were assigned by fund code to a particular department/discipline and arranged in descending order by subscription cost with a cost per use ratio included proved to be compelling information to the faculty and encouraged them to make substantial cuts of high cost/lesser used materials. I should point out here that the spreadsheets contained the same use data as had been provided previously and rejected out of hand.

As I thought about our need to have better and more comprehensive data about the use and cost of journals, in order to make wise business decisions about the cost of access versus ownership and what mix of access and delivery options to pursue, I began to discuss these issues with Dr. Kingma and asked him to think about the issues with me.

I asked him if it were possible to develop an economic model that would take into account the costs of ownership compared to access to a desired journal by some method of document delivery. We agreed that it was possible and proceeded to write a grant proposal for further cooperative work.

We proposed a cooperative study of the costs of access compared with the costs of ownership for selected high cost research journals. Using a theoretical economic model developed by Dr. Kingma, our goal was:

- to determine the cost savings, financial efficiency, and economic efficiency of local ownership compared with document delivery via a consortium of the SUNY University Center Libraries or commercial supply/delivery services, and
- to factor in not only the costs associated with these decisions for the library, but also the costs to the users served by the library.

The four SUNY University Center Libraries began the study in the fall of 1994. Interlibrary loan users on all four campuses were surveyed and financial data was collected on the costs of interlibrary loan and journal subscriptions at our four libraries.

Using his economic models and data collected through this study, Dr. Kingma developed two cost-benefit analyses of document delivery. The first analysis focused on the library cost savings of local ownership versus access via different document delivery alternatives enhanced by the use of document scanning and transmission equipment. The second analysis focused on the user's opportunity cost of the document delivery alternatives.

We believe that no one has looked at these issues in quite this way before. Our model studies not only the financial costs, but also the opportunity costs associated with ownership and document delivery. Under this model, cost per use and user satisfaction are key elements that are combined to determine the overall value of the information. Some of the costs we examined included subscription cost, labor costs associated with owning the journal, potential future use of the journal, document delivery costs, labor costs associated with document delivery, the value of the user's time, and fees associated with obtaining a journal article. This model, as far as we know, is the first time that these various factors have all been examined in determining the value of a journal.

I will now turn the podium over to Dr. Bruce Kingma who will discuss the methodology and results of our study.

Figure 1

SUNY UNIVERSITY CENTER LIBRARIES
Projects Completed for the CLR Policy and Planning Grant

Journal Overlap Study

With the assistance of OCLC, Inc., the SUNY University Center libraries developed a joint database of their serial holdings to serve as the source of data for the journal use data collection. Results from this study showed that there was an unexpectedly large number of unique journal titles (52%) in the four collections and that only approximately 48% of journal titles were duplicated by two or more University Center libraries.

Current Journal Titles Use Study

The purpose of this study was to analyze the use of journal titles duplicated at two or more of the University Center libraries in order to determine whether there were any which received sufficiently low use to justify the retention of only one copy which the other SUNY Centers could access via interlibrary loan and document delivery services. Use data was collected on current issues as well as on bound volumes of all currently received journals for one full academic year at each of the four University Centers. At the end of the study period, many members of the library staff at each of the libraries were involved in recording data on more than 10,000 titles for which over 600,000 uses were logged during the data generation period. Results showed that a significant number of titles at each campus could be considered to be low-use. The University Center libraries used the information gathered from the use study to inform collection management decisions.

The data resulting from this study was also used to develop collection management and resource sharing policies. The four University Center libraries agreed to coordinate the acquisition and cancellation of journal subscriptions, to consult before making cancellation decisions of unique journal titles, and to avoid duplication of journals not considered core to local academic programs. To a degree, discussions have been extended to the joint acquisition of electronic resources.

Interlibrary Loan Survey

This study investigated using the library journal collections of the four University Centers to meet joint document delivery and research supply needs. One of the primary objectives of the study was to examine the existing interlibrary loan journal traffic among the four libraries and to measure our collective ability to fill requests for journal articles. From our sample, we discovered at least one of the University Center libraries could provide 49% of all of the journal requests. At the time of this sample, the four libraries routinely routed only about 8% of their interlibrary loan requests to each other. The potential to fill requests was distributed fairly equally among the four University Center libraries.

As a test of the ability of the University Centers to realize the potential to supply their mutual needs, we changed our ILL procedures for a trial period. During this period, 46% of all requests were routed to another University Center library. The fill rate was a respectable 82%. Results showed that it is possible to fill a high percentage of the needs of our collective users through our combined collections. The data from this study had great significance for the University Center libraries at a time when each library has been forced to reduce journal and monographic collections. When combined with the collection use data obtained from the journal use studies, it supported significant policy changes in coordinated collection development and the planning of interlibrary loan policies and delivery systems.

The study committee recommended that the University Centers increase the use of each others' collections and develop an electronic delivery system which we subsequently called SUNY EXPRESS.

Faculty Electronic Access Survey

The fourth study was a systematic examination of current faculty access to electronic information technology, access to information resources, and current and future expectations in relation to cooperative collection development and sharing of library and information resources.

The plan and design for the Faculty Electronic Access Survey evolved from the research agenda developed at the Symposium on Cooperation. At a follow-up meeting of the University Center library directors in November 1991, the Symposium outcomes were reviewed. The results were (1) a decision to create a four-campus, faculty-administration Library Policy Advisory Council, which was convened for the first time in the fall of 1992, and (2) the decision to undertake a broadly focused study of faculty needs that would have as its objectives:

1. to produce a needs assessment and inventory of the technologies presently used and/or needed by SUNY faculty and libraries for effective access to electronic information products and networked resources;
2. to achieve an awareness of faculty needs and expectations regarding access to electronic and networked information resources;
3. to become aware of faculty perceptions of acceptable library or system performance in a resource sharing environment and for an effective document delivery system;
4. to sensitize faculty and foster their commitment to resource sharing and document delivery among the SUNY Center libraries.

The details of study design and execution can be found in the full report submitted to the Council on Library Resources in August 1993.

Meredith Butler
Dean and Director of Libraries
University at Albany, SUNY

The Economics of Access versus Ownership: The Costs and Benefits of Access to Scholarly Articles via Interlibrary Loan and Journal Subscriptions

Bruce R. Kingma
Assistant Professor, Department of Economics
School of Information Science and Policy
University at Albany

A more detailed presentation of the methodology and results from this project will appear as a special issue of the *Journal of Interlibrary Loan, Document Delivery, and Information Supply* (1996). Funding for this project was provided by the Council on Library Resources and the State University of New York, Office of Educational Technology. Acknowledgments can be found in the final report, however, I would like to thank Meredith Butler, Dean and Director of Libraries at the University at Albany, and the directors of the libraries and interlibrary loan offices at the University Libraries at the State Universities of New York at Albany, Binghamton, Buffalo, and Stony Brook for their help.

As journal subscription prices continue to escalate and commercial document delivery services, consortium agreements, interlibrary loan hardware and software continue to proliferate, it has become increasingly important for library directors to understand the economics of accessing journal articles versus owning those articles. During the 1994/95 academic year, the university libraries at the State University of New York at Albany, Binghamton, Buffalo, and Stony Brook engaged in research to determine the costs and benefits of high-priced, low-use scholarly journals.

This research focused on journals in the mathematics and sciences that historically have high prices, low levels of use, and increasing rates of price escalation. Previous studies have shown that (1) expensive journals, which have little in-house use, are better accessed through interlibrary loan than by purchase and (2) less expensive journals that patrons use frequently are best bought by subscription. The goal of this study was to more precisely determine the cost-effective choice between subscription and interlibrary loan given each journal's subscription price and level of use.

To determine the cost-effectiveness of ownership versus access this study calculates financial costs to the borrowing library and lending library of access by interlibrary loan and the financial costs to the home library of a journal subscriptions. In addition, this study measures the opportunity costs to patrons of time spent waiting when access was provided by interlibrary loan instead of a journal subscription.

Methodology

Figure 1 shows the cost-benefit matrix for providing access to journal articles via interlibrary loan versus a journal subscription. As the figure shows, there are three stakeholders in this decision: the home or borrowing library, the library patrons, and the lending library. For each of these stakeholders there are fixed and variable costs of access via the two alternatives.

The first row in Figure 1 shows the costs to patrons of access to journal articles. If access to journal articles is provided by interlibrary loan, patrons spend time filling out an interlibrary loan form and waiting for

Figure 1
Cost Matrix for Access versus Ownership

stakeholders	interlibrary loan	journal subscription
patron time	-filling out interlibrary loan form -waiting for article to be delivered	-browsing & finding journal in library -photocopying article
money	-user fee	-photocopy charges
borrowing library	-professional, clerical & student labor -supplies, postage, photocopying & long distance charges -delivery fees	-processing, binding & storing -labor for reshelving -subscription price
lending library	-labor and supplies for delivery	

the article to be delivered. At some libraries, patrons may also have to spend money to pay for delivery. However, if access is provided by the home library purchasing a subscription to the journal, patrons spend time browsing, finding the journal, and sometimes photocopying the article. If patrons photocopy the article they also must spend money on photocopy charges.

The second and third rows in Figure 1 shows the costs to the lending and borrowing libraries of providing access to journal articles. If access is provided by interlibrary loan, the borrowing library must pay for labor, supplies, and any delivery fees. The lending library supplies the labor and processing of the request. If access is provided by a journal subscription, the library must process, bind, store, and reshelve the subscription in addition to purchasing it from the publisher.

Each of the parts of the cost matrix in Figure 1 must be estimated to compare the economic efficiency of providing access via interlibrary loan versus a journal subscription. Financial data was collected from each of the four libraries to estimate the costs of interlibrary loan and journal subscriptions.

In order to estimate the value of patrons' time spent waiting for delivery at these libraries, a survey and cover letter was distributed to all interlibrary loan patrons who requested articles in the sciences or mathematics from September 1, 1994, through December 31, 1994, at the University Libraries at the State University of New York at Albany, Binghamton, Buffalo, and Stony Brook. To cover the full range of science and mathematics titles, the survey was administered to every patron who received an article requested in journals with call letters starting with Q, R, S, T, and W.

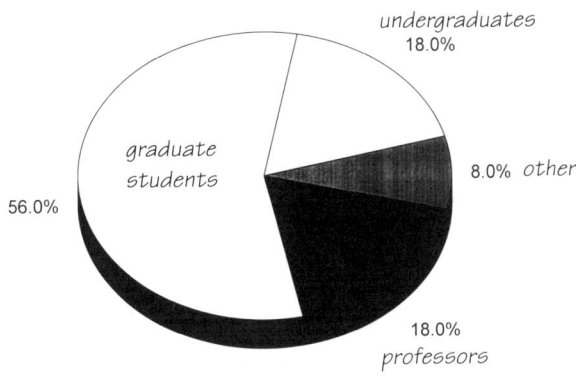

Figure 2: Percentage of Patrons by Type

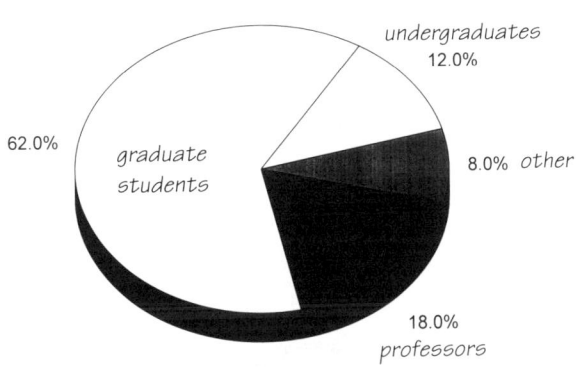

Figure 3: Percentage of Articles by Patron Type

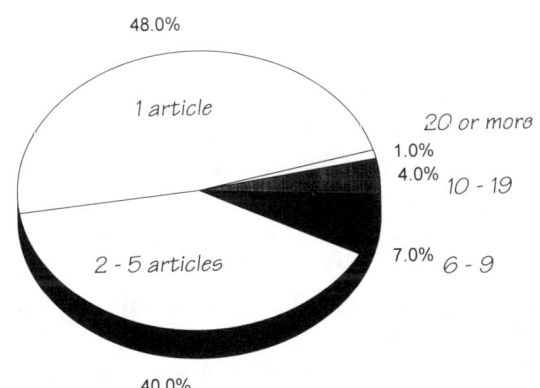

Figure 4: Percentage of Patrons by Number of Articles Requested

Survey Results and Cost Estimates

Figures 2, 3, and 4 give basic statistics on the types of patrons and numbers of articles requested from interlibrary loan at the four participating libraries. The distribution of interlibrary loan patrons and articles requested are shown in Figures 2 and 3. These figures show that interlibrary loan is used heavily by students. Graduate students submit over half of all filled articles and comprise over half of all patrons. Combining undergraduate and graduate student patrons and requests, three of every four patrons are students and three of every four requests are submitted by students.

Figure 4 shows the frequency of articles requested by individual patrons. Nearly half of the interlibrary loan patrons requested only a single article. However, a small group of patrons request large numbers of articles at each of the four libraries, with the top five patrons requesting over 60 articles each.

For all articles requested, complete information on the days of delivery, patron type, and journal requested was recorded. If a patron requested more than one article in a day, the patron received only one survey. Of 1,736 surveys sent, 830 or 47.8 percent were returned. Since several patrons received more than one survey, but did not return all surveys, returned surveys account for 2,096 (76.3 percent) of 2,747 articles requested.

Patrons were asked about their satisfaction with interlibrary loan service, their willingness to pay for priority delivery of articles from interlibrary loan, and whether they would have photocopied the article had the library owned the subscription. Patrons were asked how much they were willing to pay for one-hour delivery and one-day delivery of the article they requested. (See Figure 5.)

Figure 5

Using the following scale, indicate the quality of service with respect to this article.

1 = very satisfied, 2 = satisfied, 3 = neutral,
4 = dissatisfied, 5 = very dissatisfied

1. Timeliness of delivery

2. Quality of photocopy

3. How satisfied are you with access via interlibrary loan instead of a library subscription to this journal title?

4. If you could have received this article within 24 hours of your request, would you have been willing to pay $x for this service? 1 = yes, 2 = no

5. If you could have received this article within one hour of your request, what is the most you would have been willing to pay for this service?
   1 = $0, 2 = $2, 3 = $4, 4 = $6, 5 = $8, 6 = $10,
   7 = $15, 8 = $20

6. Had this journal been in the library, would you have photocopied the enclosed article?
   1 = yes, 2 = no

Value of "x" was chosen from the set $2, $4, $6, $8.

On average, patrons expressed a willingness-to-pay of $2.55 for one-hour delivery and $1.61 for one-day delivery of interlibrary loan. However, some patrons expressed a willingness-to-pay of over $20 for one-hour delivery and over $8.00 for one-day delivery. Willingness-to-pay for priority delivery varied by groups. Graduate students were willing to pay more for delivery than undergraduate students. Undergraduate students were willing to pay more than faculty.

While these estimates of the value of one-hour delivery to patrons are not large enough to cover the costs of priority interlibrary loan delivery, they do give us a proxy for the value to patrons of having immediate access to journal articles. In other words, a patron's willingness-to-pay for one-hour delivery can be used as an estimate of the value of providing that patron with immediate access to the journal via a subscription. (See Figure 6.)

In addition, patrons expressed that they would have photocopied 92 percent of the articles had these journals been available in the library. Given an average page length of 9.5 pages and a cost of $0.10 per page, patrons could have expected to spend $0.87 per article ($0.10x9.5x0.92) photocopying had the libraries subscribed to the journals. Patrons are not charged the cost of photocopying for articles they receive from interlibrary loan, although this is a cost to the borrowing and lending libraries.

Figure 6: Percentage of Patrons Willing to Pay for One Hour Delivery

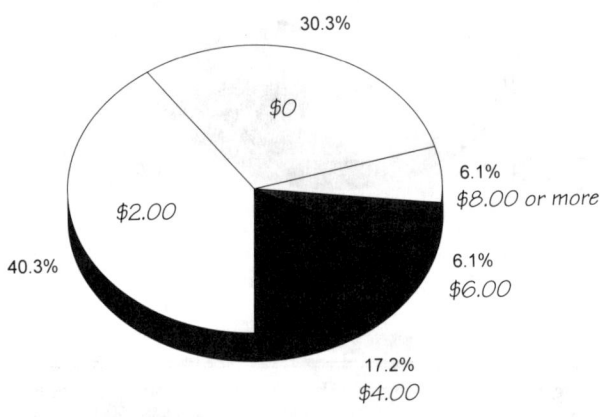

Financial Costs and Savings

The fixed costs of a journal subscription include the costs of binding, processing, and storing the subscription and depend on the number of bindings, issues, and shelf space for a subscription. These costs, on average, were estimated at $62.96 per subscription. The marginal cost of a journal subscription is the cost of student labor employed to reshelve. Student workers were timed to determine how much labor was required to reshelve journals. This cost was estimated at $0.07 per use or reshelving.

The cost per transaction for interlibrary loan include the costs to the borrowing and lending library. For the borrowing library, the marginal cost of an interlibrary loan transaction includes the cost of labor, supplies, and delivery charges and depends on the method of delivery. Estimates of this cost for the borrowing library include $18.62 per transaction which is the average cost of delivery as reported in the ARL/RLG study, $13.92 the marginal cost of delivery via Uncover, and $1.70 the marginal cost of delivery via the SUNY Express consortium when patrons submit requests which the patron has searched using the electronic catalogues of the other SUNY Express libraries. The ARL/RLG estimate of average cost is higher than the other estimates because it includes overhead and the high cost of borrowing monographs. The marginal costs of Uncover and SUNY Express were calculated by measuring the amount of staff time taken to process a request along with the cost of supplies and other expenses. The low marginal cost of SUNY Express is the result of patrons submitting printed copies of the journal entry from another SUNY Express library and student workers in the interlibrary loan office sending the request to the lending library. The marginal cost to the lending library ranges from $10.93 for the ARL/RLG average cost estimate to $3.21 for a SUNY Express library.

Figure 7: Select Cost Estimates

- patrons express a mean willingness-to-pay of $2.55 for one-hour delivery of articles, some patrons express a willingness to pay of over $20

- the mean fixed cost of a journal subscription is $62.96, the marginal cost is $0.07 per use

- the marginal cost to the borrowing library can be as low as $1.70 per article for patron-searched consortium delivery

The cost estimates for the borrowing libraries can be used to estimate the annual financial savings to these four libraries from using interlibrary loan. The annual savings from interlibrary loan at each of the four libraries are shown in Figure 8. These savings use current subscription prices and expected lifetime use of these subscriptions, based on the number of requests in a single year to all prior years subscriptions to this title, to calculate the annual savings at each of the four libraries. The interlibrary loan cost estimates use ARL/RLG average cost calculations. For each journal title accessed via interlibrary loan, the costs of purchasing and maintaining a subscription were subtracted from the financial costs of delivery of the requested articles via interlibrary loan.

Cost information from the Libraries at Albany, Buffalo, and Stony Brook was used to calculate the ARL/RLG average cost per transaction. The average cost estimate from this report is used for the University Library at Binghamton. Since the ARL/RLG report overestimates the marginal cost of interlibrary loan, the numbers in Figure 8 are conservative estimates of the annual financial savings from using interlibrary loan.

The estimated savings and savings per title are substantial. The savings are a result of the limited number of requests for any particular title. For each title that a patron requested an article from, the library saved the price of a subscription to this title and spent less providing "as-needed" access via interlibrary loan.

Figure 8
University Library Estimated Financial Savings from Providing
Access via Interlibrary Loan for Science and Mathematics Articles Requested in Fall, 1994

	journal titles	average savings per title	total savings from not purchasing 1994 subscription
Albany	535	$ 381	$203,835
Binghamton	455	$ 330	$150,039
Buffalo	275	$ 499	$137,225
Stony Brook	156	$1,674	$261,144

Notes: Journal titles are titles surveyed for which a journal price was recorded. Savings estimated based on total requests for title in 1994, average cost per borrow using ARL/RLG average cost data, and fixed and marginal costs of a journal subscription. Interlibrary loan savings estimate for University at Binghamton uses ARL/RLG average cost estimate of $18.62 per transaction.

Decision Rules for Access v. Ownership

While it is evident there are significant savings from providing access by interlibrary loan, it is important to determine what savings are possible if access by current subscriptions are replaced by access via interlibrary loan. Given the expected present value of the level of use of a journal U and the subscription price S, there are three possible decision rules that a library director can use to determine whether or not to offer access by interlibrary loan versus a journal subscription. First, there is the decision rule based on the financial cost of each alternative to the library. Second, there is the decision rule based on the economic costs to the library and the library patrons. Third, there is the decision rule based on the economic costs to the borrowing library, library patrons, and lending library. Using the cost estimates, these decision rules are illustrated in Figure 9, Figure 10, and Figure 11.

In Figures 9, 10, and 11, the lines labeled mc are the break-even combinations of subscription price and present value of use such that, given the marginal cost difference of access, the cost of providing access by journal subscription equals the cost of providing access by interlibrary loan.

In Figure 9, the line labeled "mc=$18.55" indicates the combinations of present value of use and journal subscription price such that—using the ARL estimate of average cost per transaction—the financial cost to the library of providing access via a one-year subscription to the journal equals the cost of access using interlibrary loan. The marginal cost of interlibrary loan use relative to the cost of a journal subscription is $18.55 = $18.62-$0.07. The area to the northwest of this line represents the combinations of subscription prices and present value of use such that—using the ARL estimates of cost per interlibrary loan transaction—it is more efficient to offer access by interlibrary loan rather than purchasing a subscription to this journal. For example, if the price of a journal subscription equals $800, and the present value of all future uses of the one-year subscription to the journal equals 30, it is more cost-efficient for this library to provide access by interlibrary loan. The line labeled "mc=$13.85" shows the break-even points when interlibrary loan access is provided using Uncover. In this case, there is a larger set of combinations of subscription prices and levels of use such that it is more cost efficient to provide access by interlibrary loan.

Figures 9-11

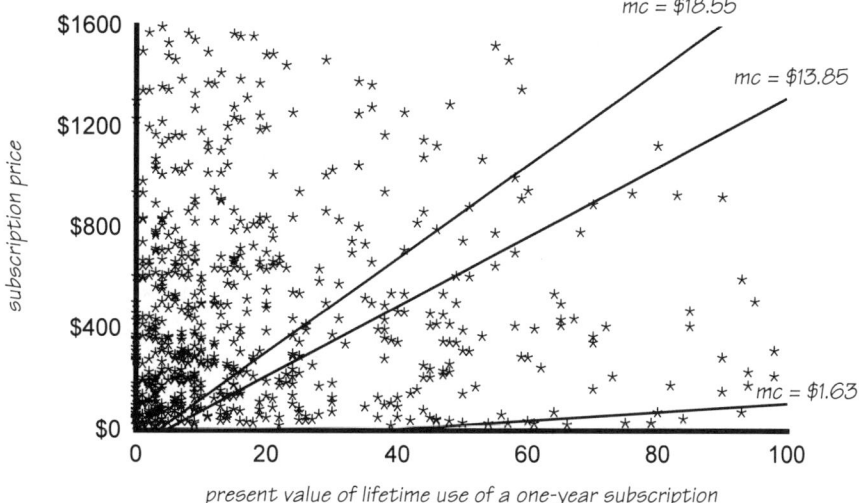

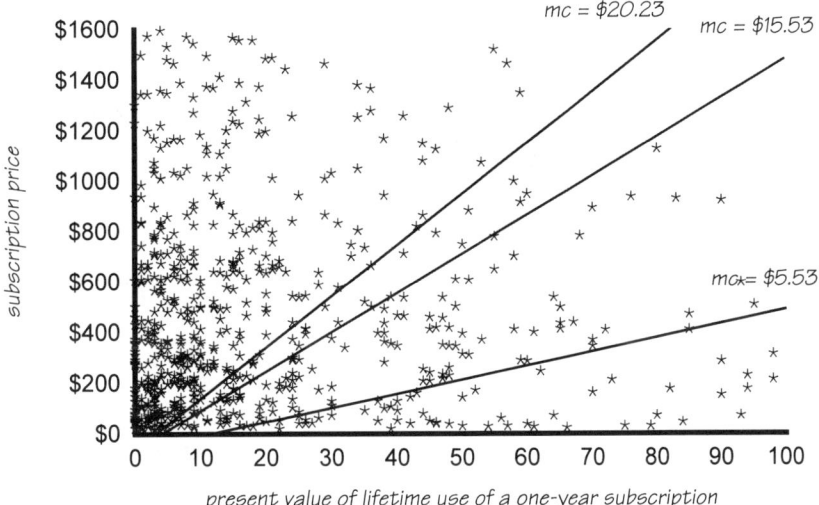

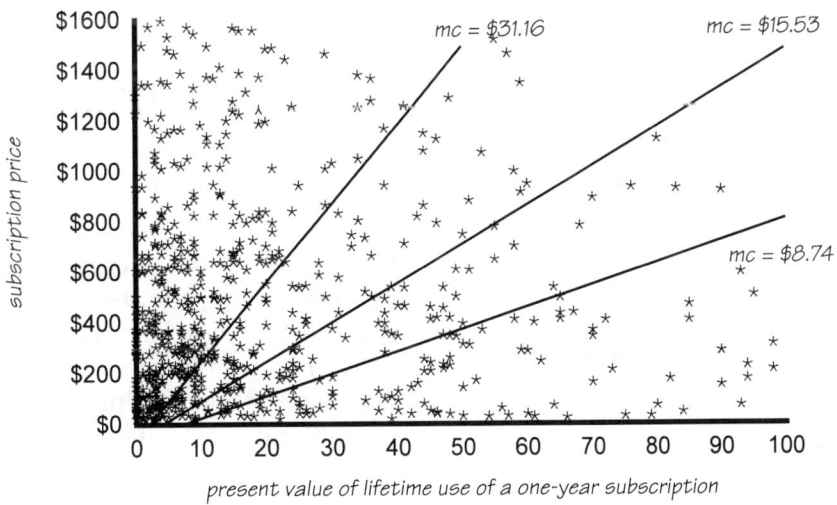

The line labeled "mc=$1.63" shows the break-even points when interlibrary loan is provided using patron-searched-SUNY-Express, the least costly method for the library.

Figure 10 illustrates the decision rules when financial cost to the library plus patron costs are considered. In this case, the patrons' marginal cost of $2.55 must be added to the cost of interlibrary loan access, while the marginal cost of $0.87 must be added to the cost of access by journal subscription. In addition, since we have not determined the opportunity cost to patrons of the patron-searched-SUNY-Express service, the marginal cost of the library-searched-SUNY-Express service is used. In this case, there is a larger area in which subscribing to a journal provides more cost-efficient access than interlibrary loan using the least-expensive method. For example, if the subscription price is $200 and the present value of use is 70, it is more cost efficient to purchase a subscription regardless of the assumption used about the cost of interlibrary loan.

Figure 11 shows the cost-decision rules when the marginal cost to the borrowing library, lending library, and the patron are considered. In this case, the marginal cost of interlibrary loan using the ARL/RLG study estimate is $31.16 (=$18.62+$10.93+$2.55-$0.87-$0.07), using Uncover is $15.53 ($13.92+$2.55-$0.87-$0.07), and using SUNY-Express is $8.74 ($3.92+$3.21+$2.55-$0.87-$0.07). Since Uncover is a commercial document delivery service, the cost of delivery includes a fee for the marginal cost by the lending library. According to Figure 11, the set of subscription prices and levels of use has increased such that purchasing a subscription is more cost efficient then providing access by interlibrary loan.

Using these decision rules, current and potential savings of providing access by interlibrary loan versus a journal subscription can be estimated. Data on current subscription prices at the University at Albany along with data from the 1992 Council on Library Resources sponsored journal use study, can be used to determine which journal titles access can be more cost-efficiently supplied by interlibrary loan.

Figures 9, 10, and 11 plot the levels of use and current subscription price to the mathematics and science journals presently subscribed to by the University at Albany. Each journal's subscription price and level use pair is represented by a '*' in Figures 9, 10, and 11. In each figure there are several '*' in each major area, indicating journal titles that would be more efficiently supplied by interlibrary loan and journal titles that are more efficiently supplied by purchasing a subscription.

Figure 12: Results

- financial and economic savings can be achieved from an increased use of interlibrary loan for access to scholarly journal articles

- consortium cost differences and current levels of journal subscription use suggest that it is not worthwhile to consider joint collection development among SUNY Express librarians

Other Factors to Consider

These decision rules provide a rough guide to the cost-efficiency of access by interlibrary loan versus a journal subscription. However, the simplifying assumptions used in the above analysis must be considered when determining which method of access is the most economically efficient. First, the decision rules used the mean number of issues per subscription year, the mean number of issues per bound volume, the mean value of immediate access to mathematics and science journals by all interlibrary loan patrons, and cost estimates based on ARL/RLG estimates or the cost of labor and other resources at the University at Albany. It is important to recognize that each of the values used will depend on the particular journal subscription being considered, the set of patrons that use that journal, the individual library, and the method of interlibrary loan used for delivery.

Second, economies or diseconomies of scale at interlibrary loan departments may result in the cost of interlibrary loan access decreasing or increasing given significant changes in the volume of transactions. As libraries become more dependent on interlibrary loan for access, these changes may be evident in the near future.

Third, if these decision rules are used by all libraries in determining what subscriptions to purchase there may be a significant decline in the number of subscriptions. The economics of journal publishing dictate that if subscriptions decline, publishers may either discontinue a subscription, or raise subscription prices and increase copyright fees. As a result, the cost to libraries that continue to purchase a subscription may increase. However, it is difficult for the library director at a single library, which has a trivial influence on the price of a journal subscription, to estimate and incorporate the possible price increase that other libraries may suffer when the library director determines whether or not to subscribe to a journal.

Fourth, the cost of a journal subscription is underestimated when articles from this journal are sent by interlibrary loan, without charge, to other libraries. Likewise, if the subscribing library charges for interlibrary loan requests by other libraries, the cost of a journal subscription is overestimated. However, while the cost of lending can be calculated, the expected cost of lending articles from a journal subscription is more difficult to determine. This cost equals the marginal cost of lending multiplied by the present value of expected uses by other libraries of the lending library's journal subscription. Accurately calculating the expected interlibrary loan requests by other libraries of the lending library's subscription to a particular journal is beyond the scope of this project.

Figure 13: Challenging Economic Assumptions

This study does not:

- account for possible economies or diseconomies of scale

- account for possible changes in subscription prices or copyright fees

- measure congestion costs

- measure the value to other libraries of the home library's subscription

Questions and Discussion

QUESTION #1: I wonder if your model took into account the benefit to patrons of using interlibrary loan or actually going into the library, retrieving the article from the shelves, and making the copy themselves, or doing it through their graduate students?

DR. KINGMA: It does take into account the fact that at these four libraries patrons get a free photocopy through interlibrary loan. And obviously they do not get a free photocopy, if they go to the shelf. And the survey included a question for the interlibrary loan transactions: Had this been on the shelf, would you have photocopied this article?

What it did not include was a time estimate of walking to the library, walking all the way to the shelf, pulling it off the shelf, retrieving it, et cetera. But there is also a time cost of interlibrary loan; the time cost of figuring out that an item is not available through the electronic catalog, walking into interlibrary loan, filling out the forms and leaving those forms.

QUESTION #2: But you don't have the second step with the SUNY Express model; right? You can do it all from a terminal.

DR. KINGMA: No. Even if you're doing it from a terminal, you have to write out an interlibrary loan request. And the terminals that provide Internet access to the electronic catalogs at the other three SUNY libraries are different from the terminals that provide access to the electronic catalog, that's in the Albany library.

QUESTION #3: So you can't actually fill out the request online.

DR. KINGMA: No. You can print out what you see on-line from the other card catalogs. Then you've got to take that printout to interlibrary loan, fill out an interlibrary loan request, staple the two together and turn them in.

QUESTION #4: from JAMES WILLIAMS: Would you take a minute and explain or describe SUNY Express so that everybody understands what happens when the patron wants to initiate a request directly?

MS. BUTLER: Yes. SUNY Express is simply an expedited delivery service among the four SUNY university centers. It can either work the traditional way or users can in essence verify their own item, which is what you were talking about.

QUESTION #5: Bruce, you cited a figure, you kind of glossed over it. There were some users who were requesting 70 to 80 articles?

DR. KINGMA: Requesting 70 to 80 articles a semester.

QUESTION #6: Did you look into the nature of that use? It seems to me that is significant demand. Are they doing survey articles or what are they up to?

DR. KINGMA: Really, I wasn't looking at or asking those kinds of questions.

MS. BUTLER: I should say Bruce didn't but our interlibrary loan librarians did.

MR. WILLIAMS: It probably illustrates a statement that someone made yesterday about the need for survey literature, that there is a crying need for a service in our libraries to provide survey literature.

QUESTION #7: It seems to me, though, that's a fundamentally different kind of use than the regular interlibrary loan demand. And regular demand is a large percentage of what's going on.

MS. BUTLER: Yes.

DR. KINGMA: I looked at the percentages of patrons and the percentages of articles. And I can give you one more number. Two thirds of all requests are generated by about 20 percent of the patrons.

QUESTION #8: How does SUNY Express deal with the CONTU guidelines or do you just pay copyright royalties for that service?

MS. BUTLER: We pay the copyright royalty for everything beyond the guidelines. We keep the same statistics that every interlibrary loan office keeps.

QUESTION #9: Bruce, your audience for this study is librarians, or at least maybe the primary audience. Librarians have learned that publishers interpret the results of interlibrary loan studies differently than perhaps librarians do. So I wonder how the results of this study will be read by publishers.

DR. KINGMA: My guess is that it's not a welcome result to publishers, because there are a number of journals at each of the sites which it would be more economically efficient to provide access to through interlibrary loan, and that implies canceling journal subscriptions. But, at the same time, all these library directors recognize that there is a difference between having an economic result that suggests these journals should be canceled and actually canceling the journal. Because then you have to face faculty and suggest that these journals must be canceled. That's a more difficult issue. The economics might show that it's worthwhile to cancel, but the politics of the individual campus might prevent the journals from being canceled. The economic result is that a lot more journals could be canceled, and that's probably a frightening result for publishers, because it implies putting competitive pressure on them. I see interlibrary loan as a competitive alternative to subscribing to a journal. And all economists know that competitive pressures typically drive down prices.

QUESTION #10: That issue was resolved in the 1976 copyright law. That's why you find it under fair use. This kind of study was done prior to that law. And the librarians established that it was less expensive for them to acquire a journal, if there were more than five uses; partly because there were low prices at that time, of course. But, if there were fewer than five uses, it was less expensive to use interlibrary loan. So they finessed the whole issue. Publishers knew about that, although I'm not sure they understood it.

QUESTION #11: Was your study or the study done by SUNY capable of distinguishing the age of the journals that were requested through interlibrary loan?

DR. KINGMA: Yes, the subscription year was included.

QUESTION #12: It would be interesting to know the demand for older journals in interlibrary loan today, especially in light of projects like JSTOR which we heard about yesterday.

DR. KINGMA: In all honesty I can't remember the distribution of requests. But both older and more current journals were requested. The majority was relatively new, the last five to ten years. But there were requests for older journals, in fact, a significant percentage.

QUESTION #13: Bruce, this is a question for you, more about the general economics of the library than about this particular case. I have to draw an analogy first. About 15 years ago the computing on our campuses was highly centralized, a monarchy. And then the PC came along and we had a "nonarchy" and a monarchy. And then we realized that we wouldn't vote for either, and so, we really had to find some middle ground. Today, a lot of the costs for computing and networking have been driven down into the department in a very rationalized model. We have paid for site licenses, or we negotiate site licenses, but the departments pay for them. They buy PCs and even pay for support for those. What I'm wondering is this. All the talk in the last few days has been built on the central model of libraries. Are any of the economists of libraries looking at a more distributed model to drive the cost out into the marketplace?

DR. KINGMA: I'm not sure I have an answer to that, but I think Don King might.

DON KING: Actually, there have been some studies done that do look at the economies of scale of library operations. And there are definite economies of scale depending on the size of the operation. But it also depends on the process that we're involved in; that is, the bibliographic verification that you have to look up, those kinds of things. Each of those processes has a different economy.

QUESTION #14: Do the graduate students use proxy cards for the faculty for whom they're working when they check out material, or is it obscured in that data that was presented whether the graduate students are checking material out for their own use or for someone else's? And did you try to control for that, Bruce, at all?

DR. KINGMA: I did on the survey. There are two ways to control for that. One is many of the graduate students will list their professor's name or whatever, in which case that was always attributed to a faculty member, not to a graduate student. And the other way is that, when the survey was sent out, it asked, "Who are you." When I got that back, I cross-matched the response with the original interlibrary loan request and used the patron's opinion of who they were; i.e., if they said they were a faculty member they were a faculty member. I think I caught a lot of what was occurring there. I don't know if I caught it all.

Part VI
Can E-Journals Save Us?

Moderator:
Ann Okerson
Director, Office of Scientific and Academic Publishing
Association of Research Libraries

Speakers:
Can E-Journals Save Us?—A Publisher's View
Lorrin R. Garson

Can E-Journals Save Us?—A Scholar's View
James O'Donnell

My two colleagues and I are here to give you a snapshot of the kind of debate that has been going on about this issue over at least the last couple of years, probably since the early '90s, mostly on the Internet but also at many learned society and library meetings. We represent a publisher, a scholar, and a librarian. Last year in a widely circulated article which was published in both a peer review journal and on the Internet, Andrew Odlyzko, who is a mathematics researcher at AT&T Bell Labs, offered some interesting calculations.[1] He wrote: "Traditional scholarly journals will likely disappear within ten to twenty years." On the basis of articles that were abstracted in the *Zentralblatt für Mathematik* and *Mathematical Review*, which are the principal sources of information and reviews of the mathematical literature, Odlyzko made some calculations about the size of the mathematical literature. These are important, because nobody else to date has done such a thing. Here's what he determined:

- The current number of math papers published per year is about 50,000.
- The number of papers in math doubles every ten years.
- On this basis, about one million mathematical papers have ever been published, half of them in the last ten years.
- If the rate of publication were to stay at 50,000 papers per year, the size of the mathematical literature would double in another 20 years.

Then he analyzed the changes in the costs of electronic storage and made the following suggestions:

- It is possible to store all the current mathematical publications at an annual cost that is much less than the subscription to a single journal.
- The one million papers previously published, if converted to electronic format at all, are likely to be converted as bit maps and page images. (Probably for obvious reasons, it's much cheaper to convert that way.)
- Compressed to current fax standards, these papers will require less than 1,000 gigabytes of storage. This is large, but it is still fewer than 150 optical disks.
- Within a decade, personal computers, let alone university departments, would be able to store all this mathematical literature, a development that alone could have startling implications for the way that a whole discipline works.
- The rapid improvement in communications networks and the impending entry of the entertainment

industry, with video and film on demand at consumer affordable prices, suggests that, if a movie to one's home costs $10, then sending much on less capacious scientific research papers over the Internet should cost pennies.

His analysis concluded, "Two centuries ago there was a huge gap between what a scholar could do and what publishers and libraries could provide. A printed paper was far superior in legibility to handwritten copies of the preprint, and it was cheaper to produce than hiring scribes to make hundreds of copies. Today these cost advantages are gone. And it is far cheaper to send out electronic versions of a paper than to have it printed in a journal. The quality advantage of journals still exists, but it is rapidly eroding."

Listening to such dialogue and reading such studies for the last five years, I conclude that we have some diverging views of the economics and functionality of the current journal publishing system. There are increasing rather than decreasing differences among the perceptions of scholars, librarians, and publishers about this topic. Today, more of the participants in the scholarly communication system no longer believe that all the parties are working together in the system's best interest, particularly on the economic issues. Thus, it seems to me that the electronic publishing systems that evolve for journals will need to reunite the needs and interests of our different parties. And if these new systems do not, they can't succeed.

Publishers

The publishers I believe have a somewhat different view to that presented by Dr. Odlyzko. From that viewpoint, if I am characterizing it correctly, the publisher's role is underappreciated and probably misunderstood. Publishing is a value-adding system that takes raw materials and turns them into products that can be sold. Selling them, in turn, assures that future products, future issues of journals, and future journals will appear in the marketplace. Scholars' writings must pass muster before becoming public, because this is the way that arts and sciences are improved and advanced. And publishers manage these portals to integrity and respectability. They manage peer review. They edit articles and turn them into shapely readable works. Without such intervention, scholarship would be much more poorly communicated and works would lack in accuracy and integrity.

Librarians

The librarian's view of all of this, I think, is more pragmatic. Librarians believe that the market for journal articles is imperfect at best. Formal scholarly communications resemble a scaled-up patronage system, more than a free market system. Researchers and their organizations pay for research from start to finish. These organizations, whether they are government agencies, research labs, or universities, pay for the time, the support of the researcher, the buildings, the systems, the librarians that provide access to the work, and the journal subscriptions that describe the results of scholarship. The library, which is paying the bills for the journals, has fewer options than a consumer would in other markets because the articles are unique.

Along with those different points of view, we have electronic technologies that are rapidly changing the way we do the business of publishing journal articles. These technologies have fostered new economic and service models for journals already, and these should continue to be nurtured and fostered.

Preprints

At the lowest "value-added" tier are electronic preprints. About five dozen of these exist today, mostly, but not entirely in science disciplines. These are no-frills services and are inexpensive to operate. They offer rapid distribution and potentially substantial feedback to authors. Electronic preprints are mounted on servers in advance of formal final article publishing. They're searchable and downloadable through public domain software. And they often link to other preprint servers and articles.

E-Journals

In the next value-added tier are refereed Internet-only journals that are being created by researchers and scholars in a number of organizations. In our ARL E-Journal database, we have identified at least a couple hundred or more such peer reviewed Internet-only journals.

For both the electronic preprints and E-Journal publications, the sponsoring institutions or organizations bear the overhead of the faculty salaries and the costs of the electronic infrastructure. Access to the end-user in both of those models currently is not charged for. And, as far as the reader is concerned, the market elements have been removed by pushing costs to the front end of production.

Traditional Print Journals Online

At the same time, today's print publishers are starting to produce electronic versions of existing print journals. Potentially such versions offer quick dissemination, save trees, and can be easily searched. Journals from cooperating publishers can be linked together. Currently no cost savings in this "traditional e-journal" model seem to be offered to subscribers. The possibilities for charging for these electronic versions of print titles include transaction-based fees or site licenses which seem to be somewhat more expensive than the equivalent print versions (thus they can pose an even larger fiscal problem for institutional subscribers). Additionally, institutional purchasers often have to invest in their own R&D, hardware, and software development, in order to utilize publishers' electronic journal tapes, because publishers may not provide local useful interfaces. So the costs of converting current print journals to electronic form seems to be high indeed.

What's going to become of e-journals then? In summary, (this is a librarian's point of view), acceptable publishing modes for journal publication will become much more diverse than they are today.

Scientists and scholars, often in partnership with their professional societies, will continue to create their own preprint site servers and journals. I believe we will continue to see a steady move to bottom-up publishing which begins on an individual scholar's home page, or as part of an aggregate site of preprints.

Publication before peer review will become increasingly common in a number of disciplines, and new types of peer review and new timing for peer review will be tested.

Institutional customers such as we represent will continue to pay for important value adding. But those values will be somewhat different. The values will include linking works together, reliable sites, powerful search engines, customized information retrieval, and good interfaces. The added value in the electronic environment shows very clearly.

Scholars will increasingly license publishers to produce their works and some will keep a copyright to their own works for themselves. This will have an impact on the economics and distribution of scholarly works, although it's too early to say quite how.

I believe there will be little economic or technical stability in the new systems we are creating, at least for awhile. And in the end a system that doesn't serve scholars or their institutions effectively and is not affordable simply won't succeed.

Introduction of Speakers

It has been my privilege in the last few years to work with a number of people on these issues, and two of them are on the podium today. **Lorrin Garson** was trained as an organic chemist. He was on the faculty of the University of Tennessee from 1967 to 1974 in the College of Pharmacy, and he joined the staff of the American Chemical Society in the Publications Division in 1974. At the ACS, he has risen in rank and responsibility and, during the past 20 years, has been involved with the development of methods to deliver chemical information electronically. He is currently the Chief Technology Officer for the ACS.

On an Internet discussion about the future of journals, Lorrin wrote something very interesting last year. He said, "I would like to suggest that publishing electronic journals is, in fact, going to be more expensive than printing. I believe most of the data we currently publish in journals today will, in the future, be acquired as coherent digital data. The collection, maintenance, and dissemination of these data will, I believe, be more costly than printing, but the information will be much more valuable. When we get to this point we will not be publishing journals. We will call the output something else."

Our second speaker is **James O'Donnell** who is a Professor of Classical Studies at the University of Pennsylvania. His scholarly work concentrates on the intellectual and cultural history of the late antique Mediterranean world. He has also innovated a variety of uses for networked information technology for scholarship and pedagogy. A number of you may know his electronic journals, the *Bryn Mawr Classical Review*, his online scholarly resources, and his advanced teaching seminars in his special fields that enroll students from around the world in four credit courses for Penn. Jim wrote on this topic the following: "There are many examples of cooperative, affordable, and sometimes seemingly for-free publication on the Internet that encourage us to dream large dreams about the ready flow of information in the future. Even if those dreams fall short of realization, it must be considered likely that the proportion of the total information economy that will be occupied by this liberal digital exchange will be larger than is now the case for print libraries. What this will mean none can say, but it will influence the market for purchase and sale of information in many ways."

---

[1] A. M. Odlyzko, "Tragic loss or good riddance? The impending demise of traditional scholarly journals," *Intern. J. Human-Computer Studies* (formerly *Intern. J. Man-Machine Studies*) 42 (1995), 71-122.

Also published in the electronic J. Univ. Comp. Sci., pilot issue, 1994
<URL:http://hyperg.iicm.tu-graz.ac.at>.

Can E-Journals Save Us?—A Publisher's View

Lorrin R. Garson
Chief Technology Officer
American Chemical Society

I take some comfort in the fact that economists have looked at the issue of publishing and have given us the same numbers that we as publishers see. Publishers too are under economic pressures. I want to convey some of these to you so you can see some of the difficulties publishers face. The American Chemical Society is a not-for-profit organization. But at the same time, as I tell many people, it's also not-for-loss. We must generate revenues to carry our program forward.

In 1995 acid-free paper went up by about 50 percent, which we had certainly not anticipated. Paper is a commodity item subject to market fluctuations. At this point we had to make the decision not to use acid-free paper, which librarians had been asking us to use for years; however, we could not bear this increase in price nor pass on the additional cost to subscribers. As it was, paper costs went up 19 percent even with ground paper stock and we had to absorb that additional expense. In 1995, postage costs went up 19 percent. Paper and postage costs are not a major expense in the dissemination of information with most scientific publishers. But nonetheless, when we see price increases like this it does have an impact on our bottom line.

From 1994 to 1995, we published 8.8 percent more pages. That is, we published from 119,000 to an estimated 130,000 pages this year in 23 journals. And by the way, this represents about five percent of the chemical information in this world, so this is not a large segment of the world's chemical information. The general rate of inflation from '94 to '95, from August to August, was 2.6 percent. Inflation right now is fairly low. Our journal prices increased on an average of 10.6 percent from '94 to '95, which is a fairly modest increase.

The thing that drives the price increase more than anything else is the increase in the amount of information we publish. Our costs are directly proportional to the number of pages we publish. Publishing in chemistry grew at an annual rate of 6.8 percent from 1990 to 1995 as published in *Chemical Abstracts*, which publishes the world's chemical information. This means there is a doubling of information every ten years, which is exactly what Ann Okerson quoted for mathematics. This is a trend that is not unique to this five-year period. This has certainly been going on all this century and probably also took place in the 19th century, and there is no hint at this point that this rate of increase is going to decrease. This probably is the single largest factor that is driving publishers, librarians, and scientists to drink.

As publishers, we have made a concerted effort to increase our productivity. We feel it is very important to do this to remain competitive. Over the last five years we have increased the number of pages we have published by 67 percent, which is an average of 13.4 percent a year. At the same time our staff involved with this activity has increased by 21 percent, an average of 4.2 percent a year. This represents a very significant increase in productivity. In 1994 we reduced staff effort by the equivalent of nine FTEs. These people weren't fired; they were assigned to do other work. Output per person has markedly increasing. This is a result of two effects. One is use of technology, the other is investment in capital primarily in computers and training of staff. Also as a consequence of this increase in productivity, we have reduced the amount of turnaround time from nine to eight weeks. That is, we have cut one week off the production cycle. That may not sound significant. But it is very important for a publisher to be competitive to one customer that we haven't talked about to a great extent, and that is the authors. Authors want things published quickly and they want them widely circulated. That is one of the bases on which they pick journals in which to publish. We publish things now in eight weeks once the peer review process is completed. When the finished manuscript comes in the door it's out in two months. A friend of mine is a Professor of Philosophy. He told me that it's not uncommon, in that discipline, to wait two years before something is published.

One of the things which has had a very significant impact on our efficiencies is the processing of softcopy manuscripts from authors. In January 1993, we had four percent of manuscripts come in as softcopy. Prior to that we probably didn't have more than a dozen manuscripts over a period of 20 years. In August of 1995, 67 percent. The second week of this month (September) was 75 percent. My expectation is it will hit about 80 percent by the end of this year and then the rate of increase will taper off.

In chemistry, processing softcopy is not an easy thing to do. If we were publishing romance novels and had only ASCII text, this would be a piece of cake. Chemistry uses a couple thousand special characters, many tables, mathematics, graphics, and it is quite a challenge to be able to do handle these kinds of data.

The issue of first copy costs has been commented on, but I want to reemphasize this. Eighty percent of our production cost is for the first copy. Twenty percent following that is whether the information is delivered by petrochemicals on crushed trees or sent electronically.

Now we come to this issue of database development and building, which Ann Okerson alluded to earlier in a comment I had made. To develop electronic products does require a fair amount of effort and capital and skill and training. It's not easy. As we learned in the CORE project with Cornell University, it's not simply a matter of taking "a file" and putting it on a computer. Within that experiment there were approximately 200 gigabytes of data that had to be handled. Universities, libraries, or publishers will find even though 200 gigabytes is not a huge amount of data, it's not a trivial amount to process. Cataloging digital data can be just as challenging as cataloging paper, if not more so. It's more subtle.

Building the database, which we started in 1974, and continue to date, has required considerable investment and effort. There are areas where delivering electronically will certainly be less expensive than on paper, one of which we are looking at now is color. Full color printing is very expensive. We charge authors a fee to do four color printing. And authors are willing to pay. They want color. Authors feel it conveys information that's very valuable to their presentation. We have a sliding fee scale for our smaller circulation journals like *Bioconjugate Chemistry*. We charge one to two thousand dollars for the author to publish in color. For *Journal of the American Chemical Society*, which has a much wider circulation, the fee is two to three thousand dollars. We feel we can publish color at a much lower cost by making it available on the Net. How much lower? I don't know. We're in the process of exploring that at this moment. But my expectation is we may offer at no charge to authors to publish, if you will, all the color they want on the Net.

Making color available electronically is turning out in experimental work to be very satisfactory. We'll see how well the community accepts it.

Yesterday Richard Lucier presented a model in which the publisher and printing was obviated by the library providing direct distribution; that is, material is obtained from authors on campus, handled by the library or some institution within the university, and returned back to the researchers. There are other models that can be followed. One which many publishers are likely to adopt, in part, is direct delivery of electronic information to their customers, whether those be libraries or to individual subscribers such as we have who are members of the American Chemical Society.

For a more complete picture I invite you to look at the ACS Publications Division Home Page, <URL:http://pubs.acs.org>. There are just two things that I want to comment on that we are doing. One is the advertised Product Information Network. Advertising provides revenues which otherwise would have to be derived from subscription sales. Advertising serves other information needs as well. We have started a program in conjunction with our traditional advertising that if customers will take out a certain number of print page ads we will put up for a fee additional product information on the Web. This product information is far more extensive than what can be included in a full-page ad in any publication. Some of these product information documents are several pages long.

You must recognize there is a certain commercial enterprise involved with chemistry which is quite significant. Our customers are not just university faculty and libraries. They're also the chemical industry worldwide which includes not only the large chemical manufacturers like DuPont, Dow, but also the pharmaceutical industry, the agricultural industry, the petroleum industry, and so forth. There is a large commercial component to publishing in chemistry. This advertising will be important and we expect to derive significant revenues from this activity.

One other thing I want to comment on is the opportunity to provide information which is not really suitable for print. In addition to the 130,000 pages that we will publish this year in the journals, we publish approximately 80,000 other pages of what we used to call supplementary material. This is data which would be far too expensive to keyboard and print but heretofore has been provided on microfiche and microfilm, which everybody hates.

We think there is a better way to do this. We have now made all this information available to subscribers over the World Wide Web. Subscribers can enter their subscriber number and then download all the information they want. At this point this material is scanned at 300 DPI and compressed. But the expectation is probably within a few years this is not going to be just scanned material. This is going to be true digital data which Ann Okerson alluded to earlier.

One activity we have is to acquire x-ray crystalographic data in what's called CIF format, CIF is an acronym for Crystalographic Information Format. This is a defacto standard ASCII format in which x-ray crystalographic data can be acquired and then used to generate molecular models, show bond distances, and bond angles—manipulation that is handled with software. Structured true digital data is far more valuable than just as tables of numeric data or bitmapped page images.

We're also looking towards acquiring other types of information such as spectra, whether these will be in Fourier Transforms, XY coordinates or something more sophisticated than that, probably the latter, I think will be available in a few years. Also within this program we are going to start publishing things look quick time movies to show molecular motion. Sound doesn't seem to lend itself terribly well to chemistry. But who knows. But showing motion certainly does. And one cannot imagine being able to convey this type of information other than electronically. It's impossible to print. But by providing it electronically, we'll significantly enhance the quality of scientific information.

In conclusion, can E-Journals save us? Well, maybe. It depends on who's being saved from what. Certainly the technology is going to be a very large factor in making the dissemination of varied types of scientific information practical for the future. If we continue to do things exactly as we have done the last 400 years, it isn't going to work, folks. We've all seen the economic problems. But there are also more fundamental challenges here; that is, authors today are able to generate far, far more data than they have heretofore, which is a consequence of computers. Instruments are no longer just outputting plots on paper. They're generating large amounts of digital data which can be very useful to subsequent investigations.

If the results of research are not conveyed and preserved, the cost of repeating the work will far exceed the cost for preserving these data companies in the pharmaceutical industry, for example, spend a great deal of money on information. They don't do that just because they like to spend money. They spend because it saves far more expensive laboratory work.

This of course applies to academic research as well. It's critically important I think, to preserve these records of research. Otherwise progress is going to be a great deal slower and more expensive.

Figure 1

Can E-Journals Save Us?

Lorrin R. Garson
Publications Division
American Chemical Society

September 19, 1995

Slide 1 of 10

Figures 2-4

Economic Pressures

- 1995, acid-free paper: ~**50%** increase
- 1995, postage: **19%** increase
- **8.8%** increase in number of pages published from 1994 to 1995 (119,463 to 130,000 pages).
- General inflation rate 1994-1995: **2.6%**

(cont.)

Slide 2 of 10

Economic Pressures (cont.)

- ACS journal prices increased an average of **10.6%** from 1994 to 1995.
- Publishing in chemistry grew at an annual rate of **6.8%** from 1990-1995 (as published in *Chemical Abstracts*).

Slide 3 of 10

Increased Productivity in Journal Production

- An increase of **67%** in pages produced in 5 years. Average **13.4%** per year.
- An increase of **21%** in staffing during the same 5 years. Average **4.2%** per year.
- In 1994, reduction in staff effort of **~9 FTEs** due to streamlined operations and new production technologies.

(cont.)

Slide 4 of 10

Figures 5-7

Increased Productivity in Journal Production (cont.)

- One week saved in journal production time from 1994 to 1995; from 9 to 8 weeks in production.
- Receipt of softcopy manuscripts a factor:
  - **4%** manuscripts in softcopy in January 1993.
  - **67%** manuscripts in softcopy in August 1995.
  - **75%** in softcopy in second week of September 1995.

Slide 5 of 10

First Copy Costs

- **80%** of production cost is for the first copy. **20%** is for distribution—whether in print or electronic delivery.
  - Mathematics
  - Tables
  - Line art and halftones
  - Database development and building

Slide 6 of 10

Color: Printing vs. Electronic Delivery

- Color printing fee paid by author
  - *Bioconjugate Chemistry*:
    - **$1,050** for 1 figure; **$2,170** for 8 figures.
  - *Journal of the American Chemical Society*:
    - **$2,050** for 1 figure; **$3,170** for 8 figures.
- Color on the Internet (WWW)
  - Cost? Much less than 4-color printing.

Slide 7 of 10

Figures 8-10

ACS Publications Division WWW (http://pubs.acs.org)

- What's New?
- Hot Articles.
- ACS Journals and Magazine Information.
- ACS Software.
- Advertised Product Information Network (PIN).

(cont).

Slide 8 of 10

ACS Publications Division WWW (http://pubs.acs.org) (cont.)

- ACS Books Information.
- Instructions for Authors and Editors.
- About ACS Electronic Editions.
- Supporting Information for Journals.

Slide 9 of 10

Can E-Journals Save Us?

- Maybe...
- If the results of research are not conveyed and preserved, the cost of repeating the work will far exceed the expense of creating and archiving the scientific record.

Slide 10 of 10

Can E-Journals Save Us?—A Scholar's View

James O'Donnell
Professor
Department of Classical Studies
University of Pennsylvania

We believe that *Bryn Mawr Classical Review* is the second oldest, by matter of a few weeks, online scholarly journal in the humanities. The clever fellows at *Postmodern Culture* seem to have beat us out onto the information highway by a whisker. We didn't know there was a competition, and at the time we began in 1990 I'm not sure that we knew we would even still be around in 1995.

We began *Bryn Mawr Classical Review* with an old-fashioned editorial insight that my colleague Richard Hamilton at Bryn Mawr College had, that there was a place in the market for timely information about new scholarly work in the classics that could be distributed cheaply, easily, and most of all quickly.

This is a world in which it is not only possible for your article to wait two years for publication, it is possible for your book to wait two or three years for a review, by which time the publisher is already looking at the stocks of it and thinking how much better they would look turned back into pulp.

We produce our reviews within six to eighteen months of a book's publication. We are already at the point of not accepting reviews any longer for 1993 publications, for example, and our work is entirely devoted to 1994 and 1995. That may sound like ordinary business practice. Within the humanities it can sound astonishing. And when we have turned down reviews submitted by very senior and distinguished scholars because they didn't get them in on time, the response is not always as warmly understanding as we wish it would be.

At the outset we began as a paper and electronic journal, and the *Classical Review* continues in both forms. We began with a small cash surplus we had from another desktop publishing operation, by giving away the new product free of charge. We had a list of 300 departments and we mailed free copies of the *Classical Review* in paper form around the country to those 300 addresses for the first year and then changed to a subscription base for the paper product of $10 per year. It has since gone up to $15 per year.

Our number of pages is going up as rapidly as it is in the discipline of chemistry. We advertise that we will give you four or five issues a year. This year it looks like we are giving you about eight. We have a certain limitation to size of issue, and so as more material comes in, more fascicles of the paper journal go out.

The electronic journal is distributed freely over the Internet and continues for the indefinite future to be distributed in that way. We have approximately 250 subscribers for our paper product. We have between the classical and medieval reviews—the medieval review is a younger sister publication that does not have a paper circulation—a total subscription for the two reviews and the overlapping subscribers of approximately 2,300 at this time.

Those subscribers may be found on every continent of the world except the one Hal

Varian mentioned has the highest Internet connectivity rate. For some reason leisured contemplation of Greek and Latin classical literature seems not to be a pastime that far south. We have our marketing people working on it. The first copy costs are still very low for this, in the very low number of thousands of dollars per year. At this point we are not passing those costs through. The operation is still being supported in the first instance by the other desktop publishing operation that works in tandem with it. We have also been fortunate enough to receive in the last year, courtesy of a program which Dr. Bowen was describing yesterday and some of its ramifications, a grant from the Mellon Foundation to study the economics of the online low overhead scholarly journal. One aspect of that is that we get a free ride for a couple of years while we see what we can do. But one of our missions under that grant is to find out how we can establish a sustainable long-term operation out of this kind of cheap, low overhead but (we think) high quality and cooperative product.

> *...[T]his is one of the kinds of Internet-based enterprises where people from around the world are able to contribute small amounts of their own intellectual time and resources to create a whole that is substantially greater than the sum of all the parts...*

We have our own technical problems in the disciplines of the humanities. Chief at the moment is that of putting fully formatted Greek text with suitable diacritical marks and accents out on the network. We're using some of the Mellon money as a small capital infusion in order to leverage ourselves up to the next level in that regard. Within the year we will have an SGML representation of the text stripped down on the fly to an HTML representation of the text in about three different ways, depending what your desktop platform is, of getting to see the Greek as actual Greek and not merely as a crude form of transliteration.

But in that regard we may simply be anticipating the technology of the marketplace by a couple of years. And when Unicode becomes the standard character set on your computer, replacing the 256 ASCII characters with 25,000 characters, all of these foreign language character sets will become much easier to handle.

We look in the medium-term to some form of institutional support for some of the costs of what we do. There is educational value, for example, for graduate students to work with us as assistants, putting the material in order. We are willing to contemplate somewhere down the line a very low level of chargeback to our customers. We hope that if we need to go to that extent we will only do so when the actual chargeback is very small. At this point if we tried to charge our Internet subscribers for the actual costs of producing the journal per year, the costs of collecting that money would substantially exceed the amount of money we would be trying to collect. At that point it's absurd to try to collect it. We hope that various Internet charging mechanisms will enable us at some point or another to charge people something on the order of 50 cents or a dollar a year for all their classical scholarship and reviews of classical scholarship.

But it must be emphasized that to a very considerable extent we depend on the kindness not only of strangers but also of friends; that we have a collaborative operation of reviewers who are contributing their time as scholarly reviewers around the world for no compensation more than perhaps getting a free copy of the book.

And if they write a bad review of the book, perhaps that doesn't always feel like compensation.

What is important to emphasize is, however, that this is one of the kinds of Internet-based enterprises where people from around the world are able to contribute small amounts of their own intellectual time and resources to create a whole that is substantially greater than the sum of all the parts and to put them together in a way that would have been impossible to put together previous to the time of Internet connectivity and computerization.

We always emphasize that even if we distributed every copy of the review in paper printed form, we still could not prepare it as we do without the Internet speeding communication back and forth between authors and reviewers. Virtually 99 percent of the reviews we get, for example, have already been keyboarded for us by their authors. This was true as well in print publication. But we don't need to rekeyboard them, and that's a very substantial saving in preparation costs.

Is there an economic model in here for how journals can be run? I would emphasize at the outset that it cannot possibly be a universal model.

Now, I have nothing to offer to Lorrin Garson as a way of replacing the preparation and distribution of 130,000 pages per year by this kind of cooperative enterprise. At the very most I think what we can hope to do is shift the center of gravity on the spectrum of what kinds of scholarly publishing take place away from the high end, high overhead, high expense products towards more collaborative enterprises. The circle of gift culture of the Internet encourages us to think that we can make communities where communities have not existed before and exploit the good will of communities in the interest of that community in order to promote, speed, and facilitate the distribution of scholarly information.

An analogy I like to use is that with the airline system. Deregulation was to the airlines what the availability of the Internet was to scholarly publication. It changed all the economic ground rules and provided possibilities of new kinds of models. I'm not quite sure that we want to be recognized as the Southwest Airlines of scholarly publication, but there are some useful points of analogy. One, the introduction of this kind of technology and this kind of transformation is disruptive to old, comfortable patterns of information production, dissemination, and reception. You're not quite sure where it's coming from. You're not quite sure where it's going, and you're not always quite sure it's going to get there. That's less disastrous anxiety in this case than in the case of the airlines.

Deregulation was to the airlines what the availability of the Internet was to scholarly publication. It changed all the economic ground rules and provided possibilities of new kinds of models.

The deregulation, that is, the electronification of journals comes with promises of better service and lower costs. As we've seen over the last decade or two with deregulation of the airlines, it's not always quite clear whether we like the level of service that we settle for, whereas we are happy that the costs we are paying get us where we want to go.

But we've also seen that there is no turning back once you go down this road, that there is inevitably a transformation in the business practices even of the high-end producers in order to adjust themselves to the new realities of the marketplace created by the introduction of low-end producers.

Whether we will like the outcome or not, I don't know. I agree with Lorrin Garson that we have no alternative but to go in this direction for purely intellectual, scientific, and scholarly reasons. The production, distribution, and consumption of information will be transformed by electronic information technologies. Vastly more information will be available and we will need to know how to manage it in one form or another.

As I sat through these last two days, the medievalist part of me has often been reminded of a line from Henry Adams. A hundred years ago in his famous book *Mont-Saint-Michel and Chartres*, his very personal meditation on the history of Romanesque and Gothic architecture, in a jaundiced mood—Henry Adams was often in a jaundiced mood—looking at some evidence in late Gothic architecture of declining quality of workmanship, fading powers of imagination, he said, "The world grew cheap, as worlds must."

Now he was as much speaking of his own time I'm sure and of the twelfth and thirteenth century. But it's a reminder that costs and benefits have long been at war in this world in which we live. The likelihood of a lasting peace and the likelihood of salvation is probably still as remote as it was in the thirteenth or the nineteenth century.

What I think we can hope for is not salvation but perhaps a little breathing room, perhaps a five or ten percent edge here and there in the costs that we need to pay, in the services that we get, and with all a less bumpy ride into the word of deregulation and the Internet than we might otherwise get if we simply sit back and wait for other people to do the job for us.

Questions and Discussion

MS. OKERSON: I heard someone say yesterday wouldn't it be nice, if there were a database of all the current digital projects that are happening? ARL does have a database of the electronic serials that are happening on the Internet, which we produce in various ways, some for sale and some for free. But an interim daily record of that is also supplied through the ARL project through an announcement called NEWJOUR, which actually happens to run at the University of Pennsylvania because NEWJOUR@CCAT.sas.UPENN.edu has over 2,000 subscribers, and we do have subscribers from the Antarctic who write to us from time to time. So if you're interested in knowing how that Internet universe is shaping up for journals, you might want to subscribe to NEWJOUR. We're posting on average now about six new titles a day. They include newsletters, journals, and magazines. This is quite an astonishing growth over the last year. And now we're starting to post notices from publishers saying we're putting everything up starting January 1996. And those kind of announcements are interesting to watch, as well.

We have a moment for questions.

QUESTION #1: It's a question to Lorrin about the reaction that he gets, if and when, he does the same kind of presentation to the chemists themselves. One of the concerns that I have is that these issues have become a problem for librarians and university administrators and perhaps the publishers. But the major players still seem to be out of the loop.

MR. GARSON: There is a broad spectrum of what you see from authors, just as there is from librarians. There are certainly librarians who are very sophisticated and understand a great deal about the whole publishing operation in general, and there are those who do not. The same with chemists. Many very prominent chemists are also heavily involved with publishing. They are editors. So you get some who are very sophisticated and understand things very well, and then you get some who are really astonishingly ignorant. There is not a nice, easy answer. It's a whole continuum. By and large we find authors are publishing longer and longer papers we suspect as a consequence of two things; word processors, which allow people to cut and paste, much more pasting than cutting, and the generation of large amounts of data. Many people in the community feel that the readability of chemistry papers is getting poorer and poorer. This is a serious problem that needs to be addressed.

QUESTION #2: One of the things that electronic publishing seems to make possible is either self-publishing by authors, in which they retain copyright, or publication by a community without involving a formal publisher. I don't know the situation in chemistry. In the social sciences and the geophysical sciences, our professional societies are actually financially dependent upon their publishing operations. There is a significant flow of income from the publishing operation to the rest of the society, even to the extent of paying for buildings. Does electronic publishing afford a real threat to the financial stability of our professional societies?

MR. GARSON: Well, I can certainly comment on that. The American Chemical Society is highly dependent upon publishing, both the primary journals, books, and also chemical abstract service. A great majority of our budget comes from publishing. I think our total budget now is around 230 million a year and publishing one way or another accounts for probably

200 million of it, which, of course, includes buildings. The ACS is much like a small college or university in terms of its size and number of employees. Now, in chemistry, at this point there seems to be very little active self-publishing probably because much of the chemical information has commercial value. One third of all patents, for example, in the United States are chemical patents. And that gives you some idea how this intertwines with publishing. Most things which were patented are also published externally, as well.

We require that authors sign over copyright to us or we won't publish it. And today we have not had a single instance where an author has said no, I won't do it, or has tried to negotiate copyrights. That is not to say that there are authors out there who, knowing this policy, would not send us papers. But we're not having a problem with tracking papers by any means. How this will change in the future remains to be seen. I just don't know. But the environment in chemistry is rather different from other disciplines in that respect.

REMARKS from DON KING: I'd like to make one comment on the economics that you and some others have mentioned. You indicated, and I think it was said twice yesterday, that 80 percent of the costs are the first copy cost. I'm sure with an average journal of about maybe five to ten thousand subscribers that's true. However, I think we have to be careful about using averages like that. Because if we're talking about a journal that has maybe a thousand subscribers, then it would be 95 percent. *Science* magazine is probably just the reverse.

Another point that I think is very important in looking at the economics of journal publishing and electronic publishing is looking at costs from the cost per reading standpoint. If you have a journal that has a thousand subscribers, then the cost per reading is very, very high. But if you have a *Science* magazine that has hundreds of thousands of subscribers, the cost per reading is very, very low. What this means is that the small journals, such as the one that we mentioned just a minute ago, lend themselves much more to electronic publishing than the very large journals. We should keep that in mind, that we shouldn't look at averages, we should look at that distribution of use, or distribution of readership. Because it will have an impact on which journals really lend themselves to full electronic publishing.

QUESTION #3: I've heard this often from publishers, that you have more papers and pages than you know what to do with. And I gather you feel an obligation to publish all those papers/pages. I just want to ask you, why you don't raise your standards and keep the pages the same.

MR. GARSON: I'm very glad you asked that question because we have wrestled with it. Let me explain why we don't. Our rejection rate is 20 to 50 percent; 50 percent in the more prestigious journals, 20 percent in the newer ones. When we look at the papers we reject, the great majority of them are published somewhere. The consequence of this is, if we don't publish them, somebody else is going to, and somebody else is likely to charge you a great deal more than we're going to charge you for that same information. The commercial publishers, because they are in business to make money, because they pay their shareholders, have to charge more for their journals. If we don't publish it and a commercial publisher does, you'll pay more for it. That stuff does get published.

Part VII
Economic Considerations for Digital Libraries

Moderator:
Thomas Galvin
Professor, School of Information Science and Policy
University at Albany, SUNY

Speakers:
**Economic Considerations for Digital Libraries:
A Library of Congress Perspective**
Hiram Davis

Cost Centers and Measures in the Networked Information Value-Chain
Paul Evan Peters

**This Little User Went to Market, This Little User Stayed Home:
What Users, Potential Users, and Nonusers Can Tell Us**
Ann P. Bishop

Introduction of Speakers

I am Tom Galvin from the University at Albany, State University of New York. The topic for this morning's session is **Economic Considerations for Digital Libraries.** While people are getting settled, I will just take a moment to share with you a reflection that came to me about midway through yesterday afternoon's presentations. As one of the clearly more aged participants in this conference, I feel a special responsibility to serve as historian and corporate memory, and to point out that the concept of the economics of libraries is hardly a new idea. Although contrary to popular belief, I was not physically present in 1883 when Melville Dewey started the first academic program for the preparation of librarians at Columbia, I do want to remind you that the terms library science and information science hadn't been coined in 1883. And Dewey had to call the school something, and he chose to call it the School of Library Economy. I suppose all that does is to validate Vico's theory of history—that history is a circle—that there really is nothing new under the sun, although there are certainly new ways of addressing old problems. And that's what we have been hearing about and will continue to hear about this morning.

We have a stellar cast of speakers who it will be my pleasure to introduce. Our first speaker is **Hiram Davis**, who since May 1994, has been Deputy Librarian of Congress. Hiram has a long and distinguished record both as an academic library administrator and as a thoughtful and articulate spokesman on the large and complex issues that confront research libraries. He came to Washington from the directorship of libraries at Michigan State University where he was a vigorous and effective advocate for networking and for electronic access to information. Hiram holds academic degrees from Missouri Valley College in economics, from Emporia State University in librarianship, and a doctorate in administration and library management from the University of Michigan.

Our second speaker is **Paul Peters,** perhaps better known to many of the people in this audience as "Mr. CNI." Paul and I first met some 20 years when we were together at the University of Pittsburgh, and Paul was involved in several forward looking research projects in library networking and resource sharing while he was completing his first master's degree.

One of the things I discovered—I was one of the first to discover—about Paul, that many of the rest of you have discovered over the last several years, is that once Paul has a target fixed in his sight, the best thing to do is to keep out of his way and sort of tag along behind him, and you will probably be moving in a very good direction.

Since the 1970s when Paul and I first met, I have followed his career with admiration. He moved from being Assistant University Librarian for Systems at Columbia University to Systems Coordinator at the New York Public Library, and in 1990 became the founding Director of the Coalition for Networked Information, which is a joint venture of the Association of Research Libraries, CAUSE, and Educom.

I know that all of you recognize what a key role Paul and the Coalition have played in advancing the cause of digital libraries and library networks, and in making sure that the needs of higher education and academic and research libraries were taken into account in planning the national information infrastructure.

In his spare time, Paul has been a leader in national professional societies. He is a regular columnist in the *Educom Review* and elsewhere, and a mainstay of the conference speaking circuit. Paul always has something interesting to say. And I know that this morning will be no exception.

This morning's third and final speaker is **Ann Bishop**, who is a member of the faculty of the Graduate School of Library and Information Science at the University of Illinois at Champaign, Urbana. At Champaign, Urbana, Ann serves as co-principal investigator for the University of Illinois' digital library initiative project, where she heads the user evaluation team. She holds master's and doctoral degrees from the School of Information Studies at Syracuse University, and has an outstanding record of participation and leadership in networked digital libraries, a topic on which she has published extensively. And to belie that old chestnut that "those who can do, and those who can't, teach," Ann is not content just to write about networks. She is the co-founder of Prairienet, a Free-Net based in Champaign.

Economic Considerations for Digital Libraries: A Library of Congress Perspective

Hiram L. Davis
Deputy Librarian of Congress

Introduction

Good morning. I am pleased to have been invited to participate in this important conference, representing the Library of Congress. Tom indicated that I majored in economics. All the references to economics and the use of such related terms the last two days made me think that I was back in Principles of Econ. 101. What he did not know, though, was that I switched from economics and went into English, thus ending my economics career.

Today's speakers have confirmed that we are indeed in the midst of economic, social, political, and technological transitions. Facing emerging and merging technologies, we have no choice but to take the best of our traditional information systems and "abandon" the rest in our organizations if we are to survive and prosper in the 21st century.[1] You will note that I did not use the "change" word. Those of you who are fans of Tom Peters understand the reason.[2]

The title of my presentation is "Economic Considerations for Digital Libraries: A Library of Congress Perspective." Time does not permit me to do more than give a thumbnail sketch of our present endeavors. My presentation will:

- Provide a framework for the Library of Congress digital library initiatives;
- Outline the Library of Congress' two-phase strategic plan designed to contribute to the development of a "national digital library"; and
- Highlight the Library of Congress' funding strategy to support the national digital endeavor.

Organizational Context

First, let me provide the organizational context within which this digital effort is taking place. I apologize to my ARL colleagues for what may be redundant, but I recognize that part of the audience consists of others who are not so familiar with the Library of Congress.

There are actually seven major units that make up the Library. They are Collection Services, Congressional Research Services, Constituent Services, Cultural Affairs, Copyright, Human Resources, and the Law Library.

We have a staff of approximately 4,600 employees. Our holdings are found on more than 530 miles of shelf space. The 100 million items include materials in more than 450 languages and in most media. There are 22 million volumes, including 5,700 volumes that were printed before the year 1500.

There are 15 million prints, photographs, and posters; four million maps, old and new; 700,000 reels of film including the earliest movies and television shows; four million pieces of music; 45 million pages of manuscripts and personal papers, including those of Presidents Washington through Coolidge; and hundreds of thousands of scientific and government documents.

The first Library of Congress was burned by the British. The second was created when Congress purchased Thomas Jefferson's collection at a cost of $23,000. There was great debate about the appropriateness of Jefferson's collection to the Congress. Can you imagine the debate that would rage today if we had to restore or create the Library of Congress? You will note from the overhead (Figure 1) that the Library of Congress of 1897 cost $126,820 as compared to today's operating budget of $324,700,000.

In concluding this organizational look of LC, an interesting question to consider is, relatively speaking, would or could the Congress make the kind of investment in 1997 that it did in 1897? A more important question is will the Congress today help build and maintain the digital library for the future? I will return to this question later in my presentation.

Figure 1

LIBRARY OF CONGRESS APPROPRIATIONS 1897/1996		
	FY 1897	FY 1996
Positions/Salaries, Library Proper	$92,020	
Purchase of Books for the Library	4,000	
Purchase of Periodicals, Serials, & Newspapers	2,500	
Purchase of Books for Law Library	1,500	
Purchase of Books for Supreme Court	1,500	
Exchanging Public Docs. for Publications of For. Govts.	1,500	
Printing & Binding	12,000	
Contingent Expenses of Library	1,000	
Total, S&E, LC, Budget	$116,020	$211,664,000
CDS Offsetting Collections		(7,869,000)
Total, S&E, LC, Appropriation	$116,020	$203,795,000
S&E, Copyright Office	10,800	30,818,000
COP Offsetting Collections		(16,840,000)
Licensing Collections		(2,990,000)
Total S&E, Copyright Appropriation	$10,800	$10,988,000
S&E, CRS		$60,084,000
S&E, Books for Blind & Physically Handicapped		$44,951,000
Furniture & Furnishings		$4,882,000
TOTAL BUDGET	$126,820	$352,399,000
Offsetting Collections		(27,699,000)
TOTAL APPROPRIATIONS	$126,820	$324,700,000

LC's Digital Library Strategy

Let me move to my second and major area of focus—LC's digital library initiatives. There was a time, not so long ago, when the library profession in general could not agree on where we were going with respect to information technology. Realization now is that the new technologies make it possible for us to travel in all directions on the information superhighway. So, this part of the information equation has been solved—today's challenge is how do we get where we need to go and who will finance the trip?

Even LC, with its $300 million-plus budget, could not apply the old economic model, the basis for how most libraries have evolved. That is, apply enough money, digitize the entire collection—the problem is solved and we can go home! Based on previous experience, we recognize that the task at hand is far more complex than simply putting everything on a chip and making it available over the Internet.

Given the size of LC's collections, which I highlighted earlier, for obvious, practical reasons, it would be inconceivable to digitize everything in our collections. Therefore, a two-phase strategy was decided upon in support of the Library's national digital effort. The first phase began with the strategic plan that started the American Memory project.

American Memory was a five-year pilot project in which unique historical collections, extensive bodies of primary-source materials of the Library were digitized. Based on the experience and success of American Memory, this project provided the foundation for the enhanced digital initiative. In the second phase, two hundred of the Library's Americana collections have been selected for digitization: unique documents about the founding of our country, photographs, sound recordings, printed matter, and motion pictures that tell the story of America from its beginnings through World War II (Figure 2).

Our goal is, by the year 2000, to have some five million items digitized, that production would reinforce the other efforts underway to provide a corpus of material in digitized format that would be accessible in every Congressional district, available to schools, public libraries, academic libraries, etc.

Figure 2

NATIONAL DIGITAL LIBRARY PROGRAM
MAJOR PHASES

Phase One (1996-1997)

The first phase of the program will be to convert the Library's Americana collections, creating a national model for sharing materials electronically among libraries.

Phase Two (1998-2000)

The second phase will be to extend that model to other libraries, vastly expanding the funding available across the country to include Americana collections from other institutions.

Creating a National Digital Library

Let's turn our attention for a moment to creating a national digital library. As any good librarian would do, I conducted a literature search for background reading in preparation for this presentation. In so doing, I was struck by the absence of citations dealing with funding specifically for digital or electronic libraries. I concluded there were two reasons for this. First, a great deal of library literature focuses on various information-related industries. Libraries are primarily viewed as receivers or agents to be supported. So from an economic standpoint, the literature deals with the economics and finances associated with the publishing industry, the technological or equipment industries, the computer industry, and the software industry, to name but a few. Second, articles concerned with the economics of the library are usually written from the perspective of the various parts, functions, and processes of the organization, i.e., cataloging, acquisitions, public services, technical services, etc.

In his book, *The Virtual Library: The Electronic Library Developing within the Traditional Library*, Harvey Wheeler pointed out that Raymond Nickerson's National Research Council Workshops has suggested "...it is important to frame questions in such a way that their answers can be stated in terms that are relatively independent... [This means] framing a discussion of the library of the future, not from the standpoint of its components but from the Virtual Library as a whole."[3]

The point being made here is that the way we write and conceptualize about libraries of the future must change. We must begin to take a far more holistic view of the entire library operation and its various environments; including in this holistic view the role of customers, suppliers, vendors, and partners if we are going to be successful in building digital libraries.

The one article that provides, I think, an excellent blueprint is by Brian Hawkins. His basic thesis is that incrementalism will simply not be enough to build the national digital library. It will require a far more concerted effort and partnerships among many entities to achieve the digital library. Let me briefly summarize Hawkins' nine "principles" (Figure 3) for building the national digital library.

Figure 3

A FRAMEWORK FOR DEVELOPING A BUSINESS PLAN FOR THE NATIONAL DIGITAL LIBRARY

- Define a business plan based on voluntarism
- Focus on institutional payment for access, not individual users
- Employ the existing infrastructure
- Increase leverage via cooperation with other stakeholders
- Work with publishers to develop models for national and international site licenses
- Define technical standards
- Support the development of tools to organize and search massive amounts of information
- Socially engineer these societal changes via tax incentives
- Leverage the trend toward common library holdings

Based on Brian Hawkins' model in "Creating the Library of the Future: Incrementalism Won't Get Us There," *The Serial Librarian*, Vol. 24, no. 3/4, pp. 17-47, 1994.

First, we need to define a business plan based on volunteerism. A single institution cannot build the national digital library; in fact, it must be a collaborative effort. Second, we must focus on institutional payment for access, not on individual users. Third, we must make use of the existing infrastructure. Fourth and fifth involve increased leverage via cooperation with other stakeholders and working with publishers to develop models for national and international site licensing. The sixth includes defining technical standards; seventh, supporting the development of tools to organize and search massive amounts of information; eighth, socially engineering these societal changes via tax incentives; and ninth, leveraging the trend toward common library holdings.[4]

At LC, I think we are incorporating six or seven of Hawkins' nine points as part of our national digital library initiative. The question then is, are we making an impact? I would say we are somewhere between "heaven and hell." On the other hand, the aforementioned principles have been incorporated into the development of the National Digital Library Federation Agreement. The agreement is among 15 large research libraries; who have agreed to:

- establish a collaborative management structure;
- develop a coordinated approach to funding;
- formulate selection guidelines that will "ensure conformance to general theme of U.S. heritage culture"; and
- identify best practices, i.e., preservation, technical standards, etc.[5]

LC's Funding Strategy for NDL

The third and final point I wanted to cover in my presentation deals with funding for the NDL. Earlier, I posed the question of whether or not the Congress would sustain the new library for the 21st century. Some time ago, the Librarian of Congress pointed out that it would not be possible for the Library to take its current appropriation and simply try to increase it to build the digital library. In fact, he said, "Creating a National Digital Library will be a coalition effort and a complex, long-term process that will bring important material to local institutions through the National Information Infrastructure."

Thus, LC adopted a two-part public/private sector funding strategy in support of the NDL. Part one is a $15 million request to the Congress to support technology infrastructure and to position LC to accelerate the processing and preservation of its collections. Part two is a private sector amount targeted at $45 million. The Congress has agreed to a multi-year funding appropriation, and approximately $20 million has been raised from the private sector.

From this funding strategy the Library of Congress hopes to 1) reach its goal of digitizing five million items by the year 2000, 2) support the digitization of treasures from other American repositories, and 3) perform a leadership role in developing public-private partnerships that can create universal access to knowledge and information for an informed society. I want to close my presentation by leaving you with the following quotes:

"In these days it is best to make a few friends."
—Omar Khayyam[6]

"I always skate to where the puck is going, not to where it's been."
—Wayne Gretzky[7]

"An organization that creates information is nothing but an organization that allows a maximum of self-organizing order or information out of chaos."
—Ikujiro Nonaka[8]

[1] "Substitute 'abandonment,'" Tom Peters, *The Tom Peters Seminar* (New York: Vintage Books, 1994), p. 3.

[2] "Change? Change!" Tom Peters, *The Tom Peters Seminar* (New York: Vintage Books, 1994), p. 8.

[3] Harvey Wheeler, *The Virtual Library: The Electronic Library*. "Raymond Nickerson's National Research Council Workshop" (Los Angeles: University of Southern California, 1987), p. 40.

[4] Brian L. Hawkins, "Creating the Library of the Future: Incrementalism Won't Get Us There!" *The Serials Librarian*, Vol. 24, no. 3/4, pp. 17-47, 1994.

[5] "Institutions Join in National Digital Library Federation Agreement" in A *periodic report from The National Digital Library Program* (Washington, DC: The Library of Congress), August 1995, no. 1, p. 4.

[6] Source unknown.

[7] George Will, "Politics: Art of Being One Step Behind," in *Chicago Sun-Times*, August 27, 1995.

[8] Margaret J. Wheatley, *Leadership and the New Science* (San Francisco: Berrett-Koehler Publishers, 1993), p. 100.

Cost Centers and Measures in the Networked Information Value-Chain

Paul Evan Peters
Executive Director
Coalition for Networked Information

I want to begin by saying how pleased I am that the Coalition for Networked Information (CNI) is a sponsor of this event. "Economic Studies and Models" is one of CNI's five major program themes. We see this conference as a major opportunity to promote clear thinking and communication in this area. Our hopes at least so far have been fulfilled. I appreciate all the work that Joan Lippincott, CNI's Assistant Executive Director, did to deliver on CNI's commitment to this program.

Introduction

I'm happy to have the opportunity of this session to provide you with a progress report on CNI's "Cost Centers and Measures in the Networked Information Value-Chain" initiative. The focus of the current phase of this initiative is capturing and analyzing how we *think* about costs. This is to say that the initiative is most properly thought of as an anthropological study of an economic subject, and a participant-observer one at that. So that places me at this conference as an anthropologist among economists.

You see, I read sociology at Columbia where the atmosphere still radiated from the fallout of the regular clashes between those titans of American social science, Paul Lazersfeld and Margaret Mead. I vividly recall how the sociologists at Columbia, my mentors, referred to the anthropologists as "the poets across campus." I shudder to imagine what the economists said of both of us. I think it started to go bad for me when I married an anthropologist (who now is a psychiatric nurse!?), but that is a story for another time and place.

Regardless, when CNI took up the question of "cost," we felt it necessary to think outside of the box of normal economics by relaxing three of the most familiar assumptions that economists commonly make:

(1) We assume that knowledge of the marketplace is *not* perfectly and equally distributed, at least not right now.
(2) We assume that technological change is *endogenous* rather than exogenous to the things we all care about.
(3) And, we assume that *irrational* behavior is the current norm.

These three assumptions influenced the design of this initiative as strongly as the mission and make-up of CNI did, and they influence where the initiative will and will not go, as well as how and when the initiative will and will not get there.

Perspective

Many, perhaps even most, of you are CNI Task Force member representatives, so I won't spend much time introducing CNI to you. But I do need to say a thing or two to set up the perspective that CNI brings to bear on this subject. First of all we were founded in March 1990 to promote scholarly and intellectually productive uses of networks.

I'll never forget how my parents responded to the news that I was leaving the New York Public Library to move to Washington, DC to establish a not-for-profit project in George Bush's America on the subject of scholarly and intellectually productive uses of networks. The question they asked me at that time was "Networks? What networks? You mean like CBS and NBC?" At that time I couldn't say "Oh, like the Internet" which is definitely something I could say now. How far we've come, and in just five short years. Of course our new problem is that many people are now surprised to hear that there *are* scholarly and intellectually productive use of the Internet.

Promoting precisely those sorts of uses is what CNI was founded to do and what we have been working on since 1990. CNI is sponsored by the Association of Research Libraries, whose Executive Director, Duane Webster, you have already heard from. I'm also pleased to say Jane Ryland and Bob Heterick, the presidents of CAUSE and Educom, CNI's other two sponsors, are also here.

CNI is driven forward by a task force of 212 research and education enterprises, of which three quarters are, generally speaking, buyers in the new marketplace of networked information technologies, resources, and services, and about a quarter are sellers. CNI tries to push the envelope of existing technologies and policies because we think they are generally underutilized in the current climate.

CNI pursues a three-dimensional program of work.

(1) The dimension that CNI was originally set up to explore was the differences in perspectives and experiences of librarians and technologists, attempting to generate a program of work on which both groups of professions could work in common.

(2) CNI very quickly started working on a second dimension: the difference in perspective and experiences between buyers and sellers.

(3) And, within the last couple of years it has become clear to us that there is third dimension to our program planning: the difference between people who are motivated by public goods and those who are motivated by private gains.

The last of these three dimensions may sound like an alternative phrasing of the second, but we believe that there are some sellers (like university presses) that share the values of most buyers, and that many buyers, at least in some situations, interact with each other as though they were sellers.

The Question of Costs

About a year ago CNI decided to undertake an initiative that would help to channel and shape the steadily growing interest in the costs of networked information resources and services, particularly as compared with the costs of equivalent printed resources and services. We believe that interest in "benefit" rather than "cost" has been the major driver of the development and use of networks and networked information. We are also painfully aware that the reward for most, if not all, of these efforts has been to increase rather than to decrease the already intense cost pressures on all of the parties they involved. (The "requirements bulge" created by new technologies, resources, and services arriving at much faster rates than old ones are departing is the culprit of this unhappy tale.)

But we are convinced that the question of costs, and whether and when they will go up or down as a result of the use of networks and networked information, is beginning to pull or to resist change. We think that, handled properly, this is a good thing; it opens a useful "second front" for the progress that's already being made as a result of how the interest in benefits is pushing or enabling change in certain directions. We also feel that something needs to be done to establish a framework for making, evaluating, and comparing claims about the cost implications of the use of networks and networked information. It seems to us that a growing number of such claims are being made, that many of these claims contradict each other, and that most are unsubstantiated by any real data. We feel that CNI can play a useful role by helping people to talk about the same things and to, eventually, make claims about costs in measurable terms.

CNI also decided to focus on "total cost," and its rate of change, rather than on "unit cost." We believe that the Internet and other information technologies have already produced tremendous gains in the unit costs of developing and providing information resources and services. It pains us that this story of steadily increasing productivity is not more widely known and acknowledged than it is. But the fact of the matter is that there is tremendous interest, to say the least, among higher education administrators and funding agents for addressing the "cost disease" in colleges and universities. We wanted to undertake an initiative that would speak to this concern for the total cost of developing, managing, and providing information products and services in higher education (and elsewhere) as well as speak to the unit cost dynamics and benefit story.

Goals and Objectives

These and other consideration led to CNI framing an initiative with five basic goals and objectives:

(1) we wanted the initiative to make sense to most (if not all) of the parties and spheres of interest that constitute the community that CNI serves;
(2) we decided to accomplish this by framing the cost question in terms of the value-chain of productive relationships that links creators and users of intellectual works, and the articulation of that value-chain became our first priority;

(3) we then established the core objective of our initiative to be the capturing of impressions about how costs are generated along that value chain, how networks and networked information are changing how costs are generated, and how to test the validity of these impressions;
(4) we also decided to take the opportunity to collect and summarize whatever cost studies we encountered along the way; and
(5) we wanted to propose a long-term strategy for doing useful work in this area.

The Value-Chain

The value-chain of productive relationships between creators and users of intellectual works is central to our initiative, and articulating that chain is our first order of business.

The conventional view of this value-chain calls attention to its five general types of *actors*:

(1) creators (authors);
(2) sellers (publishers);
(3) intermediaries;
(4) buyers (libraries); and
(5) users (readers).

CNI was not satisfied thinking of the value-chain solely in these terms. We wanted to minimize our risk of mistaking a distribution-chain for a value-chain. We also wanted to minimize our risk of conveying the impression that our actual (hidden) purpose was to protect the franchise of each of these actors, staking out "territories" in the networked information environment that are analogous to the ones they occupied in the printed information environment.

With this in mind, CNI adopted a second perspective by focusing attention on the *functions* performed by the value-chain:

(1) creation;
(2) production;
(3) distribution;
(4) protection;
(5) acquisition;
(6) organization;
(7) preservation; and
(8) utilization.

CNI believes that functions of this sort will need to be performed by the emerging system of networked scholarly and scientific communications and publications, just as they are performed by the existing system of printed communications and publications. Certainly, many of the same actors will be performing many of the same functions. But new actors will emerge, and the existing actors will change the functions that they perform or the degree to which they perform them. This two-dimensional (i.e., actors by functions) perspective on the value-chain is our basic analytical framework.

Progress To-Date

With the help of Robert Ubell Associates, in July CNI convened three expert panels (one of sellers, one of buyers, and one of intermediaries) to discuss this framework, to refine its list of actors and functions, and to capture initial impressions of which cost centers are the most significant as well as the most likely to change as a result of the spread of networks and networked information resources and services. Just over three dozen people, drawn mostly from the respondents to a "call for participation" that CNI issued earlier in the year, participated in this process, and they were divided roughly evenly between the three groups.

We set four groundrules for these expert panel discussions. These served the useful purpose of setting some boundaries for what could otherwise have turned into discussions that ranged far and wide without ever converging. I am sure we will have to revisit these groundrules later in our project (and we relaxed them at the end of each expert panel session), but I am pleased that we had the wisdom to formulate them.

(1) We asked the participants to contrast their views of the "emergent" system of communication and publication with their views of the current system, rather than to focus exclusively on the future. This turned out to be a really difficult definitional problem. We came to describe the emergent situation as the future in which users directly interact with and use information in networked environments, rather than the present situation in which sellers, intermediaries, and buyers use generally the same technologies in the production processes that delivers information in print and other non-networked forms.

(2) We asked people to focus exclusively on costs, and to ignore cost recovery mechanisms like pricing, advertising, and subsidies. We learned that this is very hard for people (particularly sellers) to do.

(3) We asked them to assume that the value-chain stays the same for the foreseeable future. There was also a lot of debate about this groundrule, but we felt it was consistent with the focus on change from the current to the emergent situation. Although there is a lot of talk about "disinter-mediation," CNI believes that the future is not as simple as most of this talk would have it. First of all, it is important to not mistake the distribution-chain for the value-chain. We believe that networks and networked information are creatively destroying the former, and that they are creatively reorganizing ("reengineering" is an even better term) the latter. CNI believes that "reintermediation" of actors (some old, many new) around different functions (again, some old, many new) is a more likely scenario for the value-chain than is disintermediation.

(4) We asked the participants to assume that "subject" and "type of material are not important." We expected to have more trouble with this than we did, because we all know for a fact that the future of the science is quite different from that of the humanities and the future of the journal is quite different than that of the monograph, if not in terms of where things are going than that at least in terms of how quickly we'll get there.

We are in the process of writing up and validating our findings from these three expert panels, but some of our findings are crystal clear already and I am pleased to share them with you:

(1) First and foremost, the participants in our expert panels indicated that they like the road that we are on with this study. Some even remarked that they arrived skeptical but left a believer. They expressed a lot of support and appreciation for our desire to re-fix the value-chain in people's minds, and then to take up the question of costs in that context.

(2) Trust is an issue. Some sellers did not participate because they could not imagine a conversation about costs that did not turn into one about prices and then into one about who is at fault for the pricing crisis of scientific and professional journals. Other prospective (and actual) participants were hesitant to share what they know, and even what they suspect, about how costs are changing because they think that that knowledge gives them a competitive advantage, both as individuals and as representatives of firms.

(3) Baseline costs are not well understood, and the ones that are understood are not understood in the same ways. Generally speaking we found that sellers do indeed understand what it costs to bring specific products and services to market, but they do not seem to have a feel for what certain value-adding activities cost across their entire product or service line. We found that, in general, buyers are more articulate about the value they add to the products and services that they buy. They too have difficulty discussing what it costs them to add these values. But we also found a lot of terminological and conceptual differences *within* the panel of buyers. Finally we learned that intermediaries presented an extreme case. They do not seem to remember the economics of "print" well at all. And, if you ask them how things are going to change for them in the future, most of them will ask in reply "What do you need?"

(4) Most people, be they sellers, intermediaries, or buyers, are still primarily motivated by market knowledge and position, rather than by cost savings. And many of them believe that the cost structure of the future will be determined by external factors more than internal ones.

Next Steps

I'm beginning to run out of time so I'll quickly tick off the next steps that we are getting ready to take on this effort:

(1) We need to validate the value-adding activities that were identified during the expert panels held in July against the participants in those panels and a group of nearly seventy-five others who have expressed interest in helping with the project.

(2) We want to use the resulting set of validated value-adding activities to start a well-moderated Internet discussion forum.

(3) We will also use the resulting set of validated value-adding activities to invite inputs, not only on value-adding activities but on costs, from participants in the TULIP Project, the Red Sage Project, the CORE Project, the DARPA computer

science technical reports project, and the AAUP/CNI "University Presses in the Networked Information Environment" initiative, among other efforts.

(4) We want to engage the participants in the July expert panels and in the Internet discussion forum, as well as other interested parties, in a discussion of the most significant cost centers in each of the most important value-adding activities and how best to measure change in those centers.

Conclusion

Taking note of the time, I'm eager to bring my remarks to a close. I'll finish by relaxing one of the rules that we set for the focus groups.

I cannot end a talk about this project without calling attention to the fact that it is focused exclusively on costs and that costs are only half of the cost/benefit equation. In CNI it's very clear to us that information systems have performance attributes other than what they cost, and that many, many people in the Internet environment are mostly focused on those other attributes.

For instance, we believe that the current Internet environment is optimized for "timeliness." People who are most interested in an information system that performs in a more timely way are the ones who adopted the Internet early. In order to get this improved timeliness they were willing to pay in terms of their personal effort and in some other ways for the lack of relevance or accuracy of many Internet information resource and services.

We believe that there are other people who are looking for an information system that's easier to use, or is more authentic, or more accurate, or costs less. Many of these people are still waiting for the Internet to demonstrate performance in those terms.

Finally, the ultimate test, when all is said and done, is whether what we are doing helps to build bridges between creators and users, and to build them quickly and easy to traverse.

Acknowledgments

I'd like to acknowledge that CNI's work in this area owes quite a debt to Don King and Nancy Roderer. I think that the last great period for this kind of thinking in the United States occurred in 1978 when Don King and Nancy Roderer published their "Systems Analysis of the Scientific and Technical Communication in the United States," a four-volume work that you can still get from NTIS. I'd also like to acknowledge the support (financial and otherwise) of the Council on Library Resources.

This Little User Went to Market, This Little User Stayed Home: What Users, Potential Users, and Nonusers Can Tell Us

Ann P. Bishop
Assistant Professor
Graduate School of Library and Information Science
University of Illinois at Urbana-Champaign

Economic Considerations for Digital Libraries: The User's View

This paper draws on user-based research to provide examples of economic considerations for digital libraries from the users' and nonusers' point of view. I use "digital library" here very broadly, to mean any collection of information accessible over a computer network. I will first present examples from national surveys that address the current income differential between users and nonusers of the National Information Infrastructure. Then, examples of new market niches and opportunities, as well as the ways that digital libraries add value and introduce new costs for their users, will be culled from the following sources:

- The research that we are conducting as part of the NSF/ARPA/NASA Digital Library Initiative (DLI) project currently underway at the University of Illinois, in which we are creating a networked collection of SGML-formatted journal articles for the academic engineering community. For more information on our DLI project, see the project homepage:
  <URL:http://www.grainger.uiuc.edu>.[1]
- A study of how artists, curators, and viewers use online galleries that I conducted this spring with Joseph Squier.[2]
- My involvement with Prairienet, a FreeNet that provides free, community-based, public access computing in Champaign, Illinois.

One thing that strikes me more and more in my own efforts to help construct online information environments is the need to consider "users" along the entire networked information value chain, remembering, for example, that when we consider national information infrastructure (NII) access, we are addressing not only who has access to networked information products but, perhaps more importantly, who has access to the means of production and distribution in the digital marketplace of ideas.

Income and NII Access, Use, and Need

One important economic consideration is the effect of income level in determining who will have access to our national information infrastructure, to the treasures we're busy digitizing, the new services we would like to sell, and to what is rapidly becoming the standard medium of communication in some scholarly disciplines.

Recent analyses of U.S. Census data reveal that the poor are restricted from entering the digital marketplace to buy, sell, barter, browse, and share ideas. On the other hand, these studies show that, where connected, the poor are often the most active users of many network services. Richard Civille compared Census data from 1989 and 1993 to show that the gap between "haves" and "have nots" is increasing.[3] He found that home computer ownership and network use are accelerating most within upper income groups. His analysis also suggests, however, that Native Americans, traditionally a low-income group, may use networked information services more extensively than any other ethnic group.

The U.S. Department of Commerce has released November 1994 Census data.[4] Its report concludes that the poor have the most difficulties in connecting to the NII, but they are among the most enthusiastic users of network services that facilitate economic advancement and empowerment. Among the findings reported is that rural and urban low-income users (with annual incomes in the $10,000-$14,999 range) are among the most likely users of online educational classes. Minority groups surpassed Whites in classified ad searches, online courses taken, and government reports accessed. These two studies of national computer and network usage suggest that the need or market for networked information exists among low-income groups. It is access that is missing.[5]

Will public libraries provide an NII safety net for the poor? Well, maybe. Unfortunately, data from a 1991 American Library Association study[6] suggest that public libraries continue to attract those with higher incomes. In addition, a study sponsored by National Commission on Libraries and Information Science[7] reported that it is our wealthy public libraries that are the most likely to provide Internet access to their patrons. About 83% of public libraries with annual operating expenses of $5 million were reported to have Internet access; the percentage drops steadily with budget—only about 12% of libraries with budgets under $100,000 have Internet connections.

While the costs of hardware and software continue to drop, I think there will always be a gap between those institutions and individuals who have access to the most advanced digital library applications and those who are unable to afford them.

To what extent do Free-Nets provide an NII safety net for libraries and individual citizens? Again, the potential seems to be there. McClure and his colleagues reported (1994) that about 6% of all public library Internet connections are provided through Free-Nets. In their study of National Capital Free-Net users, Patrick, Black, and Whalen (1995) compared the household incomes of users of the National Capital Free-Net in Ottawa with general household income patterns in the Ottawa region.[8] Their study revealed that users represent a wide range of household income levels. The largest number of Free-Net users have household incomes of $40,000-$49,000, followed by households with incomes greater than $99,000 per year. The largest discrepancies between local income levels and Free-Net use are at the extremes: people with incomes below $9,000 and over $40,000 were overrepresented as Free-Net users; people with incomes between $10,000 and 40,000 were underrepresented as Free-Net users, compared to their representation in the population at large.

The Digital Marketplace: New Niches and Opportunities

While people I have encountered in my research often express concern about the cost of access to digital information, they have also suggested a number of ways in which the technology might open new markets for them as both contributors and consumers in the information marketplace.

Artists and online gallery administrators and viewers described the advantages of what one person called the inherent "anarchy of the net" to circumvent control of the marketplace by elitist, powerful, majority-ruled institutions—ranging from museums to the National Endowment for the Arts, to agents, commercial publishers, distributors, and common taste."[9] An independent Black film producer in Great Britain noted that he had a real problem getting his work bought and disseminated by traditional distribution companies. He reported that their only concern is "will it make money?" So his films sometimes gathered dust on a shelf and were not actively promoted. He felt that he was at their mercy, because he couldn't afford to distribute his own work. He suggested that, with access to the Internet, he could advertise and disseminate his work by himself, without having to convince some institution of its worthiness or potential for market success. This artist, by the way, lacked Internet access, so he had not even seen the display of his work that had been mounted in an online gallery maintained by Joseph Squier and his colleagues at the University of Illinois.

A visitor to Squier's own virtual exhibit described, similarly, the way in which online galleries free consumers from the shackles of majority rule. He said: "Being from rural Northwest Florida (panhandle sometimes called the 'Redneck Riviera'), exposure to art exhibits that even hint of anything not 'traditional' is rare. (Monty Python's "Life of Brian" was 'banned' here...)."

Another important aspect of information technology is its potential for "dismantling discourse," in both physical and abstract terms. Using SGML allows the users of digital documents to identify and retrieve specific components of text. This suggests new modes of content representation that may be invoked by individual digital library users. Engineering faculty and students in focus groups conducted for our DLI project provided numerous examples of situations in which they would prefer to obtain only a certain piece of a journal article: an equation might be the only piece of information needed from a paper, a paper's bibliography may be more valuable than the paper itself. These potential users of our digital library testbed also provided examples of the way in which various components of an article might serve more reliably as a predictor of relevance than the traditional pieces of the bibliographic record: author, title, abstract, or subject descriptors. One engineer noted that "the abstract tells me what they wished they'd done; the tables tell me more about what they really found."

For creators of digital libraries, the implication is that the familiar units of books, articles, and pages are not necessarily their only stock in trade. While we have been astounded by the level of effort required to tag the individual components of the articles in our DLI testbed so that the retrieval of individual components is possible, there is clearly a market for this new digital library functionality. With document delivery, we have unbundled journals into articles. Now we are dealing with unbundling articles into their constituent elements and reassembling them into different packages.

While we have been astounded by the level of effort required to tag the individual components of the articles in our DLI testbed so that the retrieval of individual components is possible, there is clearly a market for this new digital library functionality.

There are hazards in this ability to atomize knowledge, of course. One undergraduate exclaimed quiet ruefully in a focus group interview: "You know, our professors won't let us just use those little summaries from the computer!" He was quite surprised at the insistence that he actually read entire articles, feeling no discomfort at, in effect, guessing at the complete content of a paper by using only the abstract. What struck me was how quickly the information technology had begun to shape norms and behaviors on a broad scale, and how seldom we consider these kinds of impacts on the growth of knowledge in our society, perhaps because such infrastructural changes tend to remain invisible.

Added Value and Costs for Digital Library Users

Who will use digital libraries—and how—is based on another type of economic consideration: who has something to gain by using them? Who has something to lose? What are the potential rewards for individuals? (In answering this question, we should recognize that reward may take the form of financial gain, recognition, reduced effort, personal satisfaction, community attention or contribution, enhanced quality of knowledge products and services, and so forth.)

One important feature of digital information environments is the manner in which they function as, or substitute for, "being there." A man who belongs to a group of families in the rural area surrounding Champaign who practice home-schooling with their children told me that they have found that the greatest advantage of Prairienet is not that it provides access to the wealth of educational resources on the Internet, but that it provides a digital "place" where their kids can "congregate" by sharing thoughts electronically between their weekly meetings and thus do not feel so isolated. On the other hand, sometimes you would just as soon *not* be there: the digital marketplace of ideas provides an environment where you do not have to congregate with others or be bothered by limiting physical constraints. One online museum visitor reported: "I don't feel like a cow off to slaughter through the corral of walls in the gallery." Another remarked: "Online art exhibits are never crowded. You never hear 'oh, Picasso's blue period' at an online art exhibit."[10]

Interviews and observations we have conducted in connection with our digital library project have suggested a number of performance problems associated with online systems. While new systems may reduce users' effort in some cases, we often minimize the scope of the problems introduced by technology. In a focus group with undergraduates, we were confronted with just how hard it is to negotiate the brittle information environment represented by our current distributed library infrastructure, a hybrid of formal and informal, online and offline resources. Students reported that they have to stand in line waiting to use the computer to find citations for a few articles. Once they get a list of potentially relevant articles, they have to run all over campus looking for the items on their list. And once they have finally located the journal volumes on the shelves, they often find that the articles they wanted have been ripped out. The irony is that the problem is so common, we often accept it as inevitable. When we asked the undergraduates to discuss the features an ideal digital library should have, we kept waiting for someone to say that the full text of articles should be available online, so that they wouldn't have to waste so much time and effort tracking down needed items. They never did. They suggested more terminals and computers that could read their minds, but when we finally suggested the possibility of retrieving entire articles online, they were dumbfounded.

Another reason our current library information infrastructure is so brittle is that people have difficulty distinguishing between different "brands" of systems—like the Web vs. the online catalog vs. indexing and abstracting databases—as if these were all just cans of beans, each much like the other except for their labels. In observations of the use of online systems in the Grainger engineering library, it became obvious that most people had little understanding of either the content or constraints of the systems they were using. People would simply "type in some words" and see what happened, trying new words or moving to the next machine if their first attempt didn't produce good results, rather than trying to find a source of information to tell them if the contents of the database were relevant to their search topic, if there was something wrong with either their terms or their search strategies, or if the system were malfunctioning.

We know that people pursue idiosyncratic paths to discover and "re-discover" useful documents, relying on word-of-mouth, scraps of paper, and remembering something about the context of the original search situation. Information moves from private to public to workgroup spheres, and we rely on both peer contacts and recommendations, as well as contact with formal information systems and intermediaries, to locate and assess particular resources. Understanding how this behavior is carried out in the digital library will help us to design better online support mechanisms for users; it also provides insights into how information seeking is being transformed, generally, in the digital environment. I am afraid that the names of our popular mall stores—like the Gap and Limited—may turn out to be just a little to apt in describing the problems faced by users in the digital information marketplace.

For example, when a high school student interviewed for our DLI project was asked to show us a particular Web site that she had mentioned, she first tried searching for it with her usual Web search engine, but was unsuccessful. She had originally heard about the Web site through a newsgroup; so she then tried accessing that newsgroup again to see if the posting that gave her the URL was still there. She couldn't find it, so she instead went back to the sent-mail log in her email account to find a message in which she had given a friend the URL of a frequently asked questions (FAQ) page on a related topic which then, *finally*, pointed her to the URL she was trying to find.

FAQ documents reduce costs for both information seekers and providers in those situations where we can predict that lots of people will need the same basic information and will be able to understand that information if it is presented in one particular format. Digital library creators and users can also reduce their costs for other kinds of information transactions that meet those same criteria. For example, local city bus maps and schedules are now available on Prairienet. One student emailed the provider of this information to say "I'm glad you have this information online now. This should keep me from missing the bus just because I'm at my computer and too lazy to walk to my office to check out the schedule." And a mass transit district administrator said in the local newspaper that he hopes it reduces their costs, too, in terms of the number of simple, repetitive phone calls they have to answer.

Finally, a number of individuals I've encountered in my research have provided examples of the way they might stand to lose by participating as information providers in the digital information environment, which is still largely "uncharted territory" as far as many people are concerned. A museum administrator who was actively exploring online exhibits, for example, noted that the Web represents a new world with no rules; norms and procedures for electronic display and distribution— "museum netiquette"— haven't been established yet. Curators know what to expect and can exert a great deal of control when they loan works, but people who copy and distribute online works often don't give credit to the "lender" and may display the work inappropriately. An engineering professor provided another example of how the new environment presented unanticipated negative consequences for information providers. She said she put up a home page listing her interests and publications, but eventually took it down because it was taking too much time to deal with the subsequent inquiries for more information or copies of documents that started coming her way.

Conclusions

The examples I have presented highlight a number of desirable performance attributes in the digital library environment, from the point of view of potential users:

- Broad and equitable access
- Easy identification and retrieval of individual document components
- Richer, more flexible and idiosyncratic retrieval mechanisms
- The ability to articulate and traverse public and private spheres, interpersonal and document sources, and online and offline media.

A more general conclusion is that user-based research helps us identify and understand new digital library services desired by knowledge creators and consumers as well as new markets in knowledge production and use. User-based research also helps us identify new costs and benefits to individuals and society and ascertain whether digital library goals are actually being met. As librarians, scholars, academic administrators, system designers, and publishers, we all need to work against simplistic assumptions about what is going on in the digital marketplace, and against romanticizing the usability of our digital library systems.

---

[1] Results presented here are drawn from research conducted by the DLI Social Science Team. I serve as team coordinator. The other members of the team are Susan Leigh Star, Laura Neumann, Emily Ignacio, and Robert J. Sandusky.

[2] Bishop, A.P. & Squier, J. (1995). Artists on the Internet. In *INET '95 Conference Proceedings* (Vol. II, pp. 1009-1018). Reston, VA: Internet Society. Available: <URL:http://www.isoc.org/HMP/proc1.html>.

[3] Civille, R. (1995). The Internet and the poor. In B. Kahin and J. Keller (Eds.), *Public Access to the Internet*. Cambridge, MA: MIT Press.

[4] U.S. Department of Commerce. (1995, July). *Falling Through the Net: A Survey of the "Have Nots" In Rural and Urban America*. Available: <URL:http://www.ntia.doc.gov>.

[5] Richard Civille and I have obtained the 1994 Census dataset and will continue his analysis of current trends in NII access and use by individuals.

[6] Westin, A.F., & Finger, A.L. (1991). *Using the Public Library in the Computer Age: Present Patterns, Future Possibilities*. Chicago: American Library Association.

[7] McClure, C.R., Bertot, J. C., & Zweizig, D. L. (1994). *Public Libraries and the Internet: Study results, Policy Issues and Recommendations, Final Report*. Washington, DC: U.S. National Commission on Libraries and Information Science.

[8] Patrick, A.S., Black, A., & Whalen, T. E. (1995). Rich, young, male, dissatisfied computer geeks? Demographics and satisfaction from the National Capital FreeNet. In D. Godfrey and M. Levy (Eds.), *Proceedings of Telecommunities 95: The International Community Networking Conference* (pp. 83-107). Victoria, British Columbia, Canada: Telecommunities Canada. Available: <URL:http://debra.dgbt.doc.ca/services-research>.

[9] Bishop, A.P. & Squier, J. (1995).

[10] Ibid.

Questions and Discussion

DR. GALVIN: I want to thank all three of our presenters for three very robust presentations and for exercising such exceptional self-discipline that we have some time left for questions from the audience. So let me invite those of you who have been sitting patiently to direct any comments, questions, concerns that you might have to one or all of the panel.

COMMENT from DON KING: I'd like to address one comment to Paul. You mentioned that libraries are buyers of subscriptions. Individuals are buyers, too. Scientists are buyers, too. As a matter of fact, there are far more individual journal subscriptions than there are library subscriptions. For scientists, at least, the number of individual subscriptions has gone from an average of about seven in 1977, down to about three at the present time. This is in science. I don't know the other fields that well. But the point is that the publishers, particularly the commercial publishers have lost that very large source of revenue. And guess what? In order to make up for that lost revenue, they have had to increase the subscription price to libraries. That's what is happening. It's a lose/lose/lose situation. It is a loss for the users, because they have to walk to the libraries now to get their subscriptions. It's a loss to the libraries, because the prices have gone up too much. And it's a loss to the publisher, because their revenue has gone down. If they priced their stuff right, it would be a win/win/win situation.

MR. PETERS: In our study, our focus groups have been drawn from the people in the pipeline because CNI's particular strength is representation of people who represent libraries, computing and publishing. The kind of buyer Don was thinking about, we have just declared as the fifth tribe of the users or the consumers of the work who may or may not need the services that the pipeline provides before or after this transition. Our hope is that we will be able to reach both authors and users more effectively through the Internet discussion, than we could through an expert panel methodology. But we hope to synergize the findings of our expert panel by using it as the material for the Internet discussion groups saying, "Does this sound like your life or not?" as a validation exercise.

When you look at what CNI is doing in this project, we are engaged in a business process reengineering effort on an industry-wide basis. Some of the material that we produce through this project we think will be very useful for people who are drawn to business process reengineering kinds of methods because it deals with functions, it deals with cost structures related to functions. But there are very few examples of a method for encouraging business process reengineering on an industry-wide basis. So we have some trepidation about that. But one of the things we're trying to do is to enable business process reengineering on an industry-wide scale against a common set of data and concepts.

DR. GALVIN: Other questions, comments?

QUESTION #1: Dr. Davis, on the conceptual model behind the national digital library, particularly given the consortium that you have described, would it be fair to say that the concept is a national digital library network, or are we talking about essentially a single centralized national digital library?

DR. DAVIS: No, we are not talking about a centralized national digital library. And I would also refer your question to Dr. Marcum because the Council on Library

Resources is providing some funding for the National Digital Library Consortium. It is conceived that each individual institution would contribute it's collections as well as resources to the effort. The hope is that there will be other institutions that will join, that this could leverage the investment and provide a level of funding that would, in turn, attract additional funding. So this is clearly viewed as a national effort.

DR. MARCUM: If I could simply add that there are now 14 institutions that have agreed to collaborate with the Library of Congress. And so far the only real agreement is that they will collaborate. We are in the process of figuring out what we need to do to make sure whatever is digitized in one institution will be available to everyone else. That's the overriding principle of the federation. But how that will be done and through what mechanisms will have to be worked out.

COMMENT by DON KING: I don't know whether people here remember it or not. But there was really some very significant studies that were funded by the Council and by ARL back in the late 1970s looking into a national periodicals center. Those were really good studies. But you probably ought to reexamine some of that when you are looking at what the Library of Congress is doing. Because at that time they were proposing to create a national periodicals center in Washington.

DR. CUMMINGS: We need to reexamine some of the early studies to see if they're relevant to digitization projects that we are talking about now.

DR. GALVIN: When our colleague from the American Chemical Society was talking this morning about the importance of journal revenue to that professional society, it reminded me of the ill-fated national periodicals center, which we thought was an idea whose time had come in 1979, but it turned out to be an idea whose time had come and gone. And we missed the opportunity. But I remember very well the day when the bottom fell out, when we had several members of the appropriate Congressional committee present for a public hearing on the national periodical center. And a gentleman who was responsible for publishing for the Audubon Society got up to speak against the notion of sharing journal resources, pointing out that if the National Audubon Society were to lose its current revenue from its magazines it would be unable to protect brood life in the national interest. It absolutely devastated the advocates for the national periodical center. How can you argue against the Audubon Society or want to do anything that would hurt them?

MR. PETERS: I just wanted to observe that the reason why I acknowledged Don King's work that came to fruition in 1978 was, because the white paper that the CNI project is producing will carry a bibliography of those previous works. I would also observe that the research we did on the literature base in the '80s found that questions of cost were being addressed at a much more component level, which is why I acknowledged the King-Roderer study as the end of the last great period of system-wide thinking. The study determined that less than a third of the cost for operating this system in the United States was in the pipeline. And, Don made this point, most of the cost was investing in readers reading and writers writing, and in the thinking process, which is why I now carry that final slide that says that if we don't hold these systems to the standard of narrowing the gap between readers and creators in all senses of the word, then we won't succeed in helping the nation with this transition.

COMMENT from the AUDIENCE: I just wanted to say I thought one of the most interesting thing to come out in this session was the set of assumptions that Paul Peters mentioned that were required of the panel of experts, the assumption to hold certain things constant. To assume that the value chain stays the same, to assume that the materials and type of content are not important, and to focus on costs and ignore possible revenue streams. One thing that's been coming through to me in the last day and a half is the potential this technology has for fracturing all of our assumptions about concepts of functionality. I think, above all, we should be not only questioning what of the value chain stays the same, but in fact which of those values themselves will survive. I think this has really been a most valuable conference, specifically because I think it raises those questions.

MR. PETERS: Briefly. I'm actually uncomfortable with those assumptions, but I will defend them as a good box to put people in when you want to focus on cost and nothing else. Because our experience in preparing for the CNI research was that in discussions of cost, frequently two people talk past each other because one is talking about the pure emergent model and the other is talking about a transitional situation. One is talking about what rate can be charged, and the other person is talking about what it takes to produce the journal. So this was our effort, to try to put people in what we felt was the cost box.

But the whole nature of our project is to describe that box in a way that draws people into it and they start talking about costs rather than these other things which are much more fun to talk about, or at least talked about much more frequently. For any one of the assumptions we used, I can spend as much time arguing against them as not. So I view them as defensible, but not necessarily convincing assumptions about this conceptualization.

QUESTION from DR. GALVIN: If I could exercise the moderator's prerogative, let me ask Ann, did you find that the level of participation in the Free-Net was high at the two extremes of the economic spectrum and low in the middle? Were middle-income people underrepresented as participants and the poor and the rich were over represented?

DR. BISHOP: Right. The greatest differential between the actual income levels and use of the Free-net was that the very low extremes of households under $9,000 were over represented, and at the very highest, households over $70,000.

DR. GALVIN: That would suggest that the rhetorical figure we are fond of using of the gap between the information rich and the information poor may be a faulty analogy.

DR. BISHOP: Yes.

Part VIII
The Economics of Information Access in Higher Education

Moderator:
Thomas W. Shaughnessy
University Librarian
University of Minnesota Libraries

Speakers:
NCLIS Remarks
Jeanne Simon
Chairperson
National Commission on Libraries and Information Science

Measuring the Costs and Benefits of Distance Learning
James H. Ryan

DR. SHAUGHNESSY: We have an addition to our agenda today, a very special guest. She was going to be here yesterday but she got called away to Illinois on an important visit. But she is with us today and she is going to say a few words now. The person I'm referring to is **Jeanne Simon**, who is the Chairperson of the National Commission on Libraries and Information Science.

JEANNE SIMON: Thank you, Mr. Ryan, for letting me share the podium. I will be brief. I am proud to be the Chairman of the National Commission on Libraries and Information Science. I'm glad that Peter Young, our Executive Director who stood in for me yesterday, will be absorbing what you are doing here today. I am not a librarian. I am a lawyer and politician who understands and loves libraries. The reason I was in Illinois yesterday is that my husband, who is retiring from the Senate and will not run again this next year, will be heading up the Public Policy Institute at Southern Illinois Institute at Carbondale. I am delighted with that because it is a bipartisan institute, where Republicans, Democrats, Independents can think about lots of things, including how we can make the world better for all of us. And my role in the announcement, which will be made more public later, is that I will be an adjunct professor at the Southern Illinois University with an office in the library. So I will be working with librarians even after we leave Washington, DC.

Right now the National Commission is developing studies on how public libraries are using the Internet. We have just recently published the study on the cost models for using the Internet. And I'm happy to say that in a recent meeting of the International Federation of Library Associations in Istanbul, Turkey I was proud to be there and to mention that the McClure study is an NCLIS study. I had really preferred to have it called the National Commission Study, but I understand that Chuck McClure has a great deal of pride in the study. As we talked in Turkey, several members in the meeting that I attended wanted copies of that study. We were very happy to send the study to them. I'm also pleased to say that people from all over the world are asking Peter for copies.

I'm sure that our current study of cost models will be equally important. We are developing right now the methodology for a future study on the use by the public of government information. We will be studying the use by the public of the Government Printing Office products.

We foresee that our budget might be reduced a little bit. I think this is in keeping with the general trend of trying to bring the budget in some kind of balance, and I agree with that. But I do think that the situation of libraries and the peril that libraries face right now is important enough for the Speaker of the House of Representatives and the majority in the Senate to see that not only our Commission continues, but that assistance to libraries at all levels must continue. If you have any input into your political process back home, and I know you do, I would urge that you talk to your legislators and convey the very powerful message that the budget is important but libraries are more important.

DR. SHAUGHNESSY: One of the sponsors of this conference is the National Association of State Universities and Land-Grant Colleges. And in your packet is a brochure from NASULGC, as it's known, a brochure on Distance Learning. We have also distributed a one-page handout that describes very briefly the Commission on Information Technologies that NASULGC established within the past two years (Figure 1). The Commission is comprised of three boards. There is a Board on Distance Education, a Board on Computing and Telecommunications, and a Board on Library Resources and Services. I happen to be Chair of the Library Resources and Services Board. The Library Board is directed by a steering committee whose membership includes Leon Raney, Dean of Libraries at South Dakota State University; Barbara Ford, Library Director at Virginia Commonwealth University; Elaine Albright, Director of Libraries at the University of Maine; and Brice Hobrock, Director at Kansas State University Libraries. These individuals have contributed their efforts to advise the NASULGC presidents on a number of important issues, issues ranging from copyright and data privacy to telecommunications legislation and a host of related issues. I would encourage those of you who have not been involved with NASULGC to consider becoming involved. In the old days NASULGC used to have as its primary focus agriculture and agricultural experiment stations. But this focus has changed and has become broader and far more inclusive. At the meeting last fall, for example, some of the topics that were discussed by the presidents and vice-presidents included the significant costs of legal support, questions about conflict of interest, faculty work load policies, responsibility centered management, re-engineering; topics that are of considerable interest to library managers and staff. In fact, these are topics that are of interest to society at large.

NASULGC presents an opportunity for librarians not only to hear what the presidents are thinking and talking about, but it is also an opportunity for librarians to try to influence their thinking on matters of information policy. So those of you who have not been involved with NASULGC, I invite you, encourage you to become involved.

Figure 1

NASULGC National Association of State Universities and Land-Grant Colleges

The Commission on Information Technologies

The Commission on Information Technologies (CIT) is one of the six key policy forming units of the National Association of State Universities and Land-Grant Colleges (NASULGC). The CIT was created to identify and develop policy positions and advisory assessments on information technology and related policy issues of concern to NASULGC members and to the nation. The use of technology is having a profound effect on the creation, preservation, and dissemination of knowledge and information. Rapid changes occurring with electronic technologies will affect learning, classroom teaching, libraries, student life, the publication process, the workplace, modes of research, and public outreach. The commission is committed to being a strong voice for public higher education by actively participating in federal initiatives relating to the development of the National Information Infrastructure.

The current commission chair is Samuel H. Smith, President of Washington State University. The Commission is steered by an executive committee consisting of the chairs of the CIT Boards on Distance Education, Library Resources and Services, and Technology Infrastructure. A fourth board consisting of university presidents and chancellors works with the CIT Executive Committee to coordinate commission policies and activities.

The Commission meets annually in the fall at the NASULGC Annual Meeting. The Boards and the CIT Executive Committee meet separately throughout the year. Members are also encouraged to communicate regularly via the CIT listservs.

All NASULGC member institutions are given the opportunity to become involved with the CIT. Each president/chancellor may appoint a voting delegate, while other individuals who work in program areas relevant to the CIT boards may participate as non-voting delegates.

The Board on Distance Education: Distance education programs have grown dramatically during the past decade within higher education, the K-12 sector, and private enterprise. In this time of budgetary constraints accompanied by projected enrollment growth, distance education has become an important component of institutional strategic planning. The Board will serve as the voice of NASULGC on federal issues which influence the direction of educational telecommunications programming.

The Board on Library Resources and Services: NASULGC members institutions are home to many of the worlds finest libraries. The Board works on behalf of these libraries by focussing on the policies needed to address a number of critical challenges, including: hyperinflation of book and journal costs, increased output and publishing for scholarly information, explosive growth of electronic formats, and declining capacity in the face of increased demand by users.

The Board on Technology Infrastructure: The Board seeks to maximize the ultimate research, education, and public service payoffs from advanced information technology investments. The Boards agenda includes tracking federal policy expressed through legislation, research funding, administrative plans, and regulatory actions.

One Dupont Circle, NW Suite 710 • Washington, DC 20036 - 1191 • (202) 778-0818 • Fax (202) 296-6456

Introduction of Speaker

Our speaker for today's program, **Dr. James H. Ryan**, serves as Vice-President and Dean of Continuing and Distance Education at Pennsylvania State University. Prior to his appointment, he was the Campus Executive for the Wilkes-Barre Campus of Penn State for nine years. He is the tenth person in the history of Penn State to head the continuing education program. Penn State's continuing education effort is one of the largest in American higher education, serving more than 170,000 credit and non-credit students at over 500 locations with participants in every state of the union and in 51 countries.

Prior to coming to Penn State, Dr. Ryan served as Director of the Division of Continuing Studies and Associate Professor of Continuing Studies and Public Environmental Affairs at Indiana University in South Bend. He received his baccalaureate, master's, and doctoral degrees from the State University of New York at Buffalo. His doctorate is in the sociology of education and higher education administration with an emphasis on organizational development. Dr. Ryan has taught, written, and lectured widely on leadership, managerial decision making, organizational change and development and the role of higher education in economic development. He has been active in many, many national community organizations where he has served in many leadership positions.

Measuring Costs and Benefits of Distance Learning

James H. Ryan
Vice President for Continuing Education
Pennsylvania State University

It is truly a pleasure to be here. As I look at the program, there is little question in my mind that you are addressing key issues. I think this is one of the most powerfully packed programs I have seen. I know some of you have made comments about the rapid pace of the sessions. Well, welcome to the 21st Century. This conference reflects the life that we have on our campuses. We're all trying to cope with change, and with learning at the exponential speed of change. I think technology is one very important tool that helps move us in that direction. I'd like to share with you my thoughts on this rapidly developing area called distance education. I will illustrate my talk with a power point presentation which not only demonstrates the technology, but represents the combined efforts of a skillful team. I have had the responsibility for distance education programs at Penn State for the last five years. I'm seeing, just as I'm sure you are, the dramatic growth in this area. I will spend the next few moments talking about the growth of distance education, its costs and benefits, and your role in helping to manage and enhance this fast growing development.

As we look at our society, we realize that there is not a sector that is not being influenced by distance education. For example, the military today is investing millions of dollars in increasing distance education capabilities by using satellite, video conferencing and online instruction, in addition to their traditional strong print programs. Reviewing the business and industry sector, we find that they are investing hundreds of millions of dollars for instruction for technicians and engineers to sales representatives and managers to enable them to improve their skills, as well as learn about how the new technology is employed. Major investments are being made to make sure people stay "state of the art," and they have highly developed skills.

Let me give you the specific example of Ford Motor Company. Ford now has a concept of survival that is driven by a fundamental premise called "outlearning the competition." They believe that by outlearning the competition, both through the latest technical and behavioral science theories, Ford will be the dominant automotive manufacturer in the year 2000. They are committed to this objective. As a result, they are building CD-ROM programs to be distributed throughout the world to managers, engineers, and technicians who need to understand how to work with a car that is microprocessor driven. If you're an engineer at Ford in the Detroit area, and you are working on a master's degree (in fact, all engineers working with Ford have to pursue a master's degree as part of their personal responsibility) you are one of the 200 engineers currently enrolled in a combination electrical/mechanical engineering master's program, and you are probably doing that from your office desktop. As the time for the class approaches, you push one key and on comes the faculty member from Wayne State providing instruction to multiple locations. The faculty member outlines the day's topic. You are then asked to push a second key. At that point, the faculty member goes into a window on your computer screen and puts an engineering simulation on the rest of the screen. You then begin to problem solve with the simulation. Every 20 minutes there is a feedback quiz to monitor comprehension since there is a performance understanding expectation written into the contract between industry and Wayne State University.

Student reactions are through a learner response pad where they are able to select an answer and provide immediate feedback to the faculty member at the master control desk. The faculty member can then decide whether or not to review the material. Or the faculty member may decide to have an online discussion at a later date. We are going to see much more of this kind of approach to instruction.

This phenomenon called distance education is extraordinary. Increasingly you will be able to chose courses from many different institutions, because location will not be a barrier. There are many exciting examples taking place throughout the country but I will talk about three institutions which will give you a good snapshot of what's going on. The first is Stanford University.

Today Stanford's College of Engineering has 5,000 students enrolled away from the university. The college offers courses leading to a master's degree in electrical engineering, computer science, and mechanical engineering and engineering economics at 220 sites, in 157 corporations, and in three countries; over 300 courses, both credit and noncredit courses are being delivered.

Project Delta from the California State system, stands for the Direct Electronic Learning Teaching Alternative. Between now and the year 2005 there is expected to be about 150,000 more students. But even today there is not enough room for enrolled students. There is also a moratorium on hiring any additional faculty or adding more buildings. There must be learning structures and methodologies to address this challenge electronically, and that's what Project Delta is doing.

At Washington State University there is an exciting vision of taking information to people through distance education technologies. Credit and noncredit courses will be made available through every county extension office in the state. From these few examples you can see that we are beginning to think about using information and taking information to people in innovative ways.

I'd like to talk about why distance education is becoming pervasive. I will briefly explore the trends, such as the need for lifelong, as well as lifewide learning. Lifelong means building on your competency set. Lifewide learning may be caused by changing careers or by learning entirely unrelated, but necessary, competencies. For example, how many of you realized 15 years ago the level of technology literacy that you would have to have to function effectively today? A second trend is the demand for quality, for accessing the best experts available, not just those closest to you. A third trend is increasing responsiveness and just-in-time learning, anywhere, anyplace, and anytime learning; the convenience of being able to access information where and when you need it. Those are some of the trends that are driving distance education.

I'd like to talk about the promise and reality of distance education. To do that, I need to start with a definition of distance education, so we all have the same foundation. First, what I'd like to emphasize is the teacher and student are not at the same location. Secondly, to be truly effective, distance education must involve two-way communication. I'm talking about the importance of interaction. Obviously technology is in the middle of all this activity. Naturally there must be evaluation of the learning. Penn State has been involved in distance education since 1892—initially through correspondence study. But today, more and more of this instructional activity is mediated in a whole variety of ways. So we need to understand that the instruction at a distance includes interaction and evaluation, and technology can facilitate that interaction. The focus must still be on learning with technology seen merely as a tool.

About five years ago I named a task force with a representative from every college at the university. I asked them to take a look at what impact technology might have on distance learning in the future and to come up with a vision of distance education at Penn State. I'd like to quote the chair of that committee, Bill Kelly, a professor of integrative arts, who had not used technology in instruction until a short time ago: "It was astounding how clearly the task force believed that distance education must become one of the central strategies in the university's future plan if the university is to seriously hold on to its national and international preeminence in teaching, research, and service."

There are a variety of compelling forces driving distance education. I would like to briefly review some of them to demonstrate how they will speed up this distance education evolution. Population decline—there is a decline in traditional college-age students and an increase in adult working students. Here we're talking about the issue of access and convenience. In a study recently done by Boston University for master's level students, the message was very clear. Adults who work full-time and take graduate courses would rather take a course through video conferencing than drive 25 miles at the end of the day to take a course at the BU campus. Given the need for continuous education, access and convenience will drive more of our clients' choice of preferred learning options.

There are a variety of economic factors, including globalization and the creation of a knowledge dependent society. It's clear that today survival in any economy really depends on how you use the latest knowledge. Motorola understands that very well. They spend more than $100 million a year through Motorola University to educate their workers throughout the world. They teach courses largely through the use of technology, and they are teaching them in 27 different languages. They invest a dedicated percentage of expenditure in every employee's professional development.

Information/knowledge is becoming a commodity and there are more players in the marketplace with innovative ways to distribute that commodity. That means much greater competition for colleges and universities.

Information/knowledge is becoming a commodity and there are more players in the marketplace with innovative ways to distribute that commodity. That means much greater competition for colleges and universities. Also, there is a lot of discussion right now about what that means for higher education role in certifying knowledge. There are some who believe that our position will never be jeopardized. Others say the marketplace will ultimately decide how competence will be certified and colleges and universities will increasingly share this role with others, including professional societies and private sector providers. In his book, *The Monster Under the Bed*, Stan Davis talks about what happens when education becomes a commodity. He provides a thought-provoking look at what happens when education becomes essential to the economic survival of a country.

As we look at the relationship of knowledge to careers, we see that the fastest growing occupations do require a college degree. As we experience the "graying" of America, we recognize that for the first time, the largest percentage of people who will be in the work force in the year 2000 are already employed. Most of our businesses and industries will not be hiring new graduates to bring in new competencies and foster change. They will need to invest in retraining and professional development of their current workforce. It is estimated by the American Society for Training and Development (ASTD) that about 80 percent of today's workforce will require some significant education. The need for lifelong learning is becoming ubiquitous and many states are mandating continuing education. You can see the extraordinary growth between 1981 and 1991 of the numbers of professions that now have some form of mandated continuing education activity.

The final force I will mention today is the increased concern about learning becoming more learner-centered, rather than faculty centered. Learning is most effective when it is active rather than passive, collaborative rather than done in isolation. Students have different learning styles and learn at different speeds. We recognize that the lecture may not be the best way of delivering information. Faculty members could work with students on synthesizing, integrating and applying information, rather than simply providing information. So this paradigm change should not come as a surprise to you. It also helps us understand that technology will increasingly play a major role in learning.

Let me comment briefly on competition. If you ask the Dean of our College of Engineering who his biggest competitor is, he will say, "I'm most concerned about Stanford." As most of us develop the technological capability, interesting things will happen in the marketplace. Pennsylvania has more than 130 colleges and universities all of whom could be competing with each other for a market share. As you think about your own universities, your own states, stop and think for a moment how many other states and great universities are offering courses, providing a wonderful array of choices to clients who traditionally, by geographic designation or location, have been yours.

There are also profit-making accredited degree-granting institutions which offer courses delivered largely online. Corporate and government training programs are growing. There is not a federal agency today that is not involved in some form of delivery of distance education or preparing to deliver distance education. From the EPA, to Agriculture, to HUD, there is a major commitment to reaching multiple employees at multiple locations through distance education. There are more purveyors of information in the marketplace than ever before. A 1990 study done by the Carnegie Commission looked at learning in the marketplace, including both college and universities, as well as others, and concluded that between 1980 and 1990, the number of both public and private organizations who provided information in the marketplace increased nine-fold. The study estimated that the supply would increase again by at least nine-fold between 1990 and 2000.

Where does the college and university, traditionally providing continuing education, lifelong learning, and master's level programming fit into this? Marv Cetron, a futurist who has written *The Educational Renaissance* and *The American Renaissance*, has a major forecasting consulting firm in Washington. He made some interesting comments about the importance of technology and instruction at a conference of the CIC institutions last year, which I'll share with you on this video.

(Video played)

Cetron's point was using technology to provide access to learning is easy when you look at the number of households that have information technologies. His data was collected in 1990. You can see that 60 percent of the homes had cable. By now, it's closer to 70 percent. But it doesn't make any difference whether you have cable or not, because for $800 you can buy a small satellite dish to give you everything that cable traditionally provides.

In the *Wall Street Journal* a few weeks ago, it was estimated that by the year 2000, about 60 percent of the households in the United States would have personal computers and 70 percent of those would have CD-ROM drives. While most of you have used Internet and experienced video compression, you may have concerns about its slowness and the quality of the video. This technology will improve dramatically. AT&T has made some assumptions about the technological future. I'm sharing these with you because it gives you a sense of how we're changing the wireless systems, its circuits, processing, and storage. What all this means is that capacity, speed and quality are increasing exponentially, and the systems are vastly improved. I was reading in the *Washington Post* in the business section that AT&T and Paradyne have announced an innovation in data compression and transmission technology which will allow two-way television signals to be sent over ordinary copper phone lines, not fiber optic. This new technology can transmit data at least 70 times faster than the fastest existing modem, meaning subscribers could get phone service and full-motion television/video over their copper phone lines at the same time.

So you see how quickly this technology is evolving. As a result of these developments and the increased demand for education, there have been many new initiatives in distance education. Prior to 1985, there were only about ten states that had significant commitments to distance education. Those were the large geographical states like Colorado, Nebraska, Maine, and others, where populations were very dispersed throughout the state. Consequently, they had to find creative ways to reach out and provide information, knowledge, and programs to their citizens. Today there is hardly a state, in fact there is hardly a major university, that doesn't have some major distance education development.

We must realize that the corporate world will have different ideas about how to access the best, not just an institution, but the best people in the discipline and how technology will allow those new developments to take place.

New developments include creating new international partnerships. There are a number of institutions partnering to develop the delivery of new degree programs at both undergraduate and graduate levels. We must realize that the corporate world will have different ideas about how to access the best, not just an institution, but the best people in the discipline and how technology will allow those new developments to take place. A partnership between Minnesota and Penn State is providing an associate degree in Russia using print and video. The interaction is done through the Internet. Within the Big Ten, the CIC institutions are looking at how to maximize unique faculty expertise, particularly at the doctoral level when there are not enough students to support some programs. Using distance education, we can have that faculty member or teams of faculty members use technology to maintain programs within a consortium of universities. We are also looking at new possibilities in the less commonly taught languages, so we can sustain faculty members and have that expertise available to students.

There are new degree patterns beginning to emerge. For example, Penn State offers a master's degree in acoustical engineering that uses a variety of delivery systems. It uses satellite, video conferencing, and online interaction. A faculty member visits the site several times a semester. Students come for two residential periods during succeeding summers. It's an exciting program. It is now being delivered to sites in the state of Washington, California, Florida, Connecticut, and Pennsylvania.

(Video played)

The tape I just shared with you is from a video compression telecast of this instruction between several sites in Washington originating from University Park, Pennsylvania.

This summer, I was in Birmingham, England attending the 21st meeting of the International Council on Distance Education where more than a thousand delegates from 100 countries were discussing distance education issues. I could have been at a NASULGC meeting, given the same level of development, interaction, and understanding of these issues with one major exception. All of the industrialized nations understood this technology and were beginning to use it. However, the underdeveloped nations were obviously using less technology and more print based distance education. This issue of technology availability between the "have and have-nots" is a worldwide challenge to which we must give some consideration. Supporting the growing interest in this area, the University of Wisconsin has been offering a conference on distance education over the last five or six years. Generally, the conference is attended by 100 to 300 people. This year, there were more than 800 people which was more than double the number they had last year. People were asked how long they had been involved with the responsibilities of distance education and more than half had assumed that responsibility only during the last 18 months. About a year ago our former university president, Dr. Joab Thomas, was asked to speak at a conference in Birmingham, Alabama. His schedule prevented him from attending in person but he was able to participate through satellite broadcast. Here is an example of the convenience of using telecommunication.

(Video played)

Our current president, Dr. Graham Spanier, has been on board for 19 days. I'd like to share with you his message to the academic community available on the Penn State home page on the Internet.

(Video played)

This is from the university's home page on the World Wide Web. The president has had six different messages for the academic community in the last 19 days, and his presentation on the State of the University was available within 24 hours on the World Wide Web. He had over 150 reactions from the academic community and alumni over the course of the next 48 hours and I would say that he's responded to all of those since that time.

Let me briefly review the benefits of distance education. First, it increases productivity. It finds new markets and opportunities. It optimizes declining resources, serves a population that is isolated and cannot access campus resources. It promotes learner-centered education. Now, with all the benefits, why isn't distance education developing even more rapidly? There are barriers. Faculty resistance, cost of technology, lack of support for instructional design, faculty development, perceived differences in quality, faculty workload, reward and recognition—those are some of the current policy issues that need to be addressed to mainstream distance education on campus. Other issues are accreditation, intellectual property, and the impact of either statewide or national information infrastructures. Issues of access, costs, and common standards are things that need our attention.

What are the implications of distance education in the future? First, the largest percentage of professional degrees will be delivered at the work-site. In 1990, I would have predicted that by the year 2000, ten percent of Penn State's professional degrees would be delivered on-site. I would now revise that estimate to say one third of our professional degrees by the year 2005 will be delivered on-site. Second, undergraduates will do more work out of the classroom. I know all of us are anxious to see that happen, because we think they'll be in the library. But that library may be in their home or in their dorm room. Third, we are going to see a decline in the distinction between residential and distance learning. As we look at the university of tomorrow, we are talking about a network of resources, increasing interaction through the technology between students and faculty, reducing constraints of time, place and space, learning more outside the traditional classroom and the changing faculty roles and responsibilities.

Historically, librarians have been both information managers and information navigators. Today technology allows more people, like myself, to become information navigators. Therefore, I think librarians become the information managers. In this environment, librarians need to help all of us with the capacity to navigate through technology, help us find out where we need to go, what we need to see, and how. Historically, librarians have provided support to the person who was in the library or someone who was connected through some information system—perhaps in your own university, your own system.

Increasingly, librarians have to find new ways to identify the databases that will be necessary to support the distance learners. Librarians will need to develop principles and standards which support the distance learner. Librarians will have to find ways to extend services to students, more vigorously and more actively, at a distance. The librarian must get involved as part of the planning team.

The planning team for a distance education course today involves a faculty member as the content provider, a technologist and an instructional designer. A librarian should be part of the curriculum delivery planning team to talk about what databases and resources can support the distance learner. People are inundated with information, from the residential learner to the distance learner. Librarians need to help students understand the difference between information and good information. Librarians need to find creative ways to be a resource to the distance learner.

What I've been talking about (and what you are experiencing in this conference) is trying to look and learn and manage at the speed of change.

Times are changing. There is great uncertainty. Some might even call that "chaos" in today's literature. People who manage chaos and manage change are people who have a sense of tomorrow, a vision, and proactively shape that vision. I am reminded of one of Margaret Mead's great comments made shortly before she died. She said, "I think we've reached a point where the past is not the best indicator of the future."

I urge you to think about what is good about

the past, what is great about the present, and how you can bring those into tomorrow, because tomorrow will be different; the paradigm will change. As we look at tomorrow, my great concern is that some institutions and professions will be as Yogi Berra prophesied, "They're going to end up somewhere, but that somewhere may not necessarily be where they wanted to be."

What I've been talking about (and what you are experiencing in this conference) is trying to look and learn and manage at the speed of change. It is a rate of change that is extraordinary and exhausting. But we need you to examine these issues and to take a major leadership role in understanding how we reach the distance learner.

References

Dillon, Connie L. & Walsh, Stephen m. 1992. Faculty: The neglected resource in distance education. *The American Journal of Distance Education*, 6(3): 5-21.

Dirr, Peter. 1990. Distance Education: Policy Considerations for the Year 2000. *Contemporary Issues in American Distance Education*. Michael G. Moore (Ed.). Oxford, England: Pergamon Press, p.397-406.

Garrison, David R. & Shale, Doublas G. 1987. Mapping the boundaries of distance education: Problems in defining the field. *The American Journal of Distance Education*, 1(1): 7-13.

Garrison, D.R. 1990. An analysis and evaluation of audio teleconferencing to facilitate education at a distance. *The American Journal of Distance Education*, 4(3): 13-24.

Kascus, Marie A. 1995. Library support for quality in distance education: A research agenda. Invitational Research Conference in Distance Education: Towards excellence in Distance Education: A research agenda, May 18-21, 1995, Penn State University. Discussion papers, 350-364.

Kascus, Maria A. 1994. What library schools teach about library support to distant students: A survey. *The American Journal of Distance Education*, 8(1): 20-35.

Keene S. Delane & Cary, James S. 1990. Effectiveness of distance education approach to U.S. Army reserve component training. *The American Journal of Distance Education*, 4(2): 14-20.

Keegan, Desmond. 1988. Problems in defining the field of distance education. *The American Journal of Distance Education*, 2(2): 4-11.

Moore, Michael G. 1994. Administrative barriers to adoption of distance education. *The American Journal of Distance Education*, 8(3): 1-4.

Moore, Michael G. 1994. Audioconferencing at a distance. *The American Journal of Distance Education*, 8(1):, 1-4.

Moore, Michael G. 1993. Interview: Speaking personally with William J. Kelly. *The American Journal of Distance Education*, 7(1): 74-82.

Moore, Michael G. 1992. Take time to design. *The American Journal of Distance Education*, 6(2): 1-4.

Olcott, Don, Hardy, Darcy Walsh, & Boaz, Mary H. Designing a university distance learning infrastructure: An application, quality, cost comparison for selecting alternative delivery systems. Eighth Annual Conference on Distance Teaching and Learning, From Vision to Reality: Providing Cost-Effective Quality Distance Education. Madison, Wisconsin, August 5-7, 1992, 113-120.

Shale, Doug. 1990. Towards a reconceptualization of distance education. *Contemporary Issues in American Distance Education*. Michael G. Moore (Ed.). Oxford, England: Pergamon Press, 333-343.

Thach, Liz & Murphy, Karen, L. 1994. Collaboration in distance education: From local to international perspectives. *The American Journal of Distance Education*, 8(3): 5-21.

Thompson, Melody M. 1994. Interview: Speaking personally with Alan G, Chute, *The American Journal of Distance Education*, 8(1): 72-77.

Part IX
The Limits of Marketplace Solutions and the Need for Collaboration

Moderator:
Barbara von Wahlde
Associate Vice President for University Libraries
University at Buffalo, SUNY

Speaker:
The Need for Collaboration to Build the Knowledge Infrastructure
Richard P. West

I'm **Barbara von Wahlde**, the Library Director at State University of New York at Buffalo. Since I didn't have a chance to make a comment during the morning presentation by Bruce Kingma, I take that opportunity now. There were just a couple of things that I would like to share with you concerning what Bruce covered. One is that we have one of those prolific researchers on our campus who I'm sure probably turns in 70 interlibrary loan requests for articles every month. She is a faculty member in material science who is highly research intensive in her work. And we do not have all the journals that she needs for her activity. So she raises the norm of the SUNY study a bit. The other thing that might be of interest to you is, that before we established SUNY Express, one of the things that we did at our university, and I don't know if it was necessary at the other three campuses as well, was that we invested more money in our interlibrary loan office staffing, prior to the establishment of SUNY Express. That upgrade in the office would not show in the costs that Bruce captured because it was done prior to our study. But we have put more money into the interlibrary loan function, primarily for student assistants.

The third point I would make is, that as the university centers have collaborated over a period of time that Meredith Butler identified as beginning in 1988, I believe we have seen a change in faculty attitudes, at least on our own campus. That is, faculty now know that we have this interdependency with the other SUNY University Center libraries and they expect us to rely on these other institutions and to receive what they need through this consortium, as well. So that has had an impact on the way faculty members express concern about our continual journal cutting and other economies that we are making.

I would also like to say in response to Dr. Ryan's talk on the economics of distance education that three of the four SUNY University Centers are engaged in a distance learning project called Enginnet with our engineering schools. And the library has been a partner in helping the project participants conceive of how library services and information would be delivered to engineering students. Also, the first distance learning classroom at the University of Buffalo has been set up just recently in the health science library. Sometimes I wish I could be cloned so that I could collaborate even more. One of the things that I notice at this conference and at others that I attend is that the need to collaborate and to work with many groups and many stakeholders seems to be increasing. And it's very difficult to widen that circle when you're just one individual trying to make contact with many. So I believe that this conference is particularly valuable both for the opportunity to engage in collaborative discussions, but also because we are studying an issue of paramount concern to me and to my boss, the economics of information.

I am concerned that when I return to campus I will be involved in what our Board of Trustees is calling "Rethinking SUNY." The State University of New York is experiencing severe financial cuts, not unlike what others have already experienced in other segments of the country. Our situation is not unique. But it will be the first time that cuts will hit us quite so hard. It's too soon to understand the implications. But we know that our Trustees are going to be mandating some cuts and changes that we must make, as well as allowing us a certain amount of latitude and creativity in thinking about ways to reduce expenditures or increase income. It will be a troublesome time and one of considerable strain and change. But, I believe that this new economic environment will only encourage the SUNY University Center libraries to continue our efforts and to expand the scope of our collaboration as well.

Introduction of Speaker

Our theme this afternoon is the **Limits of Marketplace Solutions and the Need for Collaboration. Richard West**, our speaker for this session, is particularly well educated and deeply involved on this topic. He has degrees from the University of California, from two different institutions, and his undergraduate degree was in economics. He has a Master of Business Administration degree as well. His career has been spent primarily in California, working in both the University of California system and the California State University system. Most recently, his role is Vice-Chancellor for Business and Finance in the CSU System, the largest higher education system in the United States in terms of student enrollment. At the moment there is collaboration going on between CSU, SUNY, and CUNY with some focus on our libraries. So you put those three large educational systems together, you have a sizable portion of the students enrolled across the United States.

Prior to working at CSU, Richard spent a number of years at the UCAL System where his responsibilities ranged from information systems and services to administrative services. He has continually expanded his scope of responsibilities and he's had a lot of activity related to libraries, as well as to the information technology activities on the campus. Many of us in the library world know Richard best because of his work with the Coalition for Networked Information, the Association of Research Libraries, and the Association of American Universities. He has served on the CNI steering committee since its inception, and that brings him into contact with members of EDUCOM, CAUSE, and ARL. Most recently he served as chair of the AAU task force that developed a national strategy on managing scientific and technical information. Several models and themes have emerged from that work, and I believe that they will be part of the remarks that Richard makes today. He has taught in the business school at the University of California. He's written articles that have appeared in *Educom Review* and in *Cause and Effect*. He's also served on the board of directors of the Advanced Networks and Services System.

I believe that Richard will be "weaving a tapestry" for us to unite many of the themes and the threads that we have heard in earlier sessions and position us for our next session on creating a research agenda in economics of information.

The Need for Collaboration to Build the Knowledge Infrastructure

Richard P. West
Vice Chancellor, Business and Finance
California State University System

I have found this conference to be full of particularly good sessions and very stimulating. I want now to discuss a couple of the themes and I will refer to some of the earlier discussions and comment on some of the presenters' remarks. I think that there are some extremely important points that have been made throughout this discussion. I'll also give you my own perspective on how scholarly communication is changing, what's costing less money, what might be some of the potential we see coming forth, and what some of the pitfalls might be.

Let me start by asking what is the Knowledge Infrastructure? I'll define the knowledge infrastructure from an institutional point of view but I'll also get into the entire life cycle, or as Paul Peters said, the value chain. Or stated differently, what is the sequence of events from the time that a document is created in electronic form until it's used by a variety of folks in our community. I'll define the knowledge infrastructure as made up of the following functions: collection, storage, printing/display, access, distribution (resource sharing), and integration of and presentation of information.

This is just one way of thinking about the various life cycle functions, from an institutional perspective. I would like to place particular emphasis on the last point which is the integration of resources to the user. I've always felt that this is an important issue, however it's very difficult to do when you have a variety of resources on the network. From the user's perspective, it can be very difficult to navigate the network when you don't know where these resources are. Once you do find them, just the way you interact with that information resource is a challenge. My own view is that I don't think networked information will be easy to use, until we have a more common interface for users.

The way we organize ourselves, build our technology infrastructure, acquire our information resources, and get them to the users in a networked environment is not unlike the acquisition and delivery of information in a traditional library. It has been the center of our information resource activity for academic support. I think this is really what we're trying to build with this new technology. Part of our dilemma right now is that some of our knowledge infrastructure is new, however we still rely substantially on the old information delivery system. The question becomes how to replace old approaches with new.

There is an assumption that a national and international network exists and that it operates. I think Paul Peters mentioned that we used to say it was very difficult to explain to a layperson what we were trying to do in the early stages of the NSFnet, and what the concept of networked information (content) was, because there was not an easy reference point as there is now, e.g., the Internet. It is amazing to think how far we've come in just a few years. I assume that, in a few years, we will look back and say the same thing about today. Collaboration as a requirement has been a theme throughout the conference discussions. Not only are we talking about the integration of technologies, but we are also talking about changing roles and responsibilities. The nature of technology will cause changes in those roles and responsibilities. So we look at how to combine efforts, where can we make changes? We're not going to succeed if we keep trying to do the same thing in several different parts of the organization.

One of the key pieces of information I heard earlier was the comment from Richard Lucier that at the University of California, San Francisco, library journal articles or journal subscription costs have increased by 18% per year. The annual increase in journal costs is not a new issue, but I thought there had been some moderation in price increases in the last few years. But at 18 percent, or even at ten percent as was stated in another presentation, and regardless of whether there are more pages or not, at a time when inflation is two to three percent and institutional budgets aren't staying even with inflation, our current model of access to scholarship in journals is not a sustainable economic model. As much as we have talked about this problem, we have made little progress in changing the nature of the economic market for certain types of scholarly information. We have done little, if anything, to solve the problem. We need to look at that unsustainable economic model and figure out what we have to change, because something has to change, or the marketplace will respond and tell us how to change. This is not a static environment. It's not an environment or market that is now in equilibrium.

Let's turn to the network itself. We are now in a period of rapid change. The NSFnet no longer exists. The transition from a publicly assisted and subsidized network occurred this year. As we've moved, we have transitioned the technology environment to a different management structure, so that it is a much more private marketplace structure, a very competitive environment, and we see the benefits of that competitive environment in cost reduction. What we haven't yet done is transfer this environment into a different technological infrastructure. It's still struggling with technological change. As we move into this new decentralized management structure, one of the concerns is: how easily will change be incorporated into this technologically distributed model?

There are significant potential operational concerns in this new networked environment. There is potential for outages and service problems of one type or another. These are probably inevitable in this kind of marketplace, but we are highly dependent upon the network and its resources. So this is an area that bears a lot of watching. We'll need to watch carefully as the federal government defines what its role might be. We are in a period of market regulation. Although we're moving into a marketplace environment, we still have vestiges of regulation, and there is obviously industry integration—we see that all the time—between distribution agents, whether that be telephone companies or cable industries, and content providers, whether that be Disney or a library. Part of the discussion is, as you see in the Disney/ABC example, content issues coming to the fore, but with firms trying to figure out whether a distribution mechanism gives that particular firm an advantage. How deregulated will that local telephone industry become? How regulated will cable industry be?

One of the debates in higher education now is about what strategy is in the best interest of higher education to obtain the cheapest rates for networked services? One perspective suggests that there is a tradition that certain special interests like education could obtain reserved capacity or discounted rates by law or regulation. Examples of such special rights are public access channels, broadband spectrum, or an ITFS station. Another view is that this marketplace for data communications is evolving so quickly that anyone who has economies of scale is going to be able to purchase access to the network at significant discounts. The question becomes how do we promote competition to create an environment in which costs are reduced and technology kept current? As a major purchaser of networked services, higher education would be a benefactor of such a competitive market. My view is that this is a time where the deregulation of the local environment is very important, if there is to be low cost service to higher education. A caveat to this statement is that rural areas, where there is a low concentration of volume, will make economies of scale difficult to generate. I don't think there's any doubt that, if we can get the same benefits at the local level that we've had at the long distance level, we will see a significant reduction in costs of access to the data network.

Let me turn to an analytical approach to scholarly information. (See Figures 7-11.) There are a series of functions that must be performed in any kind of scholarly communication process. Such an analytical framework allows any model of scholarly communication to be compared to another model. For each function, a technologically assisted model could serve the scholarly communications better than a model that is in traditional print format. In this analytical approach, we can examine both which of the functions are performed, and how well each of the functions are performed by different models. Finally, there are the players in each model who perform the various functions. So you have this three-way matrix that you have to think about as you examine each model. As information technology is disseminated more broadly in the scholarly communication process, the roles of the various participants will inevitably change.

What about some of the specific models? One model we see most often in today's environment is a hybrid between print and electronic-assisted distribution of scholarly information. A second model is the emergent model, which is information which does not even appear in traditional print sources. Once such a model of scholarly information becomes more prevalent, significant changes in roles and responsibilities will become more obvious. Currently, however, we are in a period of transition. The questions are, where are our cost centers now?; where should they be?; where should we restrict costs?; and where should we invest more? An essential point to remember is that any model discussed must perform all the functions of the scholarly communications process.

...[H]ow do we promote competition to create an environment in which costs are reduced and technology kept current?

Let me return to my earlier point about the high rate of increase in the costs for scholarly journals. This high rate of increase means that there is still something about the current overall scholarly communications process that has to be honored. Our current technologically-assisted models have not replaced the print based model. So where does that leave us and why? Our sessions at this conference have offered some explanations. The first requirement is to recognize the need for a change in our behavior. The challenge for us is to know how to change our behavior and how to emphasize new technologically-aided ways of providing information to our faculty, students, and staff.

I would also like to emphasize a major assumption that we all make at the campus level, as well as the regional and national level. This key assumption is that there is a data network. Although it is an assumption we have to make, it is not necessarily an easy assumption to make at the local level, because there is a need for significant investment in the technological infrastructure, the cable plant, the local network on campus. There is a desperate need for this technological investment and all institutions should keep it as a priority.

Let's now look at cost centers and the marketplace. Universities, particularly university libraries, have long been major participants in the current scholarly information marketplace. A large percentage of scholarly information is acquired from private publishers. Universities spend a lot of money to acquire information resources. So first of all, we spend a lot of money for information. Secondly, the new information data networks allow scholarly information to be stored with only one copy and that copy can be widely disseminated to many people. So all the discussion is around one copy cost, because some of the distribution costs in the new technological environment are handled by other funders or other providers of money. It's a jointly funded network. You have the intellectual and technological ability to have one copy, and you have this concept of acquisition of intellectual property rights, mostly copyrighted information, with a tradition of private acquisition. We have not done anything to change that market. We have had lots of discussion around the fair use question in a print form. There is also a debate, a significant debate, around what fair use should be in electronic form.

We have a dilemma. We have the legal property rights that limit our use, and we have the technological capability of having a single copy on the network that can be used as often as we like, by as many people as are on the network. Some of the early work CNI did with the READI Project emphasized that contractual arrangements rather than copyright arrangements would be the way we would acquire information in this new technological environment.

Agreements between two parties for buyer and supplier would be the best way to make economic arrangements for use of copyrighted scholarly information.

In this technological and legal framework, resource sharing must take on new meaning. One way of changing our thinking is to examine the cost centers or value chain of the scholarly information communication process. Most often the conventional wisdom is that offering interlibrary loan is a way that costs could be reduced. The materials budget or the acquisitions budget is the cost center that's viewed as the one that can achieve the most savings from this technological change. However, strong intellectual property rights will restrict any savings we might otherwise realize with today's technology.

In today's scholarly information market there are a variety of new pricing mechanisms that are now available for different networked information rights. Examples of different pricing approaches are: we pay per copy, per use, for the site license, or for the number of simultaneous users. In each of these approaches there are usually economies of scale that can be examined for cooperative use. Can contractual arrangements be negotiated with intellectual property owners that do not limit our benefits from that cooperative use?

One typical example of contractual license arrangements is to mount X number of journals locally on your own server, or acquire access centrally through the publisher in data networks, and make it available to your constituency, through password control or other security control. In the short run, licensed rights appear to work extremely well. The information is not acquired, but "rented." The rental approach is usually a two- or three-year contract. Often this is a successful approach and users begin to find networked information very helpful. Use of such data increases and users become enamored with it. They find it very helpful. They're hooked, basically. And you have at the end of a three-year period an interesting negotiation with your supplier. To be able to negotiate a license from the university's view there has to be reasonable substitutability for the information. Some economics research has shown that there is limited substitutability for scholarly information. The most prestigious journals are the ones that libraries need to acquire since those journals are the ones that scholars will use most often since these journals carry the most current scholarly information. Institutions can quickly be put in a box by having successful networked "rental" information.

Pretty quickly you find your institution at the mercy of the producer because you do not have a marketplace that's competitive with respect to the supply of this information. A clear example of this market condition is the rate of inflation of journal prices, 10-18 percent per year has been mentioned at this conference. One possible reason for this high rate of inflation is the lack of substitutability in the scholarly information products that we buy or rent. An economist calls this type of marketplace a producer-driven, price setting market, not a cost-driven, competitive market.

There are many things that can be done about it, however. If we tolerate the status quo, there will continue to be double digit inflation in information pricing. There are some things we can do in our institutions as well. One of the things that's clear about electronic information distribution is that there are savings on a per-unit basis on storage, access, and circulation over traditional print strategies. These price per units in storage and distribution costs should be expected to improve. Another way we can have an impact is to review collection development strategies to examine what we should share and what we should acquire? What investments should we make with respect to networked information? Should a library acquire the most often used material or the least often used? Usage drives the acquisitions costs more in the new electronic information environment than has been true in traditional print format.

Usage drives the acquisitions costs more in the new electronic information environment than has been true in traditional print format.

I've often said that librarians should become more of a portfolio manager. Usage becomes more important. One of the interesting comments earlier in this conference was that we should be driven to more of a usage-determined pattern with respect to promotion and tenure, which I don't think is the process used now. What are the implications of that from a publication and acquisition of information resources point of view? Basically, what contractual arrangement should we be making to be sure we get the best information at the cheapest costs? I think that understanding usage patterns and anticipating usage patterns are extremely important.

Fee-for-service arrangements are going to become more common in our institutions. Value-added for packaging and delivering information on the campus and to community services or other industry partners will become a necessity. Of course, no single approach will dominate in the short term.

In closing I want to leave you with several questions to contemplate. The first is similar to the question before the U.S. Congress regarding the amount of regulation or amount of competition that should occur in the local data and video (information) distribution marketplace. How many providers of distribution service should exist at the local level? Another way of stating this is, how do we create a more competitive distribution marketplace? Currently, we don't have one in local distribution of electronic networks, but we are trying to create one. One of the discussions in the public arena is whether our federal and state governments will generate and disseminate information. Will this data continue to be accessible? Obviously, it's our desire to have it accessible. But one of the features of this information society will be repackaging of information so there is value added by the way information is brought together and resold. Due to the proliferation of large amounts of networked information, this repackaging concept is going to become more and more common. Much of the reselling will be done with government information. A significant public policy question is whether we should have strong views on how that information will be repackaged or made available to our institutions.

How can we pay for double digit inflation when institutional budgets are increasing at one-third that rate?

A second question is do we retain at the institutional level the copyright of articles that are published by our faculty? What would be the impact on the scholarly communication process as we know it now? I'm not sure of the answers to this question. I think that you can imagine a couple of different scenarios. People who are comfortable with the current distribution model would say that there would not be the same amount of quality information distributed as is true now.

A third question I suggest for consideration is should promotion and tenure decisions be based on use of publications and not simply on publication? Most librarians will say there is quite a difference between what they acquire for the library and what gets used. From an economist's point of view, such a change would create a tremendously more efficient distribution system. Whether that's good from a scholarly point of view or not is an open question.

A postreview process of scholarly quality would let faculty members put on the network any material they want to publish and then the marketplace would sort out what would be used. This could cause a significant reduction in costs. But the question is at what price?

Finally, what if we assume the continuation of the current trend, that is a high rate of increase in the price of journal articles or journal subscriptions? How can we pay for double digit inflation when institutional budgets are increasing at one-third that rate? This relates to the question of how do you share and at what price. The issue is how do we create a competitive marketplace for scholarly information? If there are going to be price per unit reductions, there has to be a larger market. How do we create that? It's not clear to me that the current trajectory gets us there. I hope my questions have set the stage for the next and final session of the conference.

Questions and Discussion

MS. VON WAHLDE: Richard made three very interesting assumptions and I'm wondering if we might take a moment or two to see whether any of you would like to question those assumptions, or comment on them before we take the break? Certainly our environment is one that is not in equilibrium.

QUESTION #1: One assumption that you made is that we need to try to promote a more competitive marketplace for scholarly information. I'd like to question whether that really is desirable in dealing with a public good like scholarly information, or whether we'd actually be more efficient in distributing scholarly information on a cooperative basis among the research and scholarly community rather than trying to promote the marketplace, which obviously, from what a lot of the economists have said, would be a very artificial marketplace.

DR. WEST: Well, I think again it's the relationship to price that matters. If you pursue the more cooperative effort, someone still has to acquire the rights. If it's done in the print format, the sense that most of us have is that publishers work on a profit, or a revenue maximization and profit maximization strategy. Certainly private publishers do. So, if they are going to look for the same total revenue that they're getting now and, if there are fewer copies of whatever is acquired, the price will go up. That's the dilemma that was presented several times during this conference. You have to figure out a way, it seems to me, to cover those costs of production and all the things that the publisher does that is valued by the scholarly community. I think that's the dilemma.

QUESTION #2: Richard, you made reference to the strategy of a campus or faculty member retaining copyright. When I've discussed that with faculty members, they say they don't want to be the first to do it. They don't want to be the ones to tell the prestigious journal that they want to retain copyright and, therefore, face the possibility that their article will be turned down on that basis. On the other hand, if you look at trying to cooperate across institutions, you get into legal questions about restraint of trade, and so on. How do you get from here to there?

DR. WEST: I think that is an excellent question. It is a challenge that requires tremendous cooperation, a mutual interest which was not obvious before between the faculty and the institution or administration. I think in small discussions, when we've been able to spend enough time talking about the economic cycle that we're in, we have gotten people to this position. But unless we are able to change how our faculty judge themselves, I think we're in this dilemma, at least until there is a break point that's caused by a tremendous dislocation of cost increases which we're not able to pay. It just tells me that the providers of scholarly information know us better than we know ourselves.

QUESTION #3: Following up on your point about the system being out of equilibrium and about the non-substitutability of the source and the fact that it's producer-driven rather than cost-driven, coming from outside the library community. I have been struck by how relatively passive libraries have been in the face of the cost increases that they face. I think it's because of the reasons that you have just cited, plus maybe a couple more. What librarians do is cancel subscriptions rather than negotiate and bargain. You wouldn't do that with automobiles. If General Motors went up 18 percent you'd buy a Ford instead. But you don't have that option with a sole-source journal. So the response looks pretty passive to me. Maybe out of a commitment to scholarship and its priority and a desire not to do anything to endanger that, maybe because libraries are somewhat isolated from the procurement process by the intermediary firms that we use. But eventually, as you pointed out, this is going to endanger scholarship itself. Because the system is not in equilibrium and cannot be sustained. I'd like to see if you had further comments on that as well as on the possibility of some individual institutional effort. What, for example, would happen if a library set a budget for journals acquisition, $12 million or $120 million, and then put that out for bid and got bids from publishers, as to what journals they could supply for that $12 million?

DR. WEST: Right. It sounds good to me as the chief financial officer. My library colleagues will then spear me as I go out the door. I think part of the answer is still substitutability. The library community doesn't feel that there is good substitutability with respect to these scholarly communications. The whole point of Roger Noll's earlier remarks was that this particular marketplace is one which is driven by prestige and that the faculty want to publish in the most prestigious journals and that we have to acquire, we, the library or the institution, has to acquire those because the same faculty encourage us to do that. So a little bit is the disconnect, using a favorite word these days, or the lack of coordination with our faculty who are not on the same wavelength on these issues.

Our current economic model was a very good model for a print-based strategy. Spreading the first copy costs and the distribution costs across a large number of subscriptions worked reasonably well for a long time. As we see better sharing, as we see more technological solutions, those actually drive us to a break point of saying who is going to pick up those first copy costs? And we haven't figured out a way to share those costs institutionally that is legal and that is consistent with the relationship we have with the faculty. The promotion and tenure process is still based on number of articles published, particularly those published in the most prestigious journals. That is certainly not a usage model.

Figures 1-3

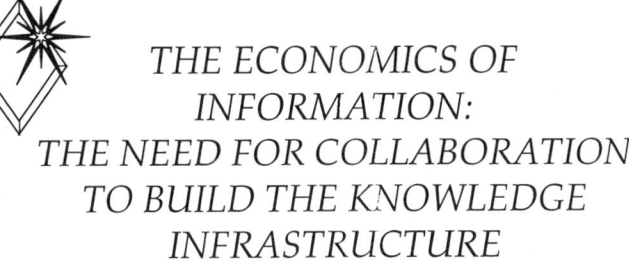

THE ECONOMICS OF INFORMATION: THE NEED FOR COLLABORATION TO BUILD THE KNOWLEDGE INFRASTRUCTURE

Richard West
California State University
Vice Chancellor
Business and Finance
September 19, 1995
Washington, D.C.

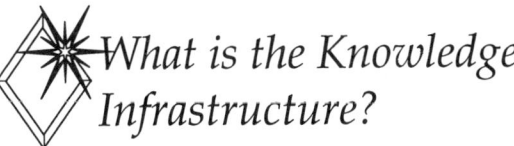

What is the Knowledge Infrastructure?

- *Collection*
- *Access*
- *Storage*
- *Distribution (Resource Sharing)*
- *Printing/Display*

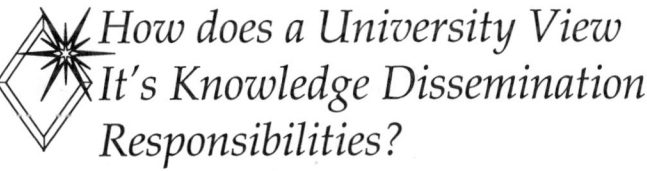

How does a University View It's Knowledge Dissemination Responsibilities?

- Functionally:
  - The Knowledge Infrastructure = The TraditionalLibrary
- Procedurally and Conceptually:
  - The Knowledge Infrastructure is Radically Different than the Traditional Library
- Need to <u>Assume</u> the Network:

Figures 4-6

National Networking Management

- Major Transition
  - Change in overall approach is now being implemented
  - Moving from Federal government managed network to a private market approach
  - Transition to be completed within the next 6 - 9 months

National Information Infrastructure

- Public Policy
  - A priority for the current administration
  - What is the National Information Infrastructure?
  - Market, regulation, industry integration

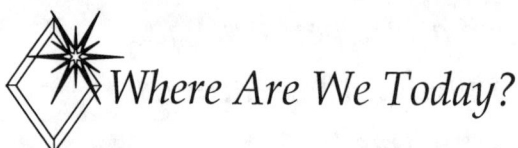
Where Are We Today?

- Operating data packet network moving to a market managed environment
- Regulated local voice network service
- Regulated local video distribution service
- Networking technology that is or soon will be highly integrated
- Content from traditional providers is beginning to be available via networks

Figures 7-9

An Analytical Approach to the Knowledge Infrastructure

- Functions of the scholarly communications process
- Attributes of performance
- Roles and responsibilities of various players

Functions of Scientific and Scholarly Communication:

- Information generation & creation
- Authoring
- Informal peer communication
- Editorial & validation
- Ownership, privacy, security
- Preservation & Archiving
- Information management
- Location & delivery
- Recognition
- Diffusion
- Access Acquisition &
- Storage
- Distribution
- Utilization of information

Performance Attributes of Scientific and Scholarly Communication:

- Ease of Use
- Accuracy
- Adaptability
- Cost
- Extensibility
- Timeliness
- Authenticity
- Relevance
- Recovery
- Responsiveness
- Predictability
- Eligibility
- Innovation

Figures 10-12

Models of Scholarly Communication

- *Classical*
- *Modernized*
- *Emergent*

Will The Knowledge Infrastructure Succeed?

- Any modernized or emergent mode must perform all functions of the scholarly communications process
- New roles and changed institutional behavior required
- Desperate need for technology infrastructure investment

Improving Technologies Enable Two Conceptual Changes in our View of Scholarly Communication

- Reconceputalization of how scholarly research will be done--the emergent model
- Does away with presumption that print performs the function of communication of results in the scholarly communication process
- Need to re-think our cost centers as more scholarly information is available in electronic form rather than print

Figures 13-15

The Marketplace for Electronic Information

- The concept of property rights
- Will the sense of Fair Use change?
- "Free" information
- Public information
- Private information
- As usual, You Get What You Pay For!

Resource Sharing Opportunities?

- Premise is often that savings (if any) from introduction of information technologies to libraries will be an extension of the inter-library loan model of resource sharing. The materials or acquisitions budget viewed as the cost center to show most savings or productivity improvement
- Due to continued strong private property rights in scholarly literature, materials budget is not likely to show savings, but in fact, is likely to increase

The New Economic Relationships of Electronic Information "Pricing"

- Different pricing approaches can mean different costs
- Variety of contractual arrangements for electronic information
    - Per copy (Traditional)
    - Per use
    - Site license
    - Simultaneous users
- Economics of scale - benefits of cooperation

Figures 16-18

The New Economic Relationships of Electronic Information "Cost Changes"

- Electronic information delivery can enable savings in storage, access and circulation over traditional library practice for scientific and technical information
- Price per unit improvements in storage and distribution costs should be expected
- Document may deliver an article for half the cost compared to the classical model's inter-library loan process
- Information collection strategy impact
- Sharing means something new

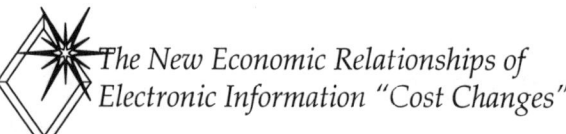
The New Economic Relationships of Electronic Information "Cost Changes"

- As material becomes available in modernized and emergent forms, savings are in access, storage, and circulation costs traditionally incurred by the library
- 60% - 70% (excluding capital costs of construction) of total library costs are in non-materials (acquisition) costs
- Goal should be to achieve savings in storage and acquisition (cataloging) costs as well as savings in distribution costs

The Implications of the "Cost Changes"

- How to make investments in electronic information rights in an increasingly networked world
- Do you retain print versions of the most often used materials on the least often used?
- Usage and content licensing arrangements will determine costs

Figures 19-21

How Will We Pay for Content Costs?

- Materials/Collections Budget
- Fee for Service
- Time Value Pricing
- Rationing of Service (Traditional)
- Productivity - Who's Cost Center (Budget) Benefits?

When Will The Future Arrive?

- No single mode is expected to dominate in next twenty years
- Concurrent models will exist for medium term period
- Cost and processes necessary to support all models will be required
- Mixed model is inevitable - strategies to recognize this environment are essential

What Should We Be Doing Next?

- Support the creation of competitive marketplaces for all components of data networking
- Support "Fair Use" concept for intellectual property in the electronically empowered network environment
- Explore cooperative continual agreements that maximize economics of scale with content providers
- Keep public information in the public domain
- Invest in local campus networking capability
- Promote efforts to maximize public and private information in electronic form
- Develop strategies to encourage a competitive market in scholarly information content

Part X
The Economics of Information and the Need for Collaboration—
Creating a Research Agenda

Moderator:
Meredith Butler
University at Albany, SUNY

Panel:
Karen R. Hitchcock
University at Albany, SUNY

Clifford Lynch
University of California

Timothy Ingoldsby
American Institute of Physics

Colin Day
University of Michigan Press

Malcolm Getz
Vanderbilt University

Richard Ekman
The Andrew W. Mellon Foundation

Deanna Marcum
Council on Library Resources

Duane E. Webster
Association of Research Libraries

MS. BUTLER: Welcome to the final session on **The Economics of Information and the Need for Collaboration—Creating a Research Agenda.** I think you will agree that we have an exceptional group of knowledgeable and committed individuals with us this afternoon to share their expertise. I have asked them to draw on key ideas from the conference and offer their thoughts on where we go from here collectively and collaboratively. How can we integrate our issues more fully into the agendas of higher education, of research universities and their faculties, their libraries, their computing centers, of professional associations, and of corporations and foundations? How can we work together most effectively on solutions, or at least on developing studies and data that help us begin to find solutions? And finally, how can we convey to our national, state, and local policymakers the urgency of public attention and support to these issues that are transforming the economic basis of our institutions and changing the way we think about education and scholarship.

It's my daunting task to keep us focused on the topic at hand and give everyone an opportunity to speak and keep us on time. So let me introduce all of the panelists to you, at least those whom you haven't met already in our conference. I will start with my immediate left.

I am very pleased to introduce **Dr. Karen Hitchcock**, Interim President of the University of Albany, SUNY. Dr. Hitchcock assumed the Albany presidency only last month, after having served for four years as the university's Vice-President for Academic Affairs. Prior to coming to Albany, Dr. Hitchcock served as Vice-President for Research and Dean of the Graduate College, Professor of Anatomy and Cell Biology, and Professor of Biological Sciences at the University of Illinois at Chicago. She received her Ph.D. in anatomy from the University of Rochester, School of Medicine and Dentistry. In her academic and administrative career, she has published numerous articles and received a good number of awards and grants. She currently serves as chair of the Council of Academic Affairs of NASULGC. Her leadership has also been instrumental in launching the Capital Region Information Service, the public network in New York's capital region, and she serves as President of its Board of Directors.

I am extremely grateful that Karen has agreed to be with us not only for this panel, but with us throughout the conference, because, of course, she is in the terrible position of being a new president in the State of New York at the moment when New York is withdrawing support of its public higher education system. And, no doubt, much too much of her time has been spent in thinking about the economics of higher education.

I have already introduced **Deanna Marcum** to you, and so I would like to move to **Clifford Lynch**. He probably needs no introduction in this audience but let me tell you a few highlights about him. Dr. Lynch is the Director of the Division of Library Automation at the University of California Office of the President. He has been at the University of California for about 15 years and has played a vital role in the national development of information technologies during those 15 years. He's a prolific author and a frequent conference speaker. He leads CNI's architecture and standards working group and is President-Elect of the American Society for Information Science.

Next we have **Colin Day**, who is the current Director of the University of Michigan Press, a position he has held since 1988. Dr. Day is a graduate of Oxford University and also holds a Ph.D. in economics. He spent several years as an academic, before joining Cambridge University Press as economics editor. Transferred to Cambridge's New York office, he later became editorial director of that press. In recent years and especially during his term as President of the Association of American University Presses, Colin has been very active in the policy debates about electronic publishing and copyright.

Next we have **Malcolm Getz**, who you saw in action yesterday as the moderator of the panel of economists. Dr. Getz has a national reputation for his work in the economics of higher education. He has been a faculty member in economics at Vanderbilt since 1973. Most of us in the library profession know him from his tenure as Director of Vanderbilt's libraries from 1984 to 1994. He also served as Associate Provost during those years and had responsibilities, not only for the libraries, but for academic computing and other information technology initiatives. Malcolm received his Ph.D. from Yale University in 1973 and has been widely recognized for his work in the economics of higher education, including the economics of the problems facing libraries.

Next we have **Tim Ingoldsby**, Director of New Product Development at the American Institute of Physics. In his current role, Tim is responsible for the process of bringing new products from the germination stage through to full fruition. Prior to assuming this position, Tim served as AIP's first Director of Information Technology. He was responsible for bringing AIP's publishing technology infrastructure up to speed. Prior to his service at AIP, Tim worked in the aerospace industry and as a physics teacher. He's been an active voice in the development of electronic publishing.

Next we have **Richard Ekman**, who is currently serving as the Secretary of The Andrew W. Mellon Foundation. From 1982 to 1991, Dr. Ekman served on the staff of the National Endowment for the Humanities, first as Director of the Division of Education Programs, subsequently as Director of the Division of Research Programs. He is currently a member of the Board of Directors of the American Association for Higher Education, the Society for Values and Higher Education, and the British American Chamber of Commerce Foundation. He received his Ph.D. from Harvard University in the history of American civilization and has had a distinguished career as a teacher, scholar, and university administrator.

Our final speaker will be **Duane Webster**. I think he needs no introduction to this audience. I'm delighted to welcome this extraordinary and varied panel of knowledgeable people.

Remarks by Karen R. Hitchcock
Interim President
University at Albany, SUNY

It's certainly a pleasure to be here. This has just been a wonderful experience these last two days. I'm sure you've all enjoyed and learned from all the presentations, just as I have. Clearly the very diversity of the topics presented, and the diversity of the attendees here at the conference itself reflect on the wide-reaching impact of information technology on all aspects of our university environment. Over the course of the conference we've heard of the transformative power of an environment of networked information technology, an environment characterized by tremendously enriched administrative practices, student services, and access to information for our students and faculty alike. David Roselle provided strong testimony to the potential such technology has to support the strategic initiatives of an institution of higher education. And Mario Morino reminded us that it is the cultural transformation enabled by this rapidly changing technology that must receive additional attention.

It is in this area of cultural transformation that I would like to focus my brief remarks. A number of the speakers over the last two days have alluded to the behavioral changes of faculty which are necessitated by new modes of scholarly communication and by new methods for information storage and retrieval. But equally important, the technologies we have been discussing will be essential in transforming the very learning environment of our institutions. More and more, inquiry and analysis, the hallmarks of the research process, are coming to define the learning experience, as well. As students become co-discovers with the faculty, the technologies and communications capabilities discussed in relationship to the scholarship of our faculty will clearly be needed to support new educational strategies, strategies which must be developed to address new demands on the academy in this period of fiscal constraint. These demands include our students' wish for anytime, anywhere education; the need to face the challenge of alternate providers, and the need to develop a learning environment which focuses on information access and information analysis skills, skills which will be essential to our students over a lifetime, given changing career options and work relationships.

Increased investment in networked information technology alone will not be sufficient to the task. Development of distance learning capabilities will also not be enough. If we are to address these new challenges, major changes are needed in the very culture of our institutions, in the role of the faculty, in the relationship of our faculty to information professionals, in the relationship of our faculty to our students, in the reward structure which determines our faculty's priorities. It is after all the faculty who must assure that the new technologies facilitate rather than drive curricular innovation. It's the faculty who must identify the ways to utilize new information technologies to meet their educational goals. As was pointed out this morning and frequently throughout this meeting, faculty must be at the table. The difficulty in bringing about such changes in pedagogy, however, cannot be underestimated.

Dr. Joseph Burke, former Provost of the State University of New York, tells a wonderful story illustrating this point. He describes an event which occurred in the theology room, a lecture hall in the University of Salamanca in Spain, an event which occurred over 700 years ago. One afternoon the lecture of a professor of theology was disrupted when civil guards burst into the hall and carried him off to prison on orders from the Spanish Inquisition. For 25 years he languished in a dungeon, pressed constantly by grand inquisitors to confess to heresy. Upon his release, people jammed the hall to hear what he would say about the evils of the inquisition, about religious persecution, about the assault on academic freedom. A hush settled over the hall as the professor, physically broken by 25 years of torture and torment hobbled to the podium. He looked at his notes and mumbled, "As I was saying."

As Dr. Burke went on, today, seven centuries later, tens of thousands of faculty still stroll to the front of the class, often to a podium, and repeat the opening words of our 13th century theologian, "as I was saying." Yes, institutions of higher education must certainly develop the long-term budget strategies to support the networked information technology critical to administrative efficiencies and enhanced information access and scholarly communication. However, as this story points out, equally important is an investment in the faculty development programs which will assure that these technologies are integrated into the campus' learning environment. Further, new coalitions are needed if such faculty development initiatives are to lead to meaningful curricular innovation. Librarians and computing professionals must be more engaged with faculty in curricular structure and content. And faculty need to be educated regarding the pedagogic potential of new technologies.

At the University at Albany we recently established the Center for Excellence in Teaching and Learning, which for both philosophic and practical reasons, was placed within our University Library. Within the center, faculty, librarians and computing professionals come together to share expertise and collaborate on curricular change. An example of such a collaboration is our new Project Renaissance. This program will strengthen and enrich the academic and campus life experiences of incoming freshman by offering them, in groups of a hundred, a unified year-long general education sequence. Team-teaching, interdisciplinary studies unified around the themes of human identity, and, technology, collaborative learning, hands-on research, discussions regarding how knowledge is created in each discipline, the development of skills in information retrieval and analysis, and the experience of participating in a living learning community are all hallmarks of this program. Each group of a hundred students will be taught by a team of faculty and information specialists. Facilitated by technology, the learning environment will be characterized by enhanced student-teacher interaction, collaborative learning teams, student responsibility for their own learning, ongoing assessment, and so forth. The instructional team will also prepare a "docuverse"—a hypertext online computer database which will contain examples of student work, course readings, and syllabi. This instructional resource will evolve overtime— enriched by all who use it.

Such experiments in pedagogy, if successful, could have a profound effect on the ways we calculate institutional costs and allocate instructional resources. Such curricular innovations cannot be assessed, regulated, or funded using current paradigms. The educational landscape, as we have been hearing, certainly has changed and many issues have emerged. New models of cost effectiveness will need to be developed. Faculty productivity measures will no longer be tied to classroom contact hours. State legislatures and university governing boards must be given alternatives to these soon to be outmoded measures. Interinstitutional instructional collaborations will test the policy assumptions of the past regarding institutional roles and missions. Faculty reward structures which recognize pedagogic innovation will need to be developed. Multiple types of learning will lead to a redefinition of the use of faculty time. Instructional teams including faculty and information specialists will challenge the current allocation of effort within our libraries and computing centers.

Professional development of our faculty will require institutional investment, if the investment in new technology is to have a real impact on the learning environment of our campuses. And clearly, we will need new economic models for, not only distance education, but also collaborative and decentralized education. Scalability and practicality must be assessed.

Curricular and pedagogic innovation facilitated by technology certainly has created a rich research agenda for all of us, an agenda which will, of course, need to address the economics of information access and scholarly communication, but an agenda which also must speak to the costs of creating and supporting a profoundly changed learning environment on our campuses. It will be an environment characterized by new faculty roles, new expectations, new partnerships. I certainly look forward to working with all the members of this conference's organizing groups; with NASULGC, with the Council on Library Resources, the Association of Research Libraries, the Coalition for Networked Information, and with our faculty to move this agenda forward.

Remarks by Clifford Lynch
Director, Library Automation
University of California

The title of this session included some discussion of a research agenda and where do we go from here. I have a couple of suggestions. First, I think that we heard two things from two different Richards over the last two days that really resonated a lot with me. Richard West reminded us that we are in an unsustainable situation. When you see growth in costs per year of the magnitude we are seeing over and over again, sooner or later something is going to break. Probably the later it happens the more dramatically it will break. I think that one of the things we're going to need to do is start looking at how it's likely to break under various assumptions. I will have more to say about that later.

The other thing we heard from Richard Lucier yesterday, who underscored the fact that we are in a situation now with a multiplicity of systems of scholarly communication operating in parallel. A lot of the issues that we're facing are issues of resource allocation among systems as well as inside a given system. How much should we be devoting to support various kinds of collaboration, electronic communication? How much should continue to go to the sort of traditional print publication channels? I think that it would be very valuable to start charting that. I'm struck by the at least anecdotal evidence gleaned from talking to people that, while we have been talking about electronic resources for a long time now, only a minuscule part of the typical acquisitions budget is going to electronic resources. It would be very interesting I think to have a better picture of how that's changing year by year by year.

I think we have got some fundamentally new kinds of content to worry about. We didn't talk about this much. For example, when we start looking at recorded distance education, we now have stuff that looks much more like performance content than anything else. This content is surrounded by a whole set of different intellectual property restrictions and may experience a whole set of different uses that I don't think we understand very well. We're certainly, for example, capturing a lot more seminars on video. These are part of our record of scholarly communication. I don't know how useful these are. I don't know whether anybody looks at them again. Video is very expensive to scan, in terms of human effort.

We focused a lot on cost. What we haven't touched on too much is the access versus cost trade-off. If something is enormously more accessible, is it worth paying more for, when, how much? This is a two-sided equation, not a one-sided equation. I think that, particularly when we're operating in a context of distance education and students who want 24-hour access to content, we really need to look at that access side of the equation as well.

We need to focus more on the role of professional societies. There's an old saying that in many cases scholars feel a stronger tie to their discipline than their home institution. One of the things that Richard West mentioned, that I think is terribly overlooked, is coherence to the user. We're looking at all these systems from the point of view of libraries and publishers. Sometimes we need to come back and recognize that users need a coherent view of information reaching them from all sources, tradition and nontraditional, published and informal. They want a much more coherent view of information. I would think that the worst nightmare of your typical consumer of information is to have this galaxy of different publishers out there all posting things randomly at a thousand Web sites they have to visit every day looking for something. And maybe we can come up with a different command language for each one and 12 or 15 different readers and viewers. This could really be horrible. Paper, as we serve it up today, has a certain consistency to the user.

We mustn't lose sight of the need to preserve that consistency. Libraries are going to have an important role in making sure that that consistency is preserved, at least I think that needs to be one of their major missions. I think we have a logical connection with professional societies. Professional societies and university presses have a great deal of commonality of interest with the universities producing knowledge. In a sense, they are governed by members of those institutions. They sit on their boards and they shape their agendas. I think that there needs to be a lot more dialogue with professional societies and with university presses about how they can help in this situation.

I'm struck that we didn't talk much about overhead costs, transactional costs. One of the things that's striking to me, even in the print world, is how transactionally we do things. We evaluate things journal by journal by journal for tens of thousands of journal subscriptions every year. It's going to get worse in the electronic environment. We can have lawyers help us negotiate license agreements for each of the ones we select. I think that in some cases we may have to look very carefully at whether there isn't a lot of transactional overhead in this system that can be reduced somehow, to think about acquiring access to large amounts of information rather than lots and lots of piecemeal acquisition. We need to spend some time seeing whether there is an advantage to be had in that direction.

We heard a number of statements to the effect that the cost of network dissemination is zero. I think that that's absolutely wrong. There is no apparent cost, but we are financing the network. In fact, if you look at our experience at the University of California with our internal network, there are two things that are driving the growth of that network. One is distance education and the other is access to information. And it's abundantly clear that this sort of T-1 local level networking, that we have been feeling very pleased with ourselves for getting installed on a reasonably broad basis, is not going to cut it in these applications. We are going to need orders of magnitude, more bandwidth before we're through. That is going to be a significant investment. I would argue that those two areas that I just mentioned, distance education and information access and dissemination, are going to be two of the broad drivers for it. We need to track those costs carefully and allocate the costs of renewing and improving and hardening that infrastructure across applications. It's not a zero cost situation.

It seems to me that there are a lot of dynamic phenomenon that are going to be happening. Richard Lucier gave us his very interesting view of how cost changes in a dual world of print and new systems, and there may be this sort of cost hump. We've raised the issue about what happens if we don't control the cost increases and the system tears itself apart and melts down. One very interesting threat I heard come up was this notion that maybe when times get really bad, there are only a small number of core journals in most fields. And maybe, if times get tough enough, we can identify those. There is another phenomenon that hasn't been commented on too much, critical mass. When we finally get enough material in a given discipline in electronic format will usage patterns suddenly and dramatically change? One of the things that may happen is that suddenly people who have gone slow in electronic distribution, publishers who have gone slow, may discover they're at an enormous disadvantage, once that critical mass effect happens. We've already seen that users will prefer easy-to-access electronic information over rummaging around for print or, God forbid, microforms. That phenomenon will get very pronounced. Yet we have very little other than speculation about any of this. Why don't we try some large scale simulations? We have pretty good technology for doing gaming and simulation with people playing the roles of various parties in complex systems. This is used a lot to try and understand, for example, the effects of other governmental and economic activities. We should be looking at trying to get some insight into how a very complex system is likely to change under the impact of forces that are only to a limited extent under our control and where we don't thoroughly understand the interactions. Those are a few reactions and thoughts about topics which might be beneficial to explore further.

Remarks by Timothy Ingoldsby
Director of New Product Development
American Institute of Physics

I'd like to thank the organizers of this conference for inviting the American Institute of Physics here as a representative of the scientific society publishing community. AIP and its member societies publish about one third of the world's physics research literature including the top journals in most of the subfields of physics. As you have learned at this conference, physics is a field in which the transformation of the scholarly communications process is occurring most rapidly. It was a group of physicists who conceived of the World Wide Web. It was another physicist who led the effort to develop Mosaic. And my society colleagues and I spend hours thinking about the changes that are coming to our profession brought on by visionaries like Paul Ginsparg of Los Alamos.

AIP also understands the pressures that have been placed on academic institutions by the spiraling cost increases of scientific literature. We are committed to ending that spiral and have reduced our annual price increases in the past two years by more than 40 percent. In one more year our price increases will be down to near inflation. How are we to survive with these self-imposed controls at a time when our commercial competitors continue to impose these double digit increases?

We believe that our survival depends on nothing less than the reinvention of the scholarly communications process in light of the changes brought about by network communication. We pledge our cooperation with the research agenda that comes out of this meeting, and, in fact, we are engaged in what will probably end up being a three-year process to totally reengineer our process of producing research literature.

As a member of this panel, I have been asked to provide two or three cogent points related to possible research agenda described during the past two days. I was very impressed by William Bowen's presentation yesterday during the lunch hour of the JSTOR project. He provided a clear description of what has been accomplished along with metrics for how it might be turned into a self-sustaining operation. I will definitely be taking this back to AIP as a potential project to consider. There will be, unfortunately, a large scaling issue, as Cliff has described, as many of our top journals have 750,000 pages in their individual archives, whereas Dr. Bowen was talking about the top ten journals in JSTOR comprising about that number of pages.

Another point that I will take from this conference is a conviction that publishers must do a better job of explaining just what it is that we do to add value to the literature that we publish. Richard Lucier's description of activities at UC San Francisco sounded very much like a rediscovery of what publishers do. He has even rediscovered the concept of page charges, as he charges back to various scientific departments for the work he publishes on their behalf. But I wonder if that library is in a position to do as much as a traditional publisher to see that the research done by a UC San Francisco scientist is widely disseminated to the entire scientific community.

Likewise, Hal Varian's description of the activities of Paul Ginsparg failed to touch on another value supplied by publishers, the improvement that can be made to a research communication by the suggestions and copy marking done by a good editor. AIP would be very interested in participating in a careful review of the economics and trade-offs involved in Ginsparg-style publishing. Now that the NSF has put a more realistic figure on Paul's operation than the ridiculous $5,000 cost that he used to claim, it is time for a careful study to assess the true costs, benefits, and shortcomings of this mode of publication.

Paul Peters asked Bruce Kingma to speculate about what might be the publisher's response to his interlibrary loan study. I will save him the trouble. The result, at least for one publisher, will be a dramatic increase in the CCC royalty fee and discussions with library consortia about site license copying fees. It also seems clear to this publisher that the culture and mores in which the CONTU guidelines for copyright were initially developed are no longer in effect. Interlibrary loan in the form of document delivery consortia such as SUNY Express should not be permitted five CONTU copies of each journal. I know it is controversial or perhaps even seditious to this audience, but it is a dialogue that needs to be initiated.

In closing, I note with interest the excited response of the audience to Mario Morino's call to arms in his keynote address. Now, perhaps my judgment was clouded by my perspective as a publisher who faces every day the fears Mario described as I try to develop new products that will be responsive to the changing marketplace. Because once the coffee break following his talk was over, we returned to the more detached academic view of the situation. I must agree with Mario, that the academic view is not what is required to survive this coming upheaval. As scholars, as publishers, we need to develop a fire to respond to these changes. Either that or we need to stick our head in the sand and hang on until we retire. I look forward to working with you to stoke the fire.

Remarks by Colin Day
Director
University of Michigan Press

I was hoping there would be a gap between the vigorous argument of the publisher's case by my colleague and my chance to be up here. It's been a very interesting conference. If you look at the agenda for this particular session we are really talking about economics. We are thinking about collaboration, and we are talking about research for the future. I will try and divide my brief remarks into those three headings.

First of all, I think it's interesting to see what we've established about the economics of information. Evidence submitted from a variety of sources established that first copy costs are dominant.

The second point that perhaps was not so strongly established but which I would like to make is that, if you contrast the Jim O'Donnell *Bryn Mawr* model this morning with the American Chemical Society model which was presented in the same session and indeed echoed Jim's comments, there clearly is an impossibility in scaling from the volunteerism kind of model of the *Bryn Mawr* approach, to the kind of scale that we're talking about in some of the major scientific journal publishing activities. I think those two things add up to a clear need to have some kind of cost recovery mechanism in place.

If we turn to Roger Noll's presentation, we see some of the problems in establishing that cost recovery mechanism. We live in a context in which there is a significant degree of market failure. One of the ways there is market failure is that the signals that come back to the publisher/creator are not complete signals of the total usage or interest in a particular publication. The signals that we're getting are unclear and certainly underestimate total demand in usual circumstances. We have a problem, therefore, of relying on the market for the kind of commodity that we are all talking about today, whether we call it information, a word which I abhor, or whether we call it knowledge, which I feel is a much more accurate reflection of the complexities of what we're talking about.

The second problem is that once we're in an electronic medium, we are in a situation where the marginal cost of a small item of knowledge is very close to zero. So any pricing structure that we construct is a complicated one and difficult to define in a way which covers all these costs. But as we think about the role of the market in this context, we also must not lose sight of something which actually rarely gets mentioned. There really is an important feedback mechanism through the price mechanism. Indeed, this is one of the virtues of the market, that customers signal back to the producer what they think about the product. They provide context in which producers can try new products out and see if they work. Some products fail and are withdrawn and others succeed.

A lot of the discussion of new economic contexts for scholarly publishing tend to lose that signaling device. It's somewhat shaky. It's not as good as one would like in the current system. But certainly we book publishers have a very clear sense of what works and doesn't work and when it doesn't work we reel back in horror and decide we won't do that again. And sometimes we look really happy and we repeat the trick because we are getting feedback from the marketplace about whether what we're doing is right or wrong. However we redesign the system, we want to have that feedback. Indeed, if possible we should be envisioning a system that strengthens that feedback.

The other kind of failure that we have, and I just very briefly want to allude to this, is what both Bill Bowen and Michael McPherson talked about as system failure. When one of the players in this research cycle (from author to reader and back again) acts to solve her/his problems it in fact exacerbates the problems of someone else in that cycle. The response of that person in the cycle is then to solve his/her problem by making it worse for the original player. The classic example is that the librarian looks at the budget, can't afford everything, cuts a subscription and decides not to buy as many books, or whatever. The publisher says, whoops, demand has fallen, our first copy costs are about constant, ups the price. So the librarian now has an exacerbated budget problem. That kind of thinking about our self interests within this complex system is extremely unconstructive. We really need to find mechanisms for talking together.

That brings me on to collaboration. I think that Michael McPherson made the point, I just want to reiterate it, we do have university presses that are actually part of the universities in which they live. We report to the same masters as the libraries. And it really is rather, I think Michael said perverse, I think it's sad perhaps, that somehow we have reached the situation where we operate hands-length and we don't exploit the benefits that there are in this institutional structure for collaboration and for undermining the systemic failures I was speaking about. The fact is that the university presses share the values of the academy. My press, and I don't think it's particularly atypical, has actually not increased prices for about two years. We're actually going to raise prices, we don't know, we're aiming for five percent, looking at the cost of paper particularly. Probably because at the margin we'll always back off and say, oh, that looks a bit too high. I suspect we'll make about three-and-a-half percent this year, and that will be the first increase for about two or three years. So we are endeavoring to restrain price increases. If you look to the Mellon Report, you will see that the university press journals were priced much more moderately, showing lower rates of inflation than commercial publishing houses. There is this institutional infrastructure in existence. We need to take more advantage of it. We need to talk more together. We need to find ways to exploit the collaborative potentials that it offers us.

I think one of the reasons for looking within the institution and looking at this institutional structure to seek some solutions to some of our problems is that I disagree with Richard West. I don't think we can avoid the fact that once any particular piece of knowledge is published, one has a monopoly; that if I publish a book it's not going to make sense for anyone else to publish that same book and, therefore, I have a monopoly in that property. If you give that to the commercial sector, which is going to pursue profit maximizing strategies, then that monopoly is going to be exploited. The advantage of the university presses and the learned societies is that we are not profit maximizers. In fact we are loss avoiders, which I thought was a wonderful phrase this morning. We're just trying to make the business work. We're trying to hold our costs down. I was impressed with the American Chemical Society's productivity improvements. But if you look at university press statistics, we have managed a comparable rise in productivity over the last decade. So there is impressive cost saving going on. And at the same time there is not that urge, not that drive to exploit the monopoly positions we have in each publication, and indeed because my master is the faculty committee. My master is also the provost. I am constrained. I am moderated in my behavior by that institutional structure in which I live.

I want to make one other general remark, which is that a lot of the time these discussions go on in terms of the collection. There is a certain staticness to the way you are thinking. I think it's very easy to slip into it. It's all that stuff there. Now, how do we get it out to people? But my perception as a publisher is very much more how do we keep the flow of new material going through the channel so that new research and new work is getting to the final reader? Mechanisms seem plausible for a static collection in a library. They're not always the right mechanisms to optimize what we should really be worrying about, which is this flow of new material.

Finally, the research agenda on which we should focus. One of the things that I am very conscious about is that we don't know how valuable academic time is. Things that cost scholars time or in some circumstances reduce their productivity, impose on them. They have to search for material rather than obtain it with a clear publisher imprint, for example, which says this is good, this is worth your attention. I think that at the core of all our questions is a failure to have any real conceptual grasp of how we talk about the value of faculty time. This would be an important valuable addition to our research agenda.

As a publisher, and I'm a book publisher rather than a journal publisher, as I launch each new product I'm testing the marketplace. Sometimes it works—usually it works. Sometimes it doesn't. So I'm always conscious of what is it the user wants. Another sort of thread weak in this conversation these last two days is the need for a real grasp of what the user out there wants? How do we best meet their needs? Market research is another part of the research agenda that we should be adopting.

Remarks by Malcolm Getz
Professor of Economics
Vanderbilt University

It will come as no surprise that I'm an advocate of prices. We have heard a lot about costs, but prices are something different than costs. There has been a variety of points of view expressed about the role of prices and how prices might be helpful and useful in rethinking how scholarly communication takes place. I'm not sure that I can piece together all of the different points of view in a coherent way. So I simply want to take my few minutes to advocate a few promising roles for prices. I think that prices empower users. So as I hear Colin talking about wanting feedback from the marketplace, those things which carry prices, in fact, give users the opportunity to vote with their dollars for what they care about. That's a very important function.

As I think about the organization of our universities, one role of prices is to be able to push decisions deeper into the organization so that they are decentralized closer to the faculty. Therefore the faculty can participate in decisions and trade-offs, increasingly complex trade-offs within the different kinds of media, different ways of communicating. The faculty can participate in a more creative aggressive way because they see real trade-offs, in terms of prices that are meaningful.

As Bruce Kingma described his study of interlibrary loan costs, it occurred to me that if the faculty on the four campuses all have access to the catalogs of the other campuses, why not have software which allows them to initiate requests from the remote libraries? Well, one reason why you would have difficulty is that such a request would impose some significant costs every time there was a fulfillment. And so it would easily be congestible; it would overrun budgets. But it would become feasible, if there was a price tag attached and if each person on a campus went to a remote source and had the opportunity of saying, well, yes, today it's worthwhile for me to make this kind of request. Colin asked how we could learn about how a faculty member values time? Well, one way to discover that would be to have a menu of choices for delivery with different price tags on them and see how people respond to them. So I think prices play a very useful role in empowering users and allowing us to discover what kinds of choices they make and, in that way, how they value different qualitative choices in the scholarly mix.

We heard a very useful distinction between first copy costs and distribution costs. And the JSTOR project focuses very aggressively and imaginitively on the distribution costs. I would like to spend my remaining moments to talk about the opportunities the electronic world makes for reducing first copy costs. We have heard some remarks from Tim Ingoldsby about the prospects for reengineering the editorial process, which I think is the heart of the whole publication process, which is the heart of the economic issue. We've heard reports from several publishers about significant productivity gains taking place in the publishing process. Many of those are in reducing the first copy costs. As I think about the way that might play out, the base line might well be Paul Ginsparg's gathering of working papers electronically. Deficiencies include the inadequate labeling of papers, the lack of support for an editorial process revision cycle, and qualitative assessments which one might then use to search the database to pull out articles that are useful.

The software (I think of it as an editorial

assistant software) that would capture the working papers, that would track the revision cycle, that would monitor, would support a variety of labeling mechanisms as the editorial process unfolds, would be the kernel of what Tim may have in mind when he talks about reengineering the editorial function at the American Institute of Physics. If it were possible to create software which would support and manage the editorial process, would it be portable across associations, and across disciplines? Is that a vehicle for dramatically reducing the first copy costs in a variety of disciplines? Is there a vendor opportunity here, maybe a software vendor perhaps?

The same process must also generate revenues for the physicist and for each association which adopts this strategy. I think there are a variety of revenue streams which can be generated. I won't go into those now. But Hal Varian suggested that one of the features that he values and that most of us as scholars value from the electronic world is the ability to follow a thread of literature, to trace from one article or one document to another, to build a bibliography, if you will, for a specific intellectual task at hand. The prospect of tracing a thread, it seems to me, is substantially enhanced the larger the database that one is working with. So one difficulty that JSTOR has at the moment is that it's a relatively small database. It will not support an extensive thread of literature through the economics discipline. There are probably two or three hundred journals in all. It might take 50 to 100 journals in that database before one would have confidence of being able to trace a significant thread.

If we are moving from journals being the core measure of the literature, to a database being what it is that we want to interact with, and we want to engage one of the two or three databases which characterize all of the physics literature in order to be able to trace the thread, then there is the risk here of substantial increase in monopoly power, substantial increase in the opportunity to drive up subscription prices and extract even more rents out of our universities. If that is the way in which the world unfolds, and it seems to be moving in that direction, then it's very important that it be the university presses and the scholarly societies who own those databases, and who are in the forefront of reengineering the editorial process in an aggressive way, so that the ownership of those databases are held in nonprofit and preferably university or learned society hands.

If that's the way the world goes, then I think there may be an advantage to introducing pay-per-view as a part of the mix. I think there should be subscriptions, of course. And part of how we get access to scholarship should be without charge on the margin in certain communities. But it occurs to me that there may be communities beyond research universities where we expect to pay for things with subscriptions who would want access without subscription, would want access to individual articles, individual elements of the research database for a use at hand. The price elasticity of demand beyond the research university for access to individual pieces of the database may be very high indeed, so that the profit maximizing mark up is quite low. So there may be a role for price on a pay-per-view with a very low mark up reflecting the very high price elasticity of demand, which would be a counterbalance to the profit maximizing high subscription rates which would come out of the database.

I pose this as a hypothesis. I don't quite have a research methodology in mind as to how to answer the question. But I think it's very important to ask if there is a big, highly elastic demand beyond the research university for access to the research literature. I think this is a researchable question. I also reiterate that prices are very important and we ought not to rule out the possibility that we would enhance our world by using prices in clever, creative ways on the margin.

Remarks by Richard Ekman
Secretary
The Andrew W. Mellon Foundation

Although the Foundation has supported research libraries for some time, in recent years our efforts have concentrated on helping libraries to come to terms with their rapidly rising operating costs. We prepared a study a few years ago which documents these costs, and now we are attempting to support a small number of demonstration projects that, we hope, will show how application of the new technologies to various stages of the scholarly communication process can change patterns of costs and patterns of use of library materials by students and faculty.

By the time we finish, a year or two from now, making grants for this purpose, we hope to have a portfolio with a reasonably diverse group of projects—including different facets of the scholarly communication process, a wide range of fields, and various types of research materials.

I confess that we bring a few biases to these otherwise "natural experiments." The first is our belief that the technology will, in the long run, lead to lower operating costs for research libraries. We also expect in these experiments not to support new technological developments, but to base projects in existing technologies.

We also believe—as Malcolm Getz has noted earlier today—that attention to pricing is critical to achieving cost-effectiveness. However, we are more skeptical than Malcolm is of pay-per-use approaches, which we fear may inhibit the kind of free-ranging intellectual inquiry which one expects to prevail in an academic setting.

Our plan is to watch our projects carefully over the next few years, and eventually to try to generalize in something we write about what we have learned. By "we," I mean the Foundation as a whole, and my colleague, Dick Quandt, and me, in particular.

Let me mention a few of the projects we've supported. JSTOR began, as you heard yesterday from Bill Bowen, as one of these, and it has become the largest and most ambitious. If you'd like a complete list of all our projects, I'll be happy to send it to you.

Also worth noting today is Johns Hopkins University's grant from the Foundation for Project Muse, an effort to create electronic versions of 40 of its existing journals in the humanities. Some of these journals are the prestigious core journals in their fields. The plan is to make available simultaneously both print and electronic versions of the journals, with a pricing scheme that encourages people to opt for the electronic version. At the end of four years, Johns Hopkins believes it will have enough information to make sound judgments as to which journals should continue to exist in print form, which to be made available in both print and electronic forms, and which to be made available henceforth only in electronic form.

Another project stems from the concern that Cliff Lynch just mentioned—and we share—that the learned societies and scholarly associations need to be involved in thinking about these issues. Our grant to Emory University and Scholars Press is for a project that deals with the journals of two learned societies, the American Academy of Religion and the Society for Biblical Literature. These journals will be made available in electronic form, along with their print versions. Both esoteric, low circulation journals and very popular ones are included.

Finally, let me mention a grant to Case Western Reserve University and the University of Akron for a "virtual chemical library." Between the two institutions, there are now subscriptions to more than 700 chemistry journals, including about 400 overlaps. The plan is to create an electronic means for access to the journals by students and faculty of these two institutions in a way that will save money. Negotiations with the publishers will assure them of revenue streams that are greater than the price of one subscription, but less than the price of two subscriptions. Because there are a great many other institutions in the Cleveland area—both nonprofit and commercial and industrial—that make extensive use of chemical journals, one can easily imagine the ways in which this project might expand regionally, and perhaps nationally.

We've begun our work by focusing on journals. (In fact, the exploration of uses of new technology in scholarly communication is more advanced with regard to journals than it is for other kinds of scholarly information.) But we are beginning to be concerned also with book-length monographs, conference proceedings, music, video, and data. To judge from Richard Rockwell's presentation at this conference about the important databases maintained by the ICPSR, it is going to be a formidable challenge to make data collections available electronically in ways that are sustainable and cost-effective.

What do we expect to learn from all this? We don't know, although some themes are already discernible. They all point to the value of collaboration. First—and most obviously—the application of technology does lead to blurring of the roles and the division of functions among scholars, publishers, and libraries. Second, if approached intelligently, the introduction of technology can serve simultaneously to advance the causes of improved teaching and improved research. This is one area in which the antagonism between teaching and research can be blunted. Third, as the techniques of digitization become more refined, it seems clear that the goals of both preservation and access can be pursued simultaneously. Fourth, insofar as technology makes possible imaginative forms of collaboration among different kinds of entities, many of the most exciting projects we hear about represent *ad hoc* efforts at collaboration among universities, publishers, libraries, learned societies, computer centers, software companies, and so on. And finally, I think it needs to be said that the nonprofit and academic sector, on the one hand, and the commercial sector, on the other, will need to discover their common self-interest in this arena. We believe that there is a common self-interest and, in the long run, that it will become more evident. What is needed—as has been said previously during this conference—is sustainable equilibrium for a fragile—and rapidly changing—system of scholarly communication.

Remarks by Deanna Marcum
President
Council on Library Resources

One of the advantages of being so near the end is that I don't have to say very much that's new because so many good ideas have come from this panel. I have taken lots of notes about ideas, and I thank all of you for that. I'm really very pleased that the Council on Library Resources had a part in this conference because it has been a wonderful opportunity for librarians and economists and technologists and faculty and university officers to interact on a very specific topic. I think that's been enormously useful. And it reminds me of the need to continue doing just that.

The Council on Library Resources started a very modest program in cooperative grants many years ago. The whole purpose was to encourage faculty members and librarians to work together to solve problems. Even though the investment was quite small in each of those projects, I was very encouraged today and yesterday when I heard so many references to the results of some of those projects that we're now seeing as much bigger projects.

The other comment I have to make wearing my preservation hat—and I always have to wear two wherever I go—as interesting as the digital projects are and as important as they are, I was very worried by late yesterday at the lack of consideration that has been given to digital archiving. In each of these digital projects, wherever you are working on them in your institutions, we have to be concerned about the long-term preservation of that digital information.

In terms of the research ideas that I came away with after listening to the presentations, I would like to see some studies that emphasize benefits as much as they emphasize costs, because I don't think we have done very much in that area. I would also be interested in seeing replications of some of the cost studies we have heard about so that we can amass data and begin to generalize with greater confidence. It is very important to find out if some of these smaller studies have the same results done in different environments. And if not, why not? I hope some of you will be interested enough in the projects you have heard about here to begin to replicate those in your own institutions. It would be very helpful if we could begin to break our results into very specific reports so that, when we are talking about the humanities, we say so, and we talk about those costs. If we're talking about the sciences, we say so, and talk about those costs. I was a little bit concerned that we didn't always define our terms very well. And I think there are vast differences in the disciplines, or at least I have been led to believe there are.

One of Bruce Kingma's findings that cooperation is expensive and maybe not worth it caught my attention because all of our rhetoric is cooperation is the answer. I hope we will study that more carefully and find out what's really involved and what we need to do to make cooperation cost effective.

Finally, I had a meeting with the AAU provosts over the weekend. We were talking to 15 provosts about technology and what it will do to institutions. Each of those provosts said, tell us what it does about teaching and learning. That's what we need to know. I hope we will pay much more attention to what these processes do for the students and for the faculty.

Remarks by Duane E. Webster
Executive Director
Association of Research Libraries

I'd like to make three points as part of my closure. One of the crucial elements that I don't think has been focused on enough is funding to support innovation. Looking to see where we are getting the money to encourage new or different practices is very important if we are going to have innovation. I say that, in part, because both the Mellon Foundation and the Council on Library Resources are literally the only two foundations that have made definite, strong and continuing commitments to support innovation in scholarly communication in libraries and in universities. We need to have more foundation support. Different types of foundations ought to be interested and involved. We ought to be finding ways to entice those other foundations. I know both Deanna and Richard have been active in talking to other funding agencies. I think more of us need to be working with them to pursue funding for innovation and foundations should be more aware and more involved in charting the future of scholarly communication.

Foundation support is particularly important now in higher education because of the drying up of federal resources that have supported us in the past. This current Congress is particularly focused on balancing the budget on the backs of some of the future investments that need to be made. The most recent development this last week with the TIIAP program is illustrative of the crisis we face in higher education. Not only do we need to argue more effectively as a community for the benefit and value of those programs to Congress, but we have got to find a way to restore that funding.

Research libraries themselves are thinking about how best to collectively fund efforts at innovation. And at the Association of Research Libraries, the membership voted four years ago to increase their dues in order to create a fund that over time will be available to reinvest in development purposes. This development fund is about a third of the way toward achieving that goal. Research libraries are committed to the innovation of scholarly communication. And they're prepared to use some of their own money to find a way to do it.

The second point concerns the electronic environment which, as yet, is an environment not dominated by the commercial publishers. Both the technology and the time is right for the development of electronic information resources that will further university education or research objectives in a cost effective fashion. We have to find ways for universities to make fresh investments in electronic publishing initiatives, particularly within the university presses and within the other not-for-profit environments. We have heard again, during the course of these two days, that it's the not-for-profit arena that gives us the best price for the publication dollar invested.

The third point I'd like to make is related to Richard Rockwell's comment about librarians being too passive when it comes to responding to double-digit increases in prices for journal subscriptions. We are in a dilemma. We are seen as passive by faculty who have not been directly involved in some of the struggles that we have been waging. They don't understand fully the complexity or the interdependencies that are present here. I think part of what we have to do is respond with a renewed effort to involve faculty in both a problem-solving process and an educational process, developing a greater awareness of the pressures that work within the scholarly communication model, and also the difficulties of working with the publishing community, particularly the commercial publishing community. But I am also reminded of Michael McPherson's comment about the danger of institutional responses to the current crises that can lead to collectively self-defeating behaviors. This posture of either responding by canceling or responding by attacking publishers can be in fact a self-defeating cycle.

When we look at the process of canceling, the studies tell us that frequently what goes are the high cost, low use items that over time diminish the commons that we have to draw upon collectively. Well, from an institutional point of view it makes a lot of sense to cancel those high cost, low use items, but collectively that strategy may be self-defeating. It seems to me that we must come up with solutions that lead to collective advancement. In that arena of collective self-advancement it is going to be investing in university-based and not-for-profit based electronic publishing where we have an opportunity to redefine and recreate the relationships between the creator, the distributor, and the user of that information.

I think the conference itself has been an extraordinary opportunity for us to bring together these several different communities to look at the set of issues that we're confronting. Clearly the issues are not strictly a library-based problem. The problems are much larger than libraries. The solutions are going to have to be drawn from a larger community. Working in this type of setting where we have representatives of several of the vested interests working to find good solutions will help us plan for a productive future.

Appendix

Conference Sponsors

Council on Library Resources

The Council on Library Resources is a private foundation established in 1956 to look toward the future on behalf of libraries, to address problems experienced by libraries in the aggregate, and to identify innovative solutions. It promotes research, organizes conferences, issues publications, and manages collaborative projects to bring about significant changes in its areas of interest. The Council is affiliated with the Commission on Preservation and Access. Together the two organizations work to ensure the preservation of the published and documentary record in all formats and provide enhanced access to scholarly information.

The University at Albany, State University of New York

Established in 1844, the University at Albany, SUNY is the oldest chartered public institution of higher education in New York. Designated as a University Center of the State University of New York in 1962, Albany has a broad mission of undergraduate and graduate education, research and public service. More than 16,000 students are enrolled in the eight degree-granting schools and colleges of the University, which is noted for its achievement of both diversity and excellence.

The University Center Libraries of the State University of New York at Binghamton, Buffalo, and Stony Brook

The four University Centers of the State University of New York, the Universities at Albany, Binghamton, Buffalo, and Stony Brook, are mid-sized, public institutions with library systems which are responsive to local, regional, state-wide, national and international needs. Their collective holdings exceed seven million volumes and serve nearly 60,000 full-time equivalent students enrolled at the four University Centers. The libraries participate actively in a variety of cooperative projects and, among them, hold membership in the Association of Research Libraries, the Research Libraries Group, and the Center for Research Libraries.

Association of Research Libraries

The Association of Research Libraries is a not-for-profit membership organization comprising 119 libraries of North American research institutions. Its mission is to shape and influence forces affecting the future of research libraries in the process of scholarly communication. ARL programs and services promote equitable access to, and effective use of recorded knowledge in support of teaching, research, scholarship, and community service. The Association articulates the concerns of research libraries and their institutions, forges coalitions, influences information policy development, and supports innovation and improvement in research library operations. ARL operates as a forum for the exchange of ideas and as an agent for collective action.

Coalition for Networked Information

The Coalition is a partnership of the Association of Research Libraries, CAUSE, and EDUCOM and was founded to help realize the promise of high performance networks and computers for the advancement of scholarship and the enrichment of intellectual productivity. It pursues its mission with the assistance of a task force of over two hundred institutions and organizations that provides focus and resources which are crucial to the ability of the Coalition to articulate and explore shared visions of how information management must change in the 1990s to meet the social and economic opportunities and challenges of the 21st century.

National Association of State Universities and Land-Grant Colleges

Founded in 1887, the National Association of State Universities and Land-Grant Colleges (NASULGC) is the nation's oldest higher education association. A voluntary association of the public research universities, all the land-grant institutions, and many state university systems, NASULGC's membership includes 189 institutions, and its campuses are located in all 50 states, the District of Columbia, and U.S. territories. Its member campuses enroll more than 2.9 million students and claim upwards of 20 million alumni. NASULGC institutions award approximately a half-million degrees annually, including about one-third of all bachelor's and master's degrees, 60 percent of all U.S. doctoral degrees, and 70 percent of the nation's engineering degrees.

Conference Advisory Committee

Meredith A. Butler
Dean and Director of Libraries
1400 Washington Avenue
University at Albany, SUNY
Albany, NY 12222
mb801@cnsvax.albany.edu

Bruce R. Kingma
Assistant Professor
School of Information Science and Policy
Department of Economics
University at Albany, SUNY
Albany, NY 12222
b.kingma@albany.edu

Karen R. Hitchcock
Interim President
1400 Washington Avenue
University at Albany, SUNY
Albany, NY 12222
krh@poppa.fab.albany.edu

Thomas Galvin
Professor, School of Information Science
and Policy
University at Albany, SUNY
Albany, NY 12222
tg504@cnsvax.albany.edu

Eleanor Heishman
Director of Libraries
Binghamton University, SUNY
Binghamton, NY 13902-6012
eleanor@library.lib.binghamton.edu

John B. Smith
Dean and Director of Libraries
State University of New York at Stony
Brook, SUNY
Stony Brook, NY 11794
jbsmith@ccmail.sunysb.edu

Barbara von Wahlde
Associate Vice President for University
Libraries
University at Buffalo, SUNY
432 Capen Hall
Buffalo, NY 14260
unlbvw@ubvms.cc.buffalo.edu

Julia Blixrud
Program Officer
Council on Library Resources
1400 16th Street, NW, Suite 715
Washington, DC 20036
http://www-clr.stanford.edu/clr.html

G. Jaia Barrett
Deputy Executive Director
Association of Research Libraries
21 Dupont Circle, NW Suite 800
Washington, DC 20036
jaia@cni.org

Joan Lippincott
Assistant Executive Director
Coalition for Networked Information
21 Dupont Circle, NW Suite 600
Washington, DC 20036
joan@cni.org

John Hamilton
Assistant Director of Federal Relations
National Association of State Universities
and Land-Grant Colleges
One Dupont Circle, NW Suite 710
Washington, DC 20036
hamiltoj@nasulgc.nche.edu

LIST OF PARTICIPANTS

Institution	Name	Title
Academic Press, Inc.	Ken Metzner	Director of Electronic Publishing
Advanced Research Technologies, Inc.	Bonnie Lawlor	Chief Executive Officer
American Chemical Society	*Lorrin Garson*	*Chief Technology Officer*
American Institute of Physics	Tim Ingoldsby	*Director, New Product Development*
Andrew W. Mellon Foundation	William Bowen	President
Andrew W. Mellon Foundation	Richard Ekman	*Secretary*
Arizona State University	William Lewis	Vice Provost for Information Technology
Association of Research Libraries	*Duane Webster*	*Executive Director*
Association of Research Libraries	Ann Okerson	*Director, Off of Scientific & Academic Pub*
Association of Research Libraries	Prue Adler	Asst Director for Federal Relations
Association of Research Libraries	Jaia Barrett	Deputy Executive Director
Association of Research Libraries	Patricia Brennan	Information Services Coordinator
Association of Research Libraries	Mary Jackson	Access & Delivery Services Consultant
Association of Research Libraries	Susan Jurow	Director, Office of Management Services
Association of Research Libraries	Martha Kyrillidou	Program Officer for Stat's & Measurement
Association of Research Libraries	Mary Jane Brooks	Office Manager
BIOSIS	James Walsh	Head, Bibliographic Control Dept.
Brigham Young University	Julene Butler	Library Use Instruction Coordinator
California State University	*Richard West*	*Vice Chancellor, Business and Finance*
California State University - Hayward	Noreen Alldredge	Library Director
California State University - Long Beach	Molly Corbett-Broad	Executive Vice Chancellor
Canada Institute for Scientific & Tech Information	Brenda Hurst	Manager, Acquisitions
CAPCON Library Network	Julia Blixrud	Director of Training and Education
CAUSE	Jane Ryland	President
Center for Research Libraries	Donald Simpson	President
Chronicle of Higher Education	Bianca Floyd	Reporter
Chronicle of Higher Education	Tom DeLoughry	Technology Editor
City University of New York	Richard Rothbard	VC for Budget, Finance & Info Services

Italics denotes speakers and moderators

209

LIST OF PARTICIPANTS

Institution	Name	Title
Coalition for Networked Information	Joan Lippincott	Assistant Executive Director
Coalition for Networked Information	Joan Cheverie	Visiting Program Officer
Coalition for Networked Information	*Paul Evan Peters*	*Executive Director*
Colorado State University	Joel Rutstein	Head, Collection Development
Columbia University	Carol Mandel	Deputy University Librarian
Columbia University	Elaine Sloan	VP for Info Services & University Lib'n
Columbia University	Angela Giral	Director, Avery Library
Congressional Information Service	Diane Smith	Director of Marketing
Cornell Information Technologies	Steven Worona	Assistant to the Vice President
Cornell University	Catherine Murray-Rust	Associate University Librarian
Council on Foreign Relations	Leigh Gusts	Director of Library Services
Council on Library Resources	Martin Cummings	Chairman, Board of Directors
Council on Library Resources	*Deanna Marcum*	*President*
Council on Library Resources	Glenn LaFantasie	Senior Program Officer
Council on Library Resources	Gail Sonneman	Program Officer
Dartmouth College	John James	Director of Collection Services
Dartmouth College	James Fries	Business and Engineering Librarian
Delaware State University	Tossie Taylor	Vice President for Academic Affairs
EDUCOM	Bob Heterick	President
Elsevier Science	Karen Hunter	VP & Assistant to the Chairman
Emory University	Charles Forrest	Director, Planning and Budget
Faxon	Bruce Heterick	Director of Sales, Eastern Region
George Washington University	Sharon Rogers	Associate VP for Academic Affairs
Georgetown University	*Sue Martin*	*University Librarian*
Georgetown University	*Leo O'Donovan*	*President*
Georgia Institute of Technology	Miriam Drake	Dean and Director of Libraries
Getty Art History Information Program	Jennifer Trant	Manager, Imaging Initiatives
Harvard University	Richard DeGennaro	Librarian, Harvard College

Italics denotes speakers and moderators

LIST OF PARTICIPANTS

Institution	Name	Title
Harvard University	Susan Lee	Associate Librarian
Harvard University - JFK School of Government	Brian Kahin	Director, Information Infrastructure Project
Inter-Univ Consortium for Political & Social Res	*Richard Rockwell*	*Executive Director*
Iowa State University	Gordon Rowley	Assistant Director for Collections
Iowa State University Computation Center	Jim Bernard	Interim Director
John Wiley & Sons	Laura Conley	Director of Research & Planning
Kansas State University	John Streeter	Director, Office of Information Systems
Kent State University	Cheryl Casper	Associate Provost
Kent State University	Jeff Gatten	Head of Collection Management
Lehigh University	Susan Cady	Associate Director for Technical Services
Lehigh Valley Association of Independent Colleges	Patricia Ann Sacks	Senior Fellow
Library of Congress	Winston Tabb	Associate Librarian for Collection Services
Library of Congress	Sarah Thomas	Acting Director, PSCMI
Library of Congress	*Hiram Davis*	*Deputy Librarian*
Miami University	Judith Sessions	Dean and University Librarian
Mississippi State University	John Gaboury	Dean of Libraries
Morino Institute	*D. Kaye Gapen*	*Senior Advisor*
Morino Institute	*Mario Morino*	*President*
Nat'l Ass'n of State Unv. & Land-Grant Colleges	Jennifer Wingard	Director, Urban and Academic Programs
Nat'l Ass'n of State Unv. & Land-Grant Colleges	John Hamilton	Asst Director for Federal Relations
National Agricultural Library	Robin Frank	Head, Information Centers Branch
National Public Radio	John McChesney	Technology Correspondent
Naval Postgraduate School	Maxine Reneker	Director, Knox Library
Naval Research Laboratory	Peter Imhof	Technical Information Officer
NE Ohio Universities College of Medicine	Jean Sayre	Director and Chief Medical Librarian
New Mexico State University	William Conroy	Executive Vice President
New York Public Library	Heike Kordish	Deputy Director of the Research Libraries
New York University	Carlton Rochell	Dean of Libraries

Italics denotes speakers and moderators

LIST OF PARTICIPANTS

Institution	Name	Title
New York University	Nancy Kranich	Associate Dean of Libraries
North Carolina A&T State University	Waltrene Canada	Director of Library Services
Northwestern University	David Bishop	University Librarian
OCLC	Donne Olvey	VP and Assistant to the President
Ohio State University	William Studer	Director of Libraries
Ohio State University	Robert Kalal	Assoc Director, Unv Technology Services
Ohio State University	Roy Koenigsknecht	Professor, Ameritech Research Fellow
Ohio University	David Stewart	Provost
Ohio University	Paul Gandel	Associate Provost
OhioLINK	Tom Sanville	Executive Director
Pennsylvania State University	Gloriana St. Clair	Associate Dean and Head, Info Access
Pennsylvania State University	*James Ryan*	*Vice President for Continuing Education*
Portland State University	Bruce Taggart	Director, Office of Information
Princeton University	Ira Fuchs	VP, Computing and Information
PRN Associates	Peyton Neal	President
Purdue University	Emily Mobley	Dean of Libraries
Readmore, Inc.	Dan Tonkery	President/CEO
Robinson and Associates	Barbara Robinson	Principal
Rochester Institute of Technology	Ron Stappenbeck	Director, Information Systems
RoweCom	Richard Rowe	President and CEO
San Francisco State University	John Gemello	Associate VP, Academic Resources
Smithsonian Institution	Barbara Smith	Director of Libraries
SOLINET	Charles Wright	Director of Business Services
South Dakota State University	B.J. Kim	Cataloger
Southeastern Universities Research Association	Dan Van Belleghem	Asst VP for Networking Applications
Southeastern Universities Research Association	Glenn Ricart	VP and Director, Network Development
Southern Illinois University	Connie Poole	Acting Director, Medical Library
Southern Illinois University at Carbondale	Carolyn Snyder	Dean of Library Affairs

Italics denotes speakers and moderators

LIST OF PARTICIPANTS

Name	Title	Institution
Roger Noll	*Professor, Dept of Economics*	*Stanford University*
Carey Hatch	Technical Manager	State University at Albany, SUNY
Stephen DeLong	Associate Vice President - Info Systems	State University at Albany, SUNY
Mike Matis		State University at Albany, SUNY
Bruce Kingma	*Director, School of Info Science & Policy*	*State University at Albany, SUNY*
Meredith Butler	*Director of Libraries*	*State University at Albany, SUNY*
Thomas Galvin	*Professor, Rockefeller College*	*State University at Albany, SUNY*
Karen Hitchcock	*Interim President*	*State University at Albany, SUNY*
Eleanor Heishman	Director of Libraries	State University at Binghamton, SUNY
Suzanne Fedunok	Asst Director for Info & Research Services	State University at Binghamton, SUNY
Stephen Roberts	Associate Director of University Libraries	State University at Buffalo, SUNY
Gary Byrd	Director, Health Sciences Library	State University at Buffalo, SUNY
George D'Elia	Professor, School of Info and Lib Studies	State University at Buffalo, SUNY
Robert Wagner	Senior Vice President	State University at Buffalo, SUNY
Barbara von Wahlde	*Assoc Vice President for Univ Libraries*	*State University at Buffalo, SUNY*
Germaine Linkins	Director of Libraries	State University at Potsdam, SUNY
John Brewster Smith	Director of Libraries and Dean	State University at Stony Brook, SUNY
Janet Potter	Director of Library Services	State University College at Oneonta, SUNY
Michael Markwith	Chief Executive Officer	Swets & Zeitlinger, Inc.
Fred Heath	Dean and Director, Evans Library	Texas A&M University
Richard Meyer	Library Director	Trinity University
Barbara Jones	Library Director	Union College
James Taaffe	Provost/Academic VP	University of Alabama
William Sibley	Vice President for Academic Affairs	University of Alabama at Birmingham
Samuel McManus	Provost & VP for Academic Affairs	University of Alabama at Huntsville
John Keating	Provost	University of Alaska - Fairbanks
Sharon West	Director of Libs and Information Tech	University of Alaska - Fairbanks
Carla Stoffle	Dean of Libraries	University of Arizona

Italics denotes speakers and moderators

LIST OF PARTICIPANTS

Name	Title	Institution
Edward Fontenette	Library Director	University of Arkansas at Pine Bluff
Verma Jones	Assistant Vice Chancellor for Academic	University of Arkansas at Pine Bluff
Ruth Patrick	University Librarian	University of British Columbia
Craig Conly	Deputy Associate Vice President	University of California
Gary Lawrence	Coordinator, Libs and Academic Computing	University of California
Martha Kendall Winnacker	Coordinator, Special Projects & Programs	University of California
Clifford Lynch	*Director, Library Automation*	*University of California*
Nancy VanHouse	Professor, School of Info Mngmt & Sytems	University of California - Berkeley
Michael Cooper	Professor, School of Info Mngmt & Systems	University of California - Berkeley
David Farrell	Assistant University Librarian	University of California - Berkeley
Hal Varian	*Dean, School of Info Mngmt & Systems*	*University of California - Berkeley*
Harvey Himelfarb	Special Assistant to the Provost	University of California - Davis
Marie Waters	Head, Reference Department	University of California - Los Angeles
Gloria Werner	University Librarian	University of California - Los Angeles
John Tanno	Associate University Librarian	University of California - Riverside
Gerald Lowell	University Lib'n and Assoc Vice Chancellor	University of California - San Diego
Richard Lucier	*Assistant Vice Chancellor*	*University of California - San Francisco*
Martin Runkle	Director of Libraries	University of Chicago
Gerry Munoff	Deputy Director of Libraries	University of Chicago
David Kohl	Dean and University Librarian	University of Cincinnati
Taylor Fitchett	Director of the Law Library	University of Cincinnati
James Williams, II	*Dean of Libraries*	*University of Colorado*
Paul Kobulnicky	Director of University Libraries	University of Connecticut
Susan Brynteson	*Director of Libraries*	*University of Delaware*
David P. Roselle	*President*	*University of Delaware*
Sharon Wheeler	Director, Office of Information Technology	University of Florida
Dale Canelas	Director of Libraries	University of Florida
John Yost	Provost	University of Idaho

Italics denotes speakers and moderators

LIST OF PARTICIPANTS

Institution	Name	Title
University of Illinois	George Badger	Associate Vice Chancellor for CCSO
University of Illinois	Burks Oakley	Professor
University of Illinois - Chicago	Elaine Martin	Asst University Lib'n for Health Sciences
University of Illinois - Urbana	*Ann Bishop*	*Professor, Dept of Library Science*
University of Iowa	Charles Shreeves	Associate Director, Collection Management
University of Kansas	Bill Crowe	Dean of Libraries
University of Kentucky	Eugene Williams	Vice President for Information Services
University of Louisville	Thomas Jenkins	Director, Academic Information
University of Maine	Elaine Albright	Dean of Cultural Affairs and Libraries
University of Maine	Marilyn Lutz	Systems Librarian
University of Manitoba	Carolynne Presser	Director of Libraries
University of Maryland	Ann Prentice	Dean of the College of Information Services
University of Maryland	H. Joanne Harrar	Executive Director for Perf Arts Lib Dev
University of Maryland	*William E. Kirwan*	*President*
University of Maryland	Brian Darmody	Asst to the President for Gov't Affairs
University of Miami	Frank Rodgers	Director of Libraries
University of Michigan	Elaine Didier	Associate Dean
University of Michigan	William Savage	Director, Dissertation Publishing
University of Michigan	Donald Riggs	Dean, University Library
University of Michigan Press	*Colin Day*	*Director*
University of Minnesota	*Thomas Shaughnessy*	*University Librarian*
University of Missouri	Charles Wurrey	Faculty Fellow
University of Missouri - Columbia	Martha Alexander	Director of Libraries
University of Missouri - St. Louis	Joan Rapp	Director of Libraries
University of Nebraska - Lincoln	Kent Hendrickson	Associate Vice Chancellor for Info Services
University of Nevada, Reno	Steven Zink	Dean of Libraries
University of New Hampshire	Walter Eggers	Provost and Vice President for Academic
University of New Hampshire	Claudia Morner	University Librarian

Italics denotes speakers and moderators

LIST OF PARTICIPANTS

Institution	Name	Title
University of New Hampshire	Michael York	Interim University Librarian
University of New Mexico	Robert Migneault	Dean of Library Services
University of New Mexico	Mary Sue Coleman	Provost and VP for Academic Affairs
University of North Carolina	Marcella Grendler	Associate University Librarian
University of North Carolina - Chapel Hill	Michael Hooker	Chancellor
University of North Carolina - Charlotte	Dawn Hubbs	Head of Documents
University of North Carolina - Greensboro	Jim Clotfelter	Vice Chancellor for Admin & Planning
University of North Dakota	Frank D'Andraia	Director of Libraries
University of Oklahoma	Sul Lee	Dean, University Libraries
University of Oregon	Pam Daener	Associate Vice Provost
University of Pennsylvania	Paul Mosher	Vice Provost and Director of Libraries
University of Pennsylvania	*James O'Donnell*	*Professor, Dept of Classical Studies*
University of Pennsylvania	Wilson Dillaway	Director, Library Information Systems
University of Pittsburgh	*Rush Miller*	*Director, University Library System*
University of South Florida	Tony Llewellyn	Director, Academic Computing
University of Tennessee	Donald King	Co-PI for SLA Research Grant
University of Tennessee - Knoxville	David Penniman	Director, Center for Information Studies
University of Tennessee - Knoxville	Paula Kaufman	Dean of Libraries
University of Tennessee - Knoxville	Jose-Marie Griffiths	Acting VC for Information Infrastructure
University of Texas at Austin	Harold Billings	Director of General Libraries
University of Vermont	Rebecca Martin	Director of Libraries & Media Services
University of Washington	Betty Bengtson	Director of University Libraries
University of Wisconsin	David J. Ward	Senior Vice President for Academic Affairs
University of Wisconsin-Madison	Mark Luker	Chief Information Officer
US Nat'l Commission on Library and Info Science	*Peter Young*	*Executive Director*
Utah State University	Glenn Wilde	Dean, Learning Resource Center
Vanderbilt University	*Malcolm Getz*	*Professor, Dept of Economics & Bus Admin*
Virginia Polytechnic Institute	Donald Kenney	Assoc Dean for Admin Services

Italics denotes speakers and moderators

LIST OF PARTICIPANTS

Name	Title	Institution
Joanne Eustis	Director of Planning and Program Review	Virginia Polytechnic Institute
Ari Palttala	Director of Marketing	VTLS, Inc.
Lizanne Payne	Executive Director	Washington Research Library Consortium
Shirley Baker	Assoc VC for Info Tech & Dean of Unv Libs	Washington University, St. Louis
Thomas LaBelle	Provost & VP for Academic Affairs	West Virginia University
Ruth Jackson	Dean, University Libraries	West Virginia University
Paul Setze	Chief Technology Officer	Whitman College
Michael McPherson	*Dean of Faculty*	*Williams College*
Scott Bennett	University Librarian	Yale University

Italics denotes speakers and moderators